# Handbook of
# SALES AND MARKETING MANAGEMENT

# Handbook of
# SALES AND MARKETING MANAGEMENT

Len Rogers

Kogan
Page

First published in 1987 by Kogan Page Ltd
120 Pentonville Road, London N1 9JN

**British Library Cataloguing in Publication Data**

Rogers, Len
   A handbook of sales and marketing management.
   1. Sales management
   I. Title
   653.8'1    HF5438.4
   ISBN 1-85091-329-3

Printed in Great Britain by
Billing & Sons Ltd, Worcester

# Contents

# List of Figures

## List of Tables

# Foreword

Some years ago, the present managing director of a company in a well-known multi-national group asked me for some advice during one of our training sessions. He had been offered the post of marketing director with another company in the group responsible for the profitable marketing and promotion of the company's range of products. The company had several millions turnover but was making a loss.

He was worried about the terms of reference. It turned out that as 'marketing director' he would be responsible for the profitable marketing of the company's products but would have no control over the product range, over sales or over the finances. It did not seem to him to be a marketing job.

I had to agree and, when I looked through the job description and specification he had been given, I advised him to turn it down. It was a non-job. He would be responsible but with inadequate authority to discharge his responsibilities. The company, despite its international reputation, was still confusing marketing and selling. The person who eventually accepted the appointment lost it after about a year.

What is the difference between selling and marketing? And, between sales management and marketing? Is marketing just a more imposing word for selling? These questions, and their many variants, always arise when people concerned with getting sales for a company gather together.

I think that there has been far too much talk about marketing, and not enough about selling. In the UK you never see the word 'Salesman' after a person's name on a visiting card, but 'Sales Representative', 'Technical Representative', 'Sales Executive', 'Area Manager', and sometimes, 'Sales Manager' even when there are no subordinates. The first chair of sales management has yet to be endowed at a UK university.

This book is for those people who are responsible for getting sales for a company; responsible for the management of those who have to find customers and satisfy them profitably; responsible for supplying the company with the means of remaining in business.

I have tried to cover those areas in which such a person must be proficient to operate satisfactorily. A number of topics within the sales manager's authority, influence or acquaintance, have had to be omitted because of limited space. A book of twice the length would hardly deal with the subject adequately. Thus, all the omissions are my responsibility.

The topics have been covered from a practical viewpoint. They will help the sales manager to get started and to develop; to organise and control the selling activities of the company. It should also help the average sales manager to become marketing-oriented.

Nearly twenty years ago (in *Sales Management*, 5th edition, ed. Len Rogers, Pitman, 1969) I wrote that

> when all the theorists and planners have had their moment and the production, finance and labour problems have been solved, or at least overcome for the time being, then someone, somewhere, has to go out and knock on someone's door and sell. It may be the door of a suburban flat or the door of a small factory; it could be the door leading to the buying agent for a foreign customer. This selling by people to people is carried out every day of the week and, because business is now a global operation, it is done 24 hours a day, year in, year out.

There are still countless marketing opportunities for people with courage, skills and techniques in selling. Britain is always in urgent need of efficient sales managers. This book is offered as a small contribution to that cause.

# 1

# Introduction

**Sales managers are the 'doers' in marketing: whether or not a company achieves its marketing objectives mostly depends on the quality of sales management. Today's managers have to embrace modern concepts, often with computerised efficiency, and combine these with skills in handling people.**

## The war room

'David! Could we spare Larry from Northern Ireland for about a week?'

John Anderson is speaking into the red phone on his command desk in the marketing war room at company headquarters. On the monitor at the UK work station the latest returns for Scotland are displayed. He looks up at the signals board on the wall next to the large-scale map of the northern region and continues.

'We've got four reds in Scotland now; that's two more since Monday and there's a good chance of a couple of the blues going red this week. I'm short on the ground at the moment because Mac's been at Bragato's HQ in Paris all week, then he's off to look at their Toulouse project.'

The sales and marketing war room is in a corner of the building furthest from the lift and stairs on the second floor of company headquarters. Access is through one large and one small office. So sensitive are the maps, displays and data in the war room that, irrespective of whether it is manned, one of the offices always has to be occupied, otherwise both must be locked.

Around the room are six work stations, one for each region. Each station has its own computer equipment, desk, telephones, wall map, signals board and filing equipment.

## Multi-national operations

This company sells specialised computer systems throughout Europe, grouped into six main regions, and each controlled from its headquarters in the UK. On entering the war room, the sales manager, knowing the meanings of the symbols, codings of the colours etc, quickly appreciates the up-to-date situation of the company's sales and marketing operations.

Three sales executives are in urgent discussion round the West German work station. By scanning the displays and listening to their decisions, one can appreciate how control in this room will affect the Stuttgart regional office later that morning, and require a technical person to fly out from Heathrow.

Company products range from around £5,000 to £250,000 and the time from initial enquiry to completion of the order is measured in months rather than weeks, and is sometimes a year or more. During this period there will be product improvements and modifications and often changes of personnel in the prospective customer's organisation.

With averages of about ten orders being processed to delivery stage, 30 in the negotiating stage, and well over 50 initial enquiries in each of the regions, management and control of company sales operations is absolutely vital for the company's success.

## Management of company sales is vital

In this company, sales management is completely involved in the marketing of its products. It monitors customer design changes, construction, assembly, delivery, installation, commissioning and running free of company supervision. Service is part of the overall marketing strategy and technical personnel are very influential in advising on 'add-ons' and upgrading of equipment.

The war room has two main activities: one is largely marketing, and the other, sales management. It is the centre for the collation, analysis and interpretation of all information received from the market and business environment; it is the centre for daily situation review and direction of the total selling operations of the company.

Companies using modern sales management techniques such as the war room* are better equipped to create and evaluate strategies for expansion, search for better-value products and services, corner specific product/market segments and develop greater executive and management effectiveness.

---

*The marketing war room, with its operational procedures, was originated by the author and has been installed in several companies.

## Confusion of selling and marketing

What customers regard as 'value', and what they buy, is decisive—it determines the nature of a company's business, what it produces, and whether or not it will prosper.

Customers are the foundation of a company; without them, it fails. This is the real purpose of marketing and selling: to find customers. Profit reflects the success of finding and satisfying them.

A company's products must be related to its target markets and attractive enough in performance and price for customers to buy. Customers are sometimes unaware of their wants and these have to be aroused. The ball-point pen was not wanted, it wasn't a yearning in customers' minds; its flexibility and advantages as compared to ink pens had to be demonstrated and a need created.

This is the essence of marketing: developing products that will satisfy specific needs of customers, and supplying them at prices that will yield profits.

Companies who give insufficient attention to customers' needs and offer them products developed in the factory rather than designed for the market, are outsold by competitors who are more aware of market needs.

Companies have discovered the need to 'market orient' their processes. Marketing received a boost in the 1960s and 1970s; many volumes were written on the subject and it was said that marketing was the reason for a company's existence. An American academic epitomised this observation by saying that *'marketing is the delivery of a standard of living'*. The scope of marketing was expanded to embrace, in one direction, the product idea long before it was manufactured and, in the other direction, the continuing satisfaction of the customer's use of the product. This new thinking required companies to adopt the 'marketing concept' and engage marketing managers. Product managers were renamed marketing managers; marketing directors were given board appointments with sales managers reporting to them.

Sales managers were still charged with the responsibility for getting sales, but with the aid of marketing. The job of the sales manager was to increase sales; the job of the marketing manager was to increase profits. The customer was all-important and company thinking had to change from 'selling products that we make' to 'making products that customers will buy'.

With all this change and development, there is no wonder that there was, and still is, confusion about the role of marketing in a company. Today, many people do not understand the difference between selling and marketing, and think that marketing is a modern term for selling. Marketing is an all-embracing activity requiring the participation, co-operation and co-ordination of all major functions in a company to satisfy customers. It may also be considered as the activity that ensures a continuing balance of production and sales over finance. Selling is the 'sharp end' of marketing; it is where company representatives are face-to-face with buyers and potential buyers.

## Meaning of sales management

Sales management is organising and controlling the sales of a company. It means managing sales and managing people. The crucial part is managing people. One of the more difficult transitions is from sales person to sales manager. Instead of getting the sales yourself, you have to obtain sales through other people. And, by the time you have agreed objectives with your subordinates, corrected their misunderstandings, checked a couple of weeks later and found that what they are doing is not what you wanted, you have had to revise the original objectives, and you find that two months later, sales are achieved at about 50 per cent of the level you could have got if you had done it yourself in the first place—within a week! But that's one of the problems of managing.

## Difference between selling and marketing

Companies have different views of marketing; these are apparent in their organisations. You may be a sales manager reporting to a marketing director, or a sales director with a marketing manager reporting to you; or a sales manager with a marketing manager on the same level as you in the organisation. Some successful marketing-oriented companies have no marketing department nor even a marketing executive in their organisations.

Marketing has two main meanings. First, it may be seen as the *total activity* of a company—the company is only in business because it is marketing; it is providing products or services to customers at a profit; it finds out what the customer really needs and then satisfies those needs. This implies that production is a service to marketing.

Determining customers' real needs costs money; obtaining raw materials and manufacturing products costs money; storing and delivering products costs money; allowing customers time to pay costs money. Finance is therefore a service to marketing and successful marketing is the reason why a company stays in business.

Second, marketing may be considered a *function* in the company in the same way that production, finance and personnel management are functions. It has certain tasks such as product distribution and market research, pricing, promotion, and so on.

The importance of marketing in a company often depends on the personalities of the executives. With a very strong production director opposed to modern marketing ideas, it will suffer. Products could be developed from the initiatives and capabilities of the production department rather than from the influence of the market place. New products proposed by a weak marketing group are sometimes resisted by a strong production department.

Thus, marketing can either be a dominant force with a company-wide influence and board-level responsibilities, or a supporting function in the quest for sales.

Marketing is sometimes a line responsibility and sometimes a staff appointment. In contrast, sales management is always a line appointment and never a staff job.

Marketing managers with no subordinates other than a secretary are not uncommon. They carry out valuable duties in promotion, advertising, publicity, exhibitions, sales literature, and product presentations to the sales organisation, but from a staff position.

A sales manager does not operate alone, but with a sales organisation. You may be appointed to this position in a newly formed company and find there are no sales people; you will be expected to build the sales organisation in line with the expansion of company business and you will be in line management and not in a staff appointment.

## Secret of sales management

The secret of successful sales management is achieving sales through other people. This is particularly relevant if you have been recently promoted from working a sales territory to being responsible for total sales. You have to change your activities from getting enquiries and orders yourself to getting them through other people. You cannot be in two places at once; you cannot see a customer in the north who is about to place a large contract, and at the same time see a customer in the south who is also giving your company a large order. You have to delegate to others.

### Delegation

You may not have sufficient knowledge of the product, and must therefore rely on others to demonstrate it. If you do have the knowledge, you won't have the time to do everything yourself; you must delegate.

Here are three meanings of delegation; which one do you think is best?

(1)  Assigning work to others while retaining the authority and accountability for results.

(2) Requiring subordinates to do assigned work in a manner that is satisfactory to you.

(3) Investing another person with the authority to act on your behalf.

In the first, the person who accepts the work has no accountability to you for carrying it out and it is not true delegation. You have offered it with one hand but kept hold of it with the other. Operating in this way will slow work down.

The second reveals that you are interested in means, not ends. You must be concerned with results and, within reason, not the way the results are achieved.

The third gives a person the right to act in your name. It is true delegation and you will be responsible for the mistakes as well as for the successes carried out in your name.

## How to delegate

When you delegate you are giving someone else the authority to act on your behalf. They will do some of your work and, doubtless, some of the things you have enjoyed doing. You cannot delegate only the unpleasant jobs.

You must organise yourself and decide what it is you are employed for. What do you have to achieve for the company? What is the main objective of your work? Until you have organised yourself you cannot organise others and delegate adequately.

Write down the specific objectives you have to achieve for the company. Examples are, 'To achieve a sales turnover of £... in twelve months', 'To increase sales to certain classes of customers by 10 per cent in twelve months', 'To achieve a minimum sales turnover of £... with certain products', 'To ensure that 95 per cent of all deliveries of products are made to customers within four working days', 'To ensure that money outstanding from customers is restricted to, or less than, an agreed percentage of total sales'.

What are the things you have to do today, tomorrow, next week? Mark those that are important, and those that are urgent. Important things are not always urgent; urgent things have to be dealt with quickly. Rank the urgent items: those to be done immediately, today, tomorrow, and so on.

Can any of these urgent things be done by anyone else? If so, break them down into tasks and estimate how long it is going to take to do them. Then, give the tasks to subordinates but ask yourself:

- Is the task reasonably simple?
- Has it been done before by the person?

- Will it take a small amount of time?
- Will I be able to check the progress made?
- If a mistake is made will it be minor?
- Am I pressed for time?

If you answer 'yes' to all of them, give the subordinate verbal instructions. If some of the answers are 'no', or:

- the task involves details
- more than one department or manager is involved
- a mistake would be serious
- you will be held responsible

put the instruction in writing, check that what you have written is unambiguous and check that the subordinate understands it.

## Delegation, responsibility, authority

To be a successful manager you must know your responsibilities and authority; especially, authority to commit the company with external organisations and to spend money. If you are responsible for profits, you must have adequate authority to take decisions to achieve the profit objectives agreed. Similarly, if your subordinates are to do their jobs satisfactorily they must know what authority they possess.

Responsibility should be given in terms of specific results to be achieved within a time period. These objectives should be agreed by the manager and subordinate and seldom, if ever, imposed.

If you are responsible for sales turnover, you need to know how many sales of which products, to which classes of customers, over what period. If you are responsible for profits, you need to know how the company defines profit, how it is calculated, and by when you are expected to achieve it.

Responsibility is the obligation to carry out a task. It is the actual work that is delegated to a person. If someone accepts the 'responsibility to carry out a task' from you, that person has become your subordinate.

Authority is the right to act in the name of a superior in an organisation. Sometimes we read that a person must have authority equal to the responsibility. This confuses different concepts: responsibility is an obligation; authority is a right or power. They are two different things.

If you hold a person responsible for carrying out certain tasks you must ensure that he or she has the means to do those tasks. A person responsible for driving a car within a speed limit must have an instrument for indicating speed as well as brake and accelerator; without these things the person cannot really be held responsible. Clearly the 'authority' of the accelerator, brake and speedometer cannot be equal to the 'responsibility' for speed limitation.

You must give your subordinates sufficient right to take decisions, if they are to be responsible to you for the tasks they have accepted.

The authority you grant must be adequate to accomplish the task you have delegated, but must not exceed your own authority. If you are responsible for restricting total sales expenses to, say, £100,000, obviously you cannot allocate expenses to your sales people to exceed this. With many other non-numerate tasks it is not so easy to define the limits of authority. Consider the tasks of maintaining contact with customers; ensuring that products are adequately displayed; ensuring that products are being used to their full advantage; ensuring that users understand the flexibility of product usage; the morale of the sales force; private use of company cars, and so on. These problems are explored in greater detail later in the book, but the following account of an actual event illustrates the difficulties of delegating.

## Responsibility for the pranged car

A sales director arrived at a customer's premises, several miles from his own office, for an important meeting. As he entered the building he realised that he had left the customer's file in his desk. Perplexed, he paused, and at that minute saw his company's office messenger coming down the stairs. He grabbed him quickly and said, 'I've left a file of documents in my desk—top left-hand drawer. It's locked. Here are my keys. I need those papers urgently. Get back to the office by the quickest possible means. See Jane. Get that file, top left drawer, and come back here as quickly as you can.'

'Right sir,' said the messenger, ran down the steps and out of the building. As he rushed out, he saw the director's car parked outside. He had been given the keys, which included the director's car keys. He had been told, 'get back by the quickest possible means'. He therefore decided to take the car. Unfortunately, in his hurry to carry out his mission, he put it into reverse and 'pranged' another car behind.

The question is: had he been given authority to take the car? Had that been delegated to him? He was told quite specifically to get back to the office *by the quickest possible means*, and given the keys which also included the car keys...

It cannot be answered neatly with a 'yes he has', or 'no he hasn't', been given authority, but it illustrates how we are often guilty of poor management and poor delegation in our business and social life. What we think we are doing and saying is often received by others in a different manner.

## Through-the-door-management

By the way in which we manage other people in an organisation will we be known. Our instructions must be clear: subordinates must know what it is they have to do and by what time. We must also be confident that they are capable of carrying out the tasks.

Over the years I have developed a technique which I call 'through-the-door-management'. However lengthy the procedures and complex the analyses we have used to arrive at our decisions, sooner or later we have to leave our office and issue instructions. When we walk out of our office, who do we tell to do what?

# 2

# Designing the Sales Force

**Your job as a sales manager. Principles you use to apply to the building of an organisation. Deciding how many people you need to have to service your customers. How to avoid too many conflicts arising from the treatment and handling of major and minor accounts.**

## Sales manager's job

The sales organisation obtains sales. Sales provide turnover; turnover provides profit. Therefore, the size, cost, and use of the sales force must eventually be related to profit. In general, you as sales manager will be faced with one of two situations: either you are starting from scratch with no sales people in the field, or you take over an existing organisation. Both situations have their advantages and disadvantages but, in whichever you find yourself, ultimately the sales organisation must be designed for the tasks of obtaining sales profitably.

The job of the sales manager is to secure results through other people. Therefore, the design of the sales organisation is vitally important.

Organisation has two distinct meanings: one is the process, the other is the end result. The process is better termed organising, and organisation the end result.

An organisation is an arrangement of functions and activities involving people, and organisation charts are often displayed on company walls. These show people and their titles in little boxes linked with lines and arranged in a pyramid shape. A well-drawn, balanced organisation chart does not imply a good organisation, but such a chart is necessary if we want a complete picture of our sales activities.

Irrespective of whether you take over an existing organisation or have to build one, certain principles apply:

- Organise activities and functions, not people.
- Provide adequate authority for responsibility.
- Balance and co-ordinate activities.
- Arrange equitable spans of supervisory control.

## Organise activities, not people

The first principle is fundamental in the design of an organisation. Sales procedures vary from company to company, so therefore, first list all the company's sales activities. Such things as customer servicing, prospecting for new customers, marketing research, product scheduling, new product development, stock control, warehousing, transportation, advertising, sales promotion, exhibitions, merchandising, forecasting, pricing, profit planning, training, credit control, etc.

Designing an organisation around functions is the most difficult principle to put into practice and, to some extent, you will have to consider people. This is obvious if you take over an existing organisation, and you will probably have a number of conflicts to resolve between functions and people. Nevertheless, the most effective organisation is one arranged for functions.

One successful company I have worked with had a unique organisation layout. At the top of the chart was the most important person in the whole operation—the customer. From this box labelled 'customer', were lines to boxes of functions dealing directly with the customer—sales person, technical service, order clerk, invoicing clerk, credit control. The result was illuminating: it clarified the various lines of communication and helped to establish responsibilities and authority.

### A dynamic entity

While organization charts serve a purpose, the modern concept of the organisation is of a living, dynamic entity, as in Figure 2.1.

*People* are grouped in formal and informal *structures* to perform *tasks*.

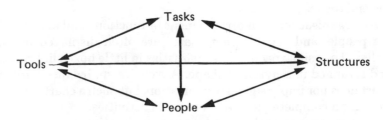

**Figure 2.1** *Modern concept of an organisation*

Their *tools* are their desks, mini-computers or computer terminals, telephones, cars, machines, etc. All four are interconnected. Modify or change any one and it affects each of the other three.

Suppose you had 30 sales people grouped in regions covering the total market calling on customers and prospects to obtain orders and enquiries. Their tools are their car, telephone, sales aids, samples, etc. They are serviced at headquarters by a number of people keeping them up-to-date with company products and procedures, confirming appointments, controlling credit, processing orders, dealing with expenses, and the many other activities of a busy sales office. If you increase the number of field staff, you will affect the regional structures, the headquarters' structure, the tasks currently being performed, and the tools. Alter the structure, perhaps by rearranging the regions, and you will affect the people, their tasks and tools.

The most important component is people. A business is built with people, not with products. When designing your sales organisation, keep Figure 2.1 in mind. It will help you to avoid some of the conflicts.

When you have your list of functions, assess the amount of time and effort each requires. One of the most important will be calling on customers to solicit orders and enquiries. This function needs special consideration.

## How many sales people?

You have to decide how many, or how few, field sales staff are needed to service all live accounts and open new ones in line with your profit objectives. The high annual cost of each sales person means that you must devote considerable time and effort to this task. Some of the factors you need to consider are:

- size of territory
- density of customers
- number of potential customers
- type of product and its applications
- time needed at each call
- frequency of purchase
- number of calls per year on each customer
- customer servicing required
- method of transport for sales people
- competitive strength

Assume that a company is to start selling an industrial product which has a repeat purchase. Although the market has many thousands of outlets, there are 4,000 buying points evenly spread throughout the country.

To open new accounts and service them requires an average of four calls each in the first year. The objective is to contact 50 per cent of the market in the first year. Therefore, $4,000 \times 4 \times 0.5 = 8,000$ calls have to be made and we estimate that each call, including travelling time, will take an hour. Thirty-five calls a week is thought to be feasible. If we allow for public and private holidays, sickness, and training, and work a 47-week year, one sales person can make $35 \times 47 = 1,645$ calls. Therefore five people are required: $8,000/1,645 = 4.9$.

If we assume that the cost of each sales person, including national insurance payments, head office supervision, travelling expenses, etc, is £20,000 a year, five people will cost £100,000. If the company works on, say, 10 per cent net profit, sales of £1 million are needed from the five to break even. If all 2,000 accounts ordered (though unlikely), this would be an average annual purchase of £500 per account. If we opened only 30 per cent of the 2,000 accounts, this would require an average annual purchase of £1,667 ($2,000 \times 0.30 \times £1,667 = £1,000,200$).

By increasing the call rate to nine per day, $9 \times 5 \times 47 = 2,115$ calls a year. This would require four sales people ($8,000/2,115 = 3.8$). We might start by employing two sales people, target 10 calls a day, monitor their performance, and if it agrees with our estimates, take on another two as quickly as possible.

## Provide adequate authority

Put the authority in writing. If you cannot commit things to paper so that they are understood, you certainly cannot do it verbally. Mismanagement will be the result. Determine what authority is necessary to carry out the task. If you give a person a task, provide the tools to do it: remember the doubtful responsibility for the damaged car described in Chapter 1. If you give a regional manager a sales quota to achieve with a sales budget, then allow that manager to hire and fire within general company regulations.

If you assign responsibility to someone for the development of a new area in the face of strong competition, give appropriate authority. This might be the right to allow special discounts to counter competition, approve credit to certain limits without recourse to head office, use local advertising facilities, entertain important clients, and any rights appropriate to the industry. Failure to give such rights to the person means inadequate authority to carry out the responsibility.

## Balance and co-ordinate activities

The most obvious balance is the work load of each sales person and is not just a matter of numbers of accounts, because territories vary in density of customers. A market consists of people, not places—people with needs, the money to spend, and willingness to spend it: ordinary individuals and professional buyers. A territory is measured by the people relevant to your product multiplied by their purchasing power. Consider geographical factors to the extent that customers and potential customers can be effectively reached by the sales force and that there are identifiable boundaries to contain advertising and publicity.

Balance the field staff with headquarters staff. Increasing the field staff probably means increasing internal staff to provide the same level of service. Balance those who get orders with those who fill them; storage, distribution and delivery facilities must keep in step with the field force.

Co-ordination is a vital consideration within the sales organisation and also with other company departments. Lay down adequate lines of communication and avoid appointing a 'co-ordinator'. An organisation with co-ordinators is suspect; co-ordination should be a normal activity in all positions and not a separate function that could develop its own empire.

## Equitable spans of control

Just how many subordinates can be controlled by one person will depend on the nature of the job and personal ability. All jobs may be considered as having a prescribed content and a discretionary content: what is prescribed is mandatory, the remainder is at the discretion of the job holder.

Supposing you had, say, six subordinates reporting to you and you intend to increase this by another four, do you give all your subordinates more discretion or more prescription? A lot depends on the job, on the subordinates and on you. How many export managers could you handle? How many office cleaners? The more discretion you give subordinates, the less you can handle. The greater the prescribed content of subordinates' work, the more you can control. How to do this is discussed in greater detail in Chapter 3.

There is a direct relationship between the span of control and number of levels of management. Suppose you have a sales organisation of about 100 people. Three regional managers report to you and each is responsible for a regional sales force of 30 people—six area managers, each with five sales people. These are three levels of management—national, regional, and area.

Increase the number of sales people reporting to each area manager from five to ten, and the nine area managers can report directly to you. The level of regional manager is removed, leaving only two levels—national and area. Too narrow a span of control means many levels of executives, higher overhead costs and communications problems. Aim for wide spans of control and a high prescribed content of all subordinates' work. Chapter 3 discusses this further.

## Planning the organisation

Your sales organisation must achieve the results for which you are responsible. Adopt the following four-stage procedure:

(1) List the objectives of the sales organisation. These should be in terms of results to be achieved in a period of time. One will undoubtedly be a certain total sales volume and value. There may also be objectives for expenses, profits, channels of distribution, advertising, pricing, discounts, etc.

(2) Place appropriate activities into major groups, such as customer servicing, new product development, marketing research, sales forecasting, advertising, promotion, warehousing, stock control, credit control, invoicing, etc. There will also be a number of relatively minor activities such as packaging, labelling, sales contests, exhibitions, etc. Marketing research and sales forecasting could be one major group; advertising, promotion, sales contests, exhibitions, another, and so on.

(3) Organise groups into workable structures related to each other: field sales people in small groups under a supervisor; supervisors grouped under second-level executives. The process continues until there is one position at the head of the whole sales organisation. Groups are arranged so that they can work together according to their importance to the company. If personal selling and advertising are of equal importance, they could work together under the control of one executive. If personal selling is much more important, then advertising might be a separate sub-group operating within it.

(4) Allocate people to specific positions. Starting from scratch will be easy; if you already have an organisation, it will take a long time, with a number of conflicts to be resolved.

## Line and staff appointments

All organisations are variations of the line and staff type. Very small companies of half a dozen people or so will normally have a pure line organisation with the owner-manager at the head. As this company grows, line assistants are hired. Beyond a certain size, specialists are appointed in staff positions. As company turnover increases there is greater demand for specialist advice and the staff positions develop their own line positions.

## Major and minor accounts

One of the commonest causes of conflict in a sales organisation arises from the classification and treatment of major accounts. As such accounts grow in importance to a supplier it is natural that they receive special consideration. They are usually serviced by a senior sales person such as a national accounts executive.

An account that has been opened by one of the sales people, and then develops into a large, major account, cannot simply be transferred to another sales person without conflict being created. The basis of classification—annual purchases—is the root cause of the conflict, because you cannot classify such accounts except in retrospect. It is better to classify 'major' accounts according to their buying procedures and geographic locations and, furthermore, to ignore their current purchases and assess their potential purchases. Thus, a company with many units throughout the country may qualify as a major account despite the fact that their current purchases from you are low.

Even more important than geographical spread are the buying procedures. If their purchases of your class of product are centrally negotiated and the details and terms subsequently circulated to their units, such an account should be handled by a major accounts executive. However, a nationally spread organisation may allow local purchasing activities, with each unit having the authority and flexibility to buy at the best terms. It would be quite natural for each of the customer's units to be serviced by an appropriate member of your field sales force.

If the customer decides to have greater control over such purchases, perhaps by negotiating centrally, it is obvious that a senior member of your organisation has to be involved. Conflict arises within the field sales force who regard this as an account, perhaps lucrative, which has been taken away from them. If the field sales force is assigned quotas or is remunerated partly by commission, the conflict is aggravated.

The key to this problem is a thorough understanding of purchasing procedures and the purchasing organisations of large customers and potential customers.

### Purchasing—selling interface

Purchasing is vitally important. Few companies get into difficulties because the sales people sell too much but, if a company buys too much, or unwisely, it soon finds itself in trouble. You should be able to answer these three questions for your main customers and large potential customers:

(1)  What steps are involved in the purchasing function?
(2)  What is the status of the buyer?
(3)  What is the buyer's responsibility for quality of purchased goods?

Your sales people must be able to distinguish the following positions in a customer's organisation:

- buyer
- chief buyer
- purchasing officer
- purchasing agent
- purchasing manager
- procurement executive
- materials management executive

## Materials management

This implies a grouping together of activities concerning the handling of all materials leading to finished products, and is increasingly evident in large organisations. The activities include:

- vendor search and evaluation
- production planning
- production scheduling
- purchasing
- storing
- transportation
- handling
- materials flow
- manufacturing

The larger the company, the larger the purchasing operation. The larger the purchasing operation, the more professional and organised it is likely to be. If your investigations reveal that a company has a materials management operation, then that company needs special consideration and should be serviced by a senior sales person.

## *Avoiding conflict*

Establish performance standards for the major accounts people as you do for field sales people. One standard should be gross sales of the major accounts or sector. Another standard should be based on the amount of central and field contact and a substantial proportion of working time should be required to be spent accompanying field sales people in major accounts follow-ups.

Ensure that your field sales people have opportunities to become major accounts executives and perceive the two types of sales jobs as complementary.

# 3

# Job Specifications

Clarifying the difference between job descriptions and job specifications. Laying down the key tasks to be accomplished and the standards that have to be achieved to do the job properly. If you set up a scheme of job specifications, you should use it to manage. An extract from a company's scheme is given with comments.

## Descriptions and specifications

A job description is a brief explanation cf a particular job, to whom the holder reports and who reports to the job holder.

A job specification is an itemised narrative of a job and what its holder has to achieve if it is to be done adequately. It is usually in three parts: the key or main tasks; the levels or standards of performance required to do the job effectively; the means by which the job holder and others can assess the performance of the job.

## The key tasks

Some of the key tasks for sales people are:

- achieving sales quotas
- maintaining regular contact with the company's customers
- active prospecting for sales
- making effective presentations of company products and uses
- preparing proposals and quotations for company products

The second part of a job specification states the levels of performance to be achieved in each of the key tasks. This is fairly straightforward for key tasks that can be quantified, such as sales quotas, but is not so easy with such tasks as making effective presentations.

## Setting standards

The achievement of company goals is the result of teamwork. Don't impose objectives on subordinates; obtain their agreement. If you set sales quotas by increasing previous results by a certain percentage, you are 'playing the numbers game'. You might be imposing objectives that are unattainable and thereby creating low morale problems. You may also be failing to exploit opportunities in the market. If sales are linked with an incentive scheme, such as variable commission, you may find an imbalance in commissions because the imposed objectives have not been adequately discussed and agreed with subordinates.

## Assessing performance

The third part of the job specification lists the means by which the performance levels can be measured. The standards should be so devised that it is possible for anyone to assess performance and arrive at similar conclusions. The specimen job specification in Table 3.1 has been taken from an existing company but with modifications to maintain anonymity; the means of measuring has also been left blank for the same reason. This column would normally have such references as weekly, monthly call schedules; weekly sales report; lost business report; monthly expenses summary; regional manager's monthly return.

It is not suggested that this job specification is an ideal one; it was as used in the company. A number of points can be noted. While the levels of performance have been detailed, many would be difficult to measure.

### Qualify where possible

1.1 lists the four quarters and three main product groups, but further objectives are needed to qualify these quotas in terms such as existing or new customers, product types, and more specific details.

1.2 would be difficult to assess because 'concentrate on' is too vague. One person might consider that adequate concentration has been achieved when half the available selling time is devoted to the four towns, whereas the intention may have been that at least 80 per cent should be in these locations.

1.3 would also be difficult to measure because of the qualitative 'strong preference' and reference to a vague expectation of future sales.

1.4 is not specific enough about the occasions when interchange with

## Table 3.1 *Specimen job specification*

| Key tasks | Level of performance | Measurement |
|---|---|---|
| 1. Achieve sales quotas | 1.1 Sales quotas by main type and quarter:<br>    Qtr 1  Qtr 2  Qtr 3  Qtr 4<br>    £000   £000   £000   £000<br>Mech:<br>Elect:<br>T/key:<br>1.2 Concentrate on the following towns: Eastown, Westown, Nortown, Southtown<br>1.3 Give strong preference for orders in excess of £xx,xxx or where there is expected to be a potential in excess of this figure within two years<br>1.4 Maintain records of closing techniques for subsequent comparison and interchange with colleagues | |
| 2. Maintain regular contacts with customers | 2.1 All users of company products in area to be visited at least four times a year<br>2.2 A User Visit Report (UVR) to be completed and mailed to HQ immediately after each visit<br>2.3 The reason for greater or lesser frequency of visit to be recorded on the UVR<br>2.4 Should a visit unearth a Red prospect situation, immediately telephone/ telex HQ | |
| 3. Maintain active, continual prospecting for sales of company products | 3.1 All appropriate publications will be scanned for leads<br>3.2 Information relative to another region to be passed to HQ<br>3.3 A pre-approach procedure will be conducted for each prospective customer<br>3.4 If it is decided to develop the prospect, copies of annual report and accounts will be obtained or requested to be obtained by regional, national, European HQ<br>3.5 An organisation chart will be drawn up of the prospect's directors, senior managers, and other appropriate personnel as thought at that time to be relevant to company products | |
| 4. Make effective presentations of company products' capabilities | 4.1 Make use of all audio-visual aids for practical presentations<br>4.2 Where appropriate, make use of satisfied customers for references, after obtaining their agreement on each and every occasion<br>4.3 Ensure ample time for complete back-up of technical assistance from HQ for demonstrations, etc | |

| Key tasks | Level of performance | Measurement |
|---|---|---|
| | 4.4 Each presentation to start with a statement of the prospect's objectives | |
| | 4.5 Each presentation should, if appropriate, contain a cost-justification of the proposed solution | |
| | 4.6 At least once a year, attend a presentation refresher course to maintain professionalism of techniques | |
| 5. Prepare professional proposals and quotations of company products | 5.1 Every proposal to a prospect should be within the company guidelines | |
| | 5.2 Every proposal should conform to the following sequence:<br>(a) Introduction<br>(b) Statement of prospect's objectives<br>(c) Company's proposed solution and costs<br>(d) Justification of the solution and an indication of savings in resources, time and money<br>(e) A closing statement assuming that the prospect is going to purchase<br>(f) Proposed timetable for implementation of solution<br>(g) Supporting documentation, references, appendices, etc | |

colleagues will take place. If these are to be during the quarterly sales meetings, this should be stated.

1.5 is too difficult to measure because it could mean all orders or only the largest orders. There is also reference to an existing company procedure where technical personnel make special visits to prospective buyers of large installations. Where such a procedure exists and takes precedence over any specific objective, it must be detailed in the specification.

2.1 to 2.4 are fairly easy to measure to assess performance.

3.1 should list the publications allocated to a sales person.

3.2 could be improved with the addition of the words 'the same day'.

3.3 makes reference to some existing company procedure and could be improved by stating the main points that have to be covered in the pre-approach procedure so that the individual cases can be assessed.

3.4 presumably relates to very large order prospects because it is unlikely that all prospective customers will merit such attention. This standard could be improved by qualifying prospects into categories that indicate their likely worth to the company.

3.5 means an organisation chart, but does not state whether these are to be prepared for all customers or only the more important.

The remainder are reasonably acceptable but need tidying up here and there, and being made more explicit. The construction of 4.2 is an example of unclear writing which will give rise to confusion later when an assessment of performance is being conducted.

5.1 and 5.2 are in conflict and 5.1 should be deleted, or expanded if it refers to items different from those relating to 5.2.

## If you do it, use it

Some years ago when I was consulting with a company, I learned that they were in the final stages of a comprehensive management-by-objectives exercise which had been occupying them for many months. Although I was not concerned with the exercise, I asked them from time to time how it was developing.

Some eight or nine months later when I enquired, the commercial director, after a moment's puzzlement, said, 'Oh! that. It's all finished. Finished about six months ago. Just a moment, I'll show you'.

He then took a thick loose-leaf volume from the top shelf of a bookcase, removed a little dust from it and, offering it to me, said, 'There it is'.

I don't think anyone had looked at it since it had been completed. The result of many months' work was a large number of job specifications enshrined in a static reference book. It was certainly not being used properly; no one was assessing performances and it was obvious that the company had little understanding of the real value of agreeing and setting standards for people to work with. I asked if they used it and was told that they did when they had to appoint someone to a new position, but not for any assessment purposes.

If you develop a set of job specifications, include only the essentials and make sure that everyone knows how the scheme is to be used. If you include a mass of details rather than the main tasks you will find that your scheme will end up on the top shelf of a bookcase somewhere.

Let your scheme grow from basic sales quotas and expenses and the ways that sales people should work their territories. To attempt to manage everything is to manage nothing. (See also Appendix II.)

# 4

# Recruiting Sales People

Recruiting good sales people is a continuing, difficult task. The need to prepare a profile of the type of person you are seeking. Ten sources of recruitment are described: five from which to maintain a 'possible' list, and five for active search. The important points to look for when interviewing candidates.

## Good sales people are rare

If you place an advertisement in the national press seeking a manager, you will receive scores of applications from managers. If you advertise for a salesman, you will be very fortunate if you get even one, from the many replies you will receive, from a salesman. So runs the old tale. It emphasises the fact that good sales people are difficult to find. Recruiting them is time-consuming and costly. As your success depends largely on the accomplishments of your sales staff, recruiting the right people must be one of your major tasks.

There are two main reasons for having to recruit a sales person: expansion and replacement. The sales organisation will be as good as its staff, the quality of field management, support, training, and motivation. When you subsequently interview applicants, you have to 'sell' the company to them. Have plenty of sound reasons to convince them that yours is a well-organised outfit.

## Expansion or replacement

When recruiting for expansion, the new recruit's territory must be capable of providing the required turnover and profit. Simply thinking that an existing territory is too large and should be split into two, or that because the company is not represented in an area someone should be recruited, are not sound expansion criteria.

Splitting an existing area should be done with the aid of reliable market research and agreement with the person currently covering the territory. Inevitably, that person will view the manoeuvre as a threat, a reduction in status, less earnings and lower potential. It is as important to gain support from the existing sales person as it is to recruit a newcomer.

Recruiting to replace someone who has been promoted can be a positive inducement to potential applicants. If replacement is because you have parted company with the previous sales person, the reasons must be investigated and understood. You must avoid recruiting another who may suffer the same fate; this would reflect on your ability as a manager.

Suppose the previous person had been discharged for failing to meet company standards such as sales quotas; the reasons why must be clear. Perhaps there isn't the potential in the territory, or competition is so firmly entrenched that the quotas were optimistic. There may have been inadequate support or training; the previous person may have needed more guidance and control. To recruit a replacement and find, after a few months, that you have the same situation, is both costly and damaging to the company.

## Benefits of good recruitment

A well-chosen sales force will be more productive than a poorly-chosen one. Do a good job of selecting and recruiting sales people and they will tend to stay with you. People who work a territory for years build up goodwill for the company; they become well-acquainted with their customers' needs and are able to give advice rooted in experience. Customers place a lot of confidence in such people.

A poorly-selected sales force inevitably means a high staff turnover and consequent low morale problems. A procession of new faces in a territory will mean inexperience of product usage, lack of knowledge about customers' requirements, and no real understanding of customers' behaviour.

## Man profile

Whether you select male or female, you need to prepare a 'man profile'. This should evolve logically from the job description and specification (see Chapter 3). Remember, however, that a true job specification is prepared partly from agreement with the job holder and should not be imposed. Some of the points that might be included in the man profile are:

- age range
- experience of products similar to the company's range
- skills and abilities
- education level
- foreign languages
- qualifications
- single or married
- current remuneration level
- appearance
- personal characteristics
- physical condition

These should be listed in terms of what is acceptable and what is preferable, as in Table 4.1. These details will also help in the preparation of the advertisement to appear in the press.

**Table 4.1** *Man profile for sales person*

|  | General | Preferred |
|---|---|---|
| Age | 26-45 | Under 30 |
| Experience | Minimum | 1 to 2 years |
| Skills | — | Ability to read blue-prints |
| Education | Minimum | First degree |
| Foreign languages | — | French or German |
| Qualifications | Minimum | Member of Institute of Sales/ Marketing |
| Single/Married | — | Married with children |
| Remuneration | — | 85% company offer |
| Appearance | Neat/tidy | M: Clean shaven, clean nails, short hair, non-smoker<br>F: Well-groomed, neat, good hands, slim, shortish hair, non-smoker |
| Personal characteristics | — | Well-spoken, well-mannered, pleasant voice, articulate |
| Physical condition | — | Able to carry and handle demonstration kit |

## Sources of recruitment

If you have a very large sales force then there is no best time for recruiting and you should maintain a list of potential sales people. This is particularly important if you have a substantial number of sales women because they are more likely to wish to leave when getting married and having children.

Sources of recruitment can be divided into two groups: sources from which to develop and maintain a list of possibles; sources to use when actively searching for people. Five of each are reviewed.

## Office and factory staff

Not a natural ground for finding good sales people, but you will have had the opportunity of observing their abilities. Frequently, such staff have a biased view of the sales person's job and their enthusiasm is misplaced. If you recruit someone from this source, give the person the opportunity of returning to her or his previous job if the selling job is not what they thought it was. Returning to the old job in this way can be a little demoralising, so therefore consider using such a person on a temporary basis from time to time: if it doesn't work out, that person will not lose face. If you do recruit someone, they are already likely to be well-acquainted with the technical aspects of the product and knowledgeable of company philosophy, policy and procedures.

## Customers

Sometimes, customers get fed up with what they are doing and leave their company to join similar organisations in sales positions. Engineers become sales engineers; designers become graphic arts sales people; computer service men become word processor salesmen; women beauticians become cosmetic saleswomen; barmen join breweries and distillers as salesmen. Such people know their particular industry well. Any customer who appears to be a potential sales person should be on your list.

## Transport and warehouse staff

A fertile source for likely sales candidates, especially transport people. They know the territories, have developed relationships with customers, and tend to like the outdoor work. You should get to know these people and, when a sales position arises, post the details on the appropriate notice boards. A sales position is a promotion for someone working in the transport and warehouse department but you must develop relationships with the managers and supervisors so that they don't hold back possible candidates because they are first-class at their current job. A van driver who becomes a successful salesman must be seen as reflecting credit on the transport manager.

*Other sales people*

Sales people who call on the company are already experienced in selling and buying procedures. Maintain regular contact with your company's buyers and encourage them to let you have details of potential applicants. A professional buyer is in a first-class position to judge the abilities and character of sales people. However, the sales person may have developed a special relationship with one of your buyers and the recommendation may not be as objective as it should. Sales people who openly indicate a desire to leave their current employment should be considered with great care. Appraise the person's company as well as the person. If you find that the company has a suspect reputation in personnel relationships, this would give support to the dissatisfied sales person. If you find otherwise, then you must treat the applicant with some circumspection.

*Competition*

Undoubtedly, sales people with competitors are a useful source, but a question of ethics arises. Attempting to take competitors' best people is not a great deal different from trying to take their best markets and customers. The practice of the former is considered unethical, while the latter is called competition.

If you are about to employ additional sales people you will probably attract applications from competitors' staff and therefore the ethical line may have to be drawn between your approaching a candidate and the candidate approaching you. If you consider that business in general and sales and marketing in particular are a form of warfare, then you may not see any real distinction between a competitor's customers and his employees.

If we forget competitors' sales people who are below average and are simply looking for a 'better job', we can assume that good sales people with competitors are only likely to move because opportunities for greater rewards and promotion exist with another company. But beware of the person who thinks that the quickest way to move up the promotion ladder is by moving from job to job.

## Prospective candidate form

If you are continually taking on sales people, you could consider a more formalised procedure for the development of your list. Encourage the use of a prospective candidate form as illustrated in Figure 4.1. (The abbreviations are 'above average', 'average', and 'below average'). Whoever is suggesting the prospective candidate would complete the form, encircling the appropriate places to indicate an initial assessment.

*Prospective Candidate*

| Name | | | | Date |
|---|---|---|---|---|
| Address | | | | Phone |
| Age group | 20-30 | 31-40 | 41-50 | |
| Appearance | AA | AV | BA | |
| Speech | AA | AV | BA | |
| Manner | AA | AV | BA | |
| How long known | 5+ | 2-5 | −2 | |
| Experience of industry | AA | AV | BA | |
| Remarks: | | | | |
| Suggested by: | | | | |

**Figure 4.1** *Prospective candidate form*

The next five sources of possible recruits are used when you are seeking people to fill a vacancy.

## Educational establishments

Few educational institutions cultivate the idea of salesmanship as a career, despite the fact that every job in a company depends on the company's customers who are sought and serviced by sales personnel. Thus, you will not find many aspiring sales people in schools, colleges and universities, but you will find educated young men and women who can be trained. Develop contacts with teachers, lecturers and tutors to ensure their greater understanding and appreciation of sales and marketing. They might be able to recommend potential candidates. But, unless you cultivate their interest and support, you might receive recommendations of people who are 'not cut out for an ordinary job but might make it in selling'!

You have to sell the selling job. You have to make people aware of the rewards in sales and marketing. Prepare a professional presentation and support it with interesting, informative literature. Educational establishments are not a source of instant sales people but of people who may satisfy future requirements. Successful applicants have to be developed and trained for future sales positions.

## Employment agencies

Whether or not agencies are a useful source of sales people is open to argument. Really dynamic sales people make things happen and do not usually wait for opportunities to arise. On the other hand, a general business recession has disastrous effects on many companies who are forced to scale down their operations and make many otherwise excellent people redundant. Lists of perfectly competent sales people can be obtained from agencies and you should appreciate that some sales people who may be first-class at selling a company's products may be reluctant or unable to sell themselves.

## Trade associations

Every business has one or more associations and institutes devoted to stimulating trade. You and your subordinates should support your association or institute, attend the occasional meeting or function, and keep in touch with its permanent staff. In addition to the occasional introduction to a possible sales recruit, they are an excellent source of industry news and personnel movements.

## Situations wanted

The appropriate columns in national press, trade, technical and professional journals should always be read. Occasionally, sales people seeking greater opportunities will advertise their interest and availability.

## Advertising

While this is the most important source of recruits, it is not a means of getting sales people quickly. It is a lengthy process and needs special consideration. Normally, advertisements produce large numbers of applicants and, although the general quality is low, the cost of reaching likely recruits is also low. The quality of the respondents can be increased by careful media selection and by the information in the ad. If you use a trade or professional journal rather than a national newspaper, this will automatically focus your appeal.

The information you give also acts as a screen and attracts only those applicants who consider they meet the requirements. Perhaps the first important decision is whether or not a company's name is to appear in the ad. There is a tendency for low grade companies to conceal their identities so as to attract respondents who might not bother if they knew the name of the company. Therefore, it is better to name your company and do a good selling job for it in the ad. This means that the emphasis must be on what the company can offer the new recruit as well as on what can be expected in return.

When the national press is used, there is sometimes argument as to which day is best. Some national papers now have a certain day for sales and marketing appointments. This makes your choice easier because likely applicants will be looking at these special editions. Always use the medium where readers are looking for ads rather than have your ads looking for readers.

Another question is the size of the ad. Should it be a classified or display? Consider the type of applicants you are seeking; if you wish to screen them, this can be done with a display ad but is difficult with a classified. If you intend to 'sell' the company and attract really first-class people, this cannot be done adequately with a classified ad. Good sales people looking for posts are interested in joining a good company and will have a hierarchy of ads to which they will write—the best, most impressive and attractive being top of their list.

Don't make the mistake of listing the optimum, or even desirable, qualifications and characteristics looked for in candidates. List the minimum you are prepared to accept. You may be seeking a sales person in the 30-35 age range but willing to employ someone in the 23-48 age group, if otherwise acceptable. If you state the optimum requirements, you may have eliminated some first-class possibilities.

It is best to regard your display ad as if you were selling one of the company's products. Although you are seeking something, you have something to offer, something of considerable value. Sell it well in the ad and be prepared to run the ad over two or three successive weeks to ensure wide readership.

## Application forms

Process applications as they are received. Some you can reject immediately. To these people, write a standard letter thanking them for their interest in the company but saying that there are other applicants whose experience and qualifications more closely match the requirements of the company. This letter must also sell the company as a first-class organisation and not make the applicant feel completely despondent at being turned down so quickly.

To the others, send a formal application form and a personalised letter. Explain that the applicant is being considered further but, in view of the large number of applications, it may take some time to process them. This will give you time to consider all likely applicants.

Start with the assumption that the person you eventually select will decline or will have accepted another offer. Do not turn any possible candidate down until after the selected applicant has accepted.

The application form should be short and used as an initial screening device with the essentials requested: name, age, address, marital status, contact telephone number, current employment, education standard reached, professional qualifications, languages. State clearly that every-

thing is in confidence and no references will be taken up until the applicant has given permission in writing. Do not limit the information asked
for to that required for initial screening because this might be obvious to
an applicant. You should include some questions that are not pertinent
but which will conceal the vital information you are seeking.

For example, you may be looking for a married person over 30 years
old, educated to first degree standard or equivalent, and with at least two
years' experience in the industry. If these are the minimum criteria you
will accept, it is easy to screen applicants with a short application form.
However, you must take care with such minimum requirements. Supposing you received an application form from a divorced man of 28 and not
quite two years' experience in the industry: he might be the very person
you need in the territory.

## Selecting for interview

It should be possible to select candidates for interview from initial application forms. Candidates who are called for a first interview should be
asked to complete a more comprehensive application form, offered an
interview date, informed of the location and given an expenses form to
bring with them. Don't expect applicants to pay their own expenses for
interviews; make it clear exactly what they can claim for.

This leads to the question of where to hold interviews. It is less costly
for company personnel to visit convenient towns and hold local interviews rather than have all initial interviews at one place.

If you have a large organisation with regional or area managers, the
territory executives can carry out the preliminary screening work. A
manager could select a few prospective candidates, any of which he or she
would be prepared to work with. The final decision as to who is appointed
should be yours. But avoid developing a power of veto. This would under-
mine the morale and confidence of the field managers. You may interview
the candidates on your own but the decision as to which person is offered
the job must be taken with the territorial manager under whom the new
recruit will work.

## The interview

All interviews should be structured to obtain certain information. The
structure may be extensively patterned with a complex questionnaire
and spaces to record the applicant's responses and interviewer's opinions. Highly detailed interview forms are normally developed within
individual companies but all follow a similar pattern. In addition to the
main details (education, previous employers, social interests, etc), the

key points usually listed in the screening interview form are personal appearance, physical characteristics, voice, poise, articulation, alertness, personality. These are characteristics that can be observed or brought out in conversation. Usually, they are listed on the left-hand side of the form and each has a set of suggested descriptions and scores. Here are examples taken from one company:

| *Personal appearance* | Untidy | Lack of attention to detail | Neat and clean | Well dressed | Immaculate in dress and person |
|---|---|---|---|---|---|
| | (1-2) | (3-4) | (5-6) | (7-8) | (9-10) |
| *Voice* | Irritating | Thick dialect, difficult to understand | Actor's or announcer's timbre | Clear, easy to under-stand | Compelling, unusual quality |
| | (1-2) | (3-4) | (5-6) | (7-8) | (9-10) |

An interesting point is that, in the five statements for 'voice', this company does not rate an applicant with a voice like a BBC announcer very high. They are in the construction industry and prefer their sales people to have what they describe as an ordinary voice.

A second interview often makes use of a highly patterned form with up to 30 or more key points to be observed or discussed and rated. The scores are added to give an overall rating for the applicant. Some companies use more than one interviewer who, individually, rate the applicants. Candidates who obtain a high total are then short-listed.

In companies where the interview is not highly patterned, the following list of characteristics and qualities includes all that I have seen in their various interview procedures:

| | |
|---|---|
| 1. Appearance | 11. Enthusiasm |
| 2. Handshake | 12. Numeracy |
| 3. Courtesy | 13. Flexibility |
| 4. Friendliness | 14. Health (smoker?) |
| 5. Poise | 15. Knowledge |
| 6. Speech | 16. Originality |
| 7. Self-control | 17. Persuasiveness |
| 8. Handwriting | 18. Mental alertness |
| 9. Ambition | 19. Interest in job |
| 10. Curiosity | 20. Self-starter |

During the interview there is no formal scoring but the first eight are observed or easily extracted. Such qualities as numeracy, knowledge, mental alertness and flexibility cannot be determined by simple questions, and more searching ones need to be prepared before the interview. One company introduces a new product during the interview, the use of which is deliberately obscure. The interviewer hands it to the applicant and asks, 'What do you think this would sell for?'.

The usual response is, 'What is it?', to which the reply is, 'Have a guess, but how much would you think it would sell for?'.

Applicants are reluctant to state a price without knowing its use but their responses help the interviewer to appraise their curiosity, flexibility, originality and mental alertness. This company explores candidates' ability to handle figures by having the interviewer say, 'Actually, it's not one of our products but we have been considering it. It's a control device and should sell for about 500 pounds,' adding, disarmingly, 'If you had to carry this line, how many would you need to sell a year to cover your salary of, say, (naming a figure)?'.

The replies indicate whether the applicant is able to think in figures, realises that profit is important and suggests a profit figure, and is able to calculate a simple sum.

Interviews must be conducted so that candidates are not exposed to each other and, as you are 'selling' the company and the job, you should be thoroughly equipped and be seen to be well-organised. You will need to have your interview schedule, watch, candidate's application forms, copy of the advertisement, interviewer guide or questionnaires, map of the vacant territory, company literature, a sales kit if appropriate, and samples or photographs of the product.

## Short-listing

Candidates who are potential employees are short-listed and notified as soon as possible. You should give a date to all candidates by which time they will have heard from you. People who are short-listed must be progressed quickly and invited for further interview. Once the decision has been taken to offer a job to a candidate, this must be put in writing. Only when it has been accepted in writing, references taken up, and perhaps even the candidate reported for duty, should you notify the unsuccessful candidates. You could also ask them whether they would be interested in joining the company when future posts are being considered.

## References

During the interview you should confirm to the candidates that no references will be taken up until their permission has been given. This should be obtained in writing. Seldom, if ever, will you receive an adverse reference from a referee. First, the candidate will offer only referees who will provide a good reference. Second, referees are unlikely to write anything detrimental to a person; it is often necessary to 'read between the lines'. Telephone references to previous employers are very useful because the tone of the voice of the referee often reveals more than what is said about the candidate. Of the various telephone reference lists used by companies, the following points are the most common.

Talk only to the referee; introduce yourself, your company, and the reason for phoning; and find out: dates of employment; nature of job; approximate remuneration; opinion of supervisors and managers; reasons for leaving; strong points; weak points; whether applicant would be rehired.

Selecting new sales and marketing people is a very rewarding but difficult task. It is much easier to measure people once they are working than to select them, but the costs of doing this are often very high.

# 5

# Training the Sales Force

Sales people need education and training; often, they can contribute to the analysis of their own needs. It is important to establish objectives before training is undertaken, and the results should be monitored on the job. Advice is given on programme content and structure, and a number of tips are described, including how to use the expert, but boring, speaker.

## Education and training

There is often confusion between the meanings of education and training. The difference can be better understood from the suggestion that you wouldn't mind a daughter of yours receiving sex education, but you would certainly object to her having sex training! Sales people need both education and training.

No sales person can hope to sell successfully without possessing a good knowledge of the product and its uses. This requires product education and training: education about the origin of the product, its constituents or components, how and where it is made, how it compares with similar products and its various applications; training in the use of the product to achieve a skill in handling and manipulating it.

Sales training is not just a combination of product knowledge and selling techniques; there are many different selling situations, each requiring a different set of skills. The job of the sales person must be analysed before an adequate training programme can be devised.

## Selling situations

At one extreme in selling, the sales person calls on small shopkeepers and takes regular orders for goods that are frequently purchased by the shopkeepers' customers. New lines and special offers are introduced from time to time.

At the other extreme, the sales person has an initial discussion with a company executive; a further meeting with, perhaps, two or three other specialists in the company; makes an appointment for an initial demonstration at the company's premises; arranges a visit for them to see the product being assembled or otherwise developed at the factory; and subsequently, makes a presentation, which might include a comprehensive financing package, to the company's board of directors.

No amount of training in closing techniques is likely to be of much use to the second sales person, and training the first one in contribution analysis or discounted cash flow is not going to increase the size of the order from the shopkeeper. Develop all training from an analysis of the job and the person doing the job.

## Responsibility for training

Training is a line management responsibility and although you, as sales manager, cannot be expected to carry out the training personally, you are responsible for the performance of the sales organisation.

While you will need to delegate the task of training to others, you must retain an active interest in the content of the programmes, the training methods and, most important and most difficult, implementation. What is learned in training should be used in actual selling situations, otherwise there is little point in training people. All training should therefore be related to the job specifications of the sales people and, ideally, you should maintain a continuous analysis of training needs for each person. This will not only highlight the areas for individual training, but will ensure that the performance of sales people is regularly monitored.

## Sales skills survey

You can also encourage your sales people to contribute to their own training programmes. Figure 5.1 is a basic skills analysis form used by one company to survey these needs.

## Programme content

If you maintain an ongoing survey of training needs, evaluate the overall performance of the sales organisation, and study territorial managers' reports, you will get to know what type of training is required. It is not a one-off activity, but a continuous process that reflects changing markets

---

*Sales skills survey*

Over the next year we will be running several training courses. Please indicate the subjects in which you consider you would like to have further training and dates when you are not available.

( )   1. Prospecting
( )   2. Pre-approach
( )   3. Approach
( )   4. Presentations
( )   5. Demonstrations
( )   6. Dealing with objections
( )   7. Closing
( )   8. Report writing
( )   9. Analysing customer potential
( ) 10. After-sales service
( ) 11. Territory planning and management
( ) 12. Letter writing

Other subjects:

Preferred months:

Dates not available:

---

**Figure 5.1** *Basic skills analysis form*

and product development. New staff will always require courses in product knowledge and company procedures. Depending on their experience, they may need training in selling techniques. External, open courses on basic techniques are ideal for new, inexperienced sales people. From time to time, more advanced external courses help to keep experienced sales people in touch with any new selling techniques and other companies' activities, and to 'recharge their batteries'.

# Training objectives

Agree with the trainers the objectives to be achieved for training. These should be 'enabling' objectives: each is assumed to be prefaced with the words 'After attending this course, participants will be able to...'. This requires that all objectives must be specific, attainable, and able to be measured. Here are some examples of enabling objectives.

After attending the course participants will be able to:

● analyse their sales territory, identify prospective customers, classify them into potential grades

- establish a call plan to visit them during the next six months
- present the new product to customers and demonstrate its uses

Course assessments should be linked with the objectives. This can be done immediately at the end of the course and later when assessing the degree of implementation on the actual job. Participants are not necessarily the best judges of course content and their comments should always be subject to qualification. They often need injections of training which they don't enjoy. Compare this with the man about to visit the tropics who suffers misery for two days after essential inoculations. He doesn't want them, but he certainly needs them!

## Training methods

The real test of training is the extent to which the subject matter is implemented in real life. If the content is not applied to the job, it may not be appropriate or the methods of training may be inadequate. Always monitor the performance of your sales force after training sessions; ideally, this monitoring should form part of the training.

You cannot actually teach anyone to do anything; you can only create the conditions in which they learn. Training requires a great deal of professional skill and experience. The best method has three main steps: teach, try, test.

*Teach* by preparing the candidates with suitable preamble to receive the new material. Present and illustrate the new material; demonstrate it; discuss it to make sure that it is understood.

*Try* the new learning under controlled conditions or under supervision. Does it work? Does it need to be modified to suit the candidate? Are the trainees able to handle it? Role playing is one way of trying out new skills.

*Test* what has been learned in the market place and monitor over a period to see whether it is being used effectively.

Teach, try, test. This three-step method is simple but comprehensive and virtually fool-proof.

Over the years, I have developed a number of things that help people to learn: not only in sales training but in all training. I have taught many of my own staff and several thousands of others the arts and crafts of business. This has been face-to-face and in writing. The points and hints that follow are based on this experience.

## Learning

Learning is an individual assimilation process that normally proceeds at the trainee's own rate. It can be speeded up with the application of pressure, but the number of failures tend to correlate with the degree of pressure applied. If you need trained people fast, then exert pressure and be satisfied with the survival of the fittest. But, you may not get the best. The people who always have the highest marks, who are always in 'the first twenty', may not be as good, in the long run, as those in 'the second twenty'. Learning is not as easy for this second group; they have to work for success and this stimulation tends to stay with them as a habit. Second-twenty groups usually contain the people with the facility to stick at a job to see it through.

Of the various learning situations—lectures, individual exercises, small group work, open-ended plenary discussions, cases, demonstrations, films, etc—the best learning situation is small group work. Small groups, called syndicates, work on a problem that is concise and devoid of unessential things, but is capable of being analysed quantitatively and qualitatively. The learning environment is excellent: there is a more intimate atmosphere in discussions between four, five or six people than in the large plenary sessions; syndicates are able to adjust their rate of discussion; there is strong group loyalty and a highly developed sense of competition with other syndicates. Individuals who are reticent to say anything in plenary session speak more readily in small groups. Those quick at quantitative analysis have to explain their calculations to other syndicate members, and this, in itself, is good training.

Presentations are made by the syndicates in plenary session and defended against criticism and attack from other syndicates. Spokesmen are chosen by the groups and even the most reluctant are usually encouraged to make a presentation before the end of the course.

There must be a minimum of 'number crunching' and participants must not spend too large a proportion of their time calculating. If the calculations and analyses would normally be available in real life, they should be supplied. Such calculating should only be introduced if it is part of the learning process. For example, to illustrate the work of cost accountants and their value to sales and marketing people, I frequently use an exercise that requires delegates to apportion overhead costs in different ways to three products. They have to decide what prices they would set for each of the three products and these, of course, will vary considerably depending on the method they choose to recover overheads.

## Syndicate presentations

When syndicates make their presentations in plenary session they seldom win support from other syndicates unless there is a large area of mutual agreement. There is a strong entrenchment of opinions. Attempts by syndicates to persuade others to agree with their views, which are different, always fail.

If one of the objectives of sales training is to develop a consensus of opinion on certain actions, syndicate work appears to run counter to this and creates more dissension than agreement.

I have overcome this in a number of ways. First, I do not allow discussion of each presentation as it is made, but only questions that seek elucidation such as, 'Did you say that all sales staff would carry the new product?' or, 'Is the profit projection before, or after, tax?' or, 'Is it Mr Brown or Mr Green who is appointed?'. I restrict answers by delegates to those that relate to specific points in their presentations to remove doubt as to what was said, and to these questions the answers could be, 'I didn't say', or, respectively, 'yes', 'before tax', and, 'Mr Green'. If the questioner persists and tries to follow with further points, I intervene and disallow discussion at that stage. If discussion were permitted after the first presentation, many points that might be made by other syndicates could be explored and the impact of their presentations reduced.

If you chair a training session with syndicate presentations, before the syndicates start, announce that there will be no general discussion until after all the presentations. Only permit questions of fact to clear up any misunderstanding or clarify a point; tell them to take notes for the subsequent discussion.

Sometimes, after all the presentations have been made and before the general discussion, I ask each syndicate to tell me what were the main points made by another syndicate, and give them a couple of minutes or so to decide. This is an excellent way of ensuring their attention in future presentations and it is not unusual, the first time I do this, for a syndicate to admit that they were not listening properly. Occasionally, a personality will emerge and the person is able to respond elegantly and eloquently. Such people should be watched as possible suitable material for development in the company.

A variation is to ask each syndicate in turn what they liked most about the presentation of another syndicate. These ploys can only be done once or twice on the same course but are helpful in making people listen.

Another useful exercise is to ask all syndicates to decide on a product they would like to market and give them wide scope in their choice of a product: industrial or consumer; company or non-company; serious or amusing. For each syndicate, another syndicate is nominated as their marketing team. The client syndicate has to brief its marketing team on the product, the production capabilities, costs, and any other relevant details. I stress that they must have adequate knowledge of the chosen product so that they can brief their marketing team thoroughly. Company products are not often chosen but serious products are often selected because someone in the syndicate has a good knowledge of that product. Amusing products are favourites; the briefing takes longer because various fictitious production rates and costs have to be devised by the client syndicate.

The list of lighthearted products I have heard is very long. Some of the more notable were: electronic cockroach catcher, electronic cuff links, various sexual aids, a device for changing the channel when the TV adverts appeared, many automatic gadgets operated by heat, light, rain or sun, plastic coffins, electric mouse and rat trap, and a doggy pooper-scooper for people walking their dogs to keep the pavements clear. Although much mirth was extracted during these sessions, the ease with which syndicates applied sales and marketing techniques, some un-known by them previous to the course, was remarkable.

This project is only really feasible with courses of a week or more because about four days is necessary for the briefing and preparation, much of which is done in delegates' free time.

Before the marketing teams start their presentations to the clients, I nominate a third syndicate to each as the advertising agency. Based on what they hear from the marketing presentation, they have to present an advertising plan to the client and its marketing team the following day.

## Programmed lectures

Programmed lectures are much more interesting and instructive than ordinary lectures. They are based on specially prepared texts that have blanks and spaces to be filled in by delegates during the presentation and discussion. By carefully organising the blanks, omitting various figures and explanations, the interest and learning of the delegates can be controlled and considerably extended. It also helps to get over the problem of 'switching off'.

People switch off quite normally for two reasons: they are bored or interested. When the presentation is dull, switching off soon starts with people thinking about other things. If the presentation is stimulating, people switch off because they start to think about applying what they are hearing to real life.

## Timing

Timing is very important in training. Participants must know the starting and finishing times of all sessions. Don't let them sit in chairs all day. Give them plenty of movement. I work to 1½-hour periods throughout the day, leaving the evenings for syndicate work: 0900-1030; 1100-1230; lunch; 1400-1530; 1600-1730. The morning and afternoon breaks are important for personal reasons, refreshment, and the inevitable dis-cussions.

Sometimes it is necessary to extend the afternoon session beyond 1730, but always get agreement from the group. This strict adherence to start and stop times is also appreciated by the catering staff.

If you have a visiting speaker, ensure that he or she knows the time the session is due to stop. If the speaker is important enough, or the content of the input is particularly relevant to the group, the session should be at the end of the day so that over-running is not so disruptive.

It could be argued that over-running is poor speaking or organising. However, groups vary so much that the same speaker on the same topic can have totally different receptions. One group will wish to prolong the session with point after point, all pertinent to the job; another group will quite happily break up at the appointed time.

Ensure that the day is controlled and not allowed to get out of hand with subjects not covered and everyone being continually pressed for time. Leave adequate time for questions and discussions after every presentation.

## How to use the boring expert

Inevitably you will be using experts in the company on training courses. Sometimes these experts can be very entertaining and informative; often they can be dull and boring. Listening to one mediocre presentation after another is extremely tedious for participants. When you know your experts, you can arrange the programme so that a poor but important speaker is sandwiched between more interesting events.

A method I use with some experts who are unable to give interesting presentations is to get them to prepare a paper on their topic, raising relevant questions if appropriate. This paper is circulated to delegates before the course, with a note telling them to read it prior to the session, at which questions will be dealt with. When the expert appears, all that he or she has to do is to answer questions from the delegates. It is remarkable how an expert can answer questions in a reasonably interesting way but be unable to make a good presentation. You should take the chair at these sessions and start by putting a question first; you should also seed three or four questions in the group.

## Continuity

The course should be structured so that there is continuity throughout its whole length; each day linked with the next. In general, the inputs during the day are used as a basis for syndicate work on cases and exercises in the evenings. Syndicates should not be expected to work into the small hours but they should have their presentations ready at the appointed time. How and when the work is done is a syndicate matter.

Distribute as much of the course material as possible on the first day. Every hand-out should be numbered and delegates given an index of hand-outs and a programme of what hand-outs will be used when. While the hand-outs can be filed numerically in a loose-leaf binder, they do not have to be used in numerical order. Only the index and the programme need to be updated in order to maintain this flexibility.

Avoid having a course with a series of people giving lectures and presentations one after another. I call these 'briefcase lectures': a succession of people appear before a group, open their briefcases, take out their notes, talk for their allotted period, answer questions and leave, never to be seen again. This is not training but dissemination of knowledge and experience.

## A syndicate exercise

A useful day can be developed with the following exercise. Divide the delegates into syndicates of four or five and give each syndicate a large flip chart and a thick, black felt-tipped pen. (A minor, but important point: use thick black felt-tipped pens and not thin ones. These invite small writing which makes for poor presentation to those at the back of the room.) Give them an hour and a half to answer the question: 'Why do our customers buy from us?'. After a break, syndicates make their presentations, which are summarised and collated into one set of reasons.

After lunch, the same syndicates are asked to answer the question: 'Why do customers buy from our competitors?'. Again, there is a collation of responses and conclusions. The plenary session will then attempt to agree what action is to be taken.

## Role of chairman or tutor

A chairman, or tutor, has an important role in most training courses. This person, who may also lecture, acts as a unifying presence. Each day is evaluated and the relevance of the input related to delegates' jobs; any specific points that may not have been adequately covered are highlighted; any areas required by the delegates are explored; each day is rounded off with a general discussion; finally, the whole course is assessed and any implementation required, agreed.

## Course structure

For courses with a high training content, it is useful to have two themes running through the courses: from morning to evening the subject matter varies from general to specific; from the first day to the last, the content is from simple to more complex. Thus, starting on the first day, the topics are general and simple; towards the end of the last day, the topics have become complex and particularly relevant to the delegates' work.

Do not have too many delegates on a training course and, in general, the more advanced the course, the smaller the number of participants. For advanced work, keep the number to a maximum of 12, subdividing them into four syndicates. If the work is involved, a maximum of nine, subdivided into three groups. For advanced work, I often work with four to six people.

Basic selling courses can have 20 or more people but, if there is a good deal of participation—as there should be—20 is too large. With highly participative courses such as developing executives' presentation skills, I limit the number to nine and run the course over four days. Each member is then able to make at least six presentations which are videoed, viewed and analysed during the course and again subsequently.

There will always be exceptions and you must learn to adjust to situations. When I travel to India, the Far East and beyond, I frequently have to run high-level courses for 30 or more and for up to three weeks.

## Room layout

Arrange the training room with delegates' tables in a horseshoe shape. Allocate members to syndicates and get them to sit in their syndicates round the room. Allow space between each group of two or three tables containing the syndicates. Thus, if you have 16 delegates divided into four syndicates, each group of four would sit at two tables with space between them and the next syndicate. It gives the room a much more open appearance than if the tables are set in a solid 'U' shape. It enables you to walk round each syndicate and avoids making the room look like an arena.

Do not have plastic-covered chairs: they cause undesirable personal discomfort; insist on firm, fabric-covered chairs. Smoking should not be permitted and 'no smoking' notices prominently displayed. No phone calls should be permitted unless there is an emergency.

## Presentations

Syndicate presentations are exercises in themselves. Ask them to adopt the following five-point plan:

- what is being proposed
- where it will take place
- when it will happen

- costs of the proposal
- benefits, cash and non-cash

It may be necessary to add a couple of supplementary points such as, who will do what is being proposed, and how it will be done. The important advice is to keep the presentations simple and communicable. All too often I hear presentations, sometimes in real-life job situations, that are unstructured and vague. If necessary, these five points can be reduced to three:

- What are you suggesting we do?
- How much will it cost?
- How soon before we get our money back?

# 6

# Remuneration and Incentives

It is important to construct a remuneration package that provides adequate finance for sales people, and rewards effort. Examples of good and poor use of a commission scheme are illustrated.

## Two main aims

Your sales organisation has two main aims: to find customers and to service customers. However, these two broad aims conceal a number of different and separate activities. Finding customers can be as simple as 'calling on every shop in the village', or as complex as developing a series of negotiations with different people in an organisation over a period of many months, with the possibility of landing business in a year or two.

If you join a company as head of their existing sales organisation, you will probably inherit a compensation plan. The costs of maintaining a sales force are so great that control is vital and, if you are to achieve the profit objectives for the company, you will need to look very closely at the existing scheme. Broad calculations should convince you of the importance of this advice.

## Break even

The annual cost of a good sales person for personal remuneration, car, travelling, hotel and other expenses, head-office and, perhaps, regional supervision, social security and insurance payments, sales aids, etc, is many thousands of pounds. If your company operates on, say, 5 per cent net profit then, to break even on the cost of a sales person requires twenty times his or her cost. Table 6.1 gives some of the annual sales necessary to break even on the annual cost of the sales organisation at various net profit percentages. From this table you can see that if your company is working on an average of, say, 15 per cent profit, to pay for a sales organisation that costs £75,000 a year requires an annual turnover of £500,000.

Table 6.1 *Turnover required to meet annual cost of sales force*

| | Annual cost of sales force (£) | | | | |
|---|---|---|---|---|---|
| Profit | 20,000 | 50,000 | 75,000 | 100,000 | 300,000 |
| 5% | 400,000 | 1,000,000 | 1,500,000 | 2,000,000 | 6,000,000 |
| 10% | 200,000 | 500,000 | 750,000 | 1,000,000 | 3,000,000 |
| 15% | 133,333 | 333,333 | 500,000 | 666,667 | 2,000,000 |
| 20% | 100,000 | 250,000 | 375,000 | 500,000 | 1,500,000 |

You can calculate your own company's break-even figure for the cost of the sales force by dividing 100 by your average profit percentage, and multiplying this by the annual cost of the sales organisation. For example, if your company is making an average 8 per cent profit, and the sales organisation costs £750,000 a year, you need an annual turnover of £9,375,000 to pay for the sales organisation: $(100/8) \times 750,000$.

## Five long-term objectives

A good remuneration and incentive scheme will achieve the following five basic objectives:

- attract competent sales people
- retain profitable sales people
- facilitate management control
- stimulate selling efforts
- ensure adequate customer servicing

### Attracting good sales people

Companies develop reputations as employers for being good or poor payers. If you want to attract the best recruits you must have an attractive compensation scheme. Inherent in any scheme is the starting salary, which should compare at least equally with the starting income for similar jobs in other companies.

## Retaining good people

Often, the value of a good sales person is not realised until that person submits a letter of resignation. All companies experience this situation: a new person is trained and developed to a level of profitable activity and is then attracted to another company. The cost in time, effort and money to recruit and train a replacement is great indeed.

The sales person with several years of practical experience of your company, its products and customers, is very valuable. Because of this experience, such a person is also of value to competitors who may be willing to offer a more attractive compensation package for their services. As your sales people become proficient and effective in achieving profitable sales, this should be reflected in the overall compensation plan. If you wish to retain good sales people you must create a situation that makes an offer from a competitor for your good people less attractive.

## Facilitate management control

If you fail to construct the compensation plan with possible future developments taken into consideration, you may lose control of it when unexpectedly large orders arise. I used to be with a large group when terms of employment were not as regulated as they are today, and the compensation plan for our export sales manager included a modest percentage commission on sales. He landed an order from a mining group in Belgium which entitled him to a commission of over five times his annual salary. Such a possibility had not been foreseen and, after an appropriate discussion with the tough but short-sighted chairman, the export manager reluctantly agreed a lower commission rate and received a much reduced sum. Within six months, he landed a huge order from Poland and, even on the lower commission rate, was entitled to a commission of over 17 times his annual salary!

Needless to say, such were employment conditions at the time, he had another discussion with the chairman on the 'folly' of having such a large commission payment, and settled for a greatly reduced amount. These incidents, the products of badly constructed compensation schemes, became widely known at the time and created a poor image for the company as employers. These were also crucial factors that subsequently made it difficult to obtain good people.

With current employment legislation such events are probably not possible but the remuneration scheme you devise for your organisation should allow for considerable turnover growth and, at the same time, be controllable. It is very easy at the start of a selling operation to fail to appreciate the extent to which turnover could develop.

For example, a salesman opens an account with a chain of retail outlets and succeeds in selling a product to the first half-dozen or so. What is the position when all 2,000 branches start to order? Does he get commission on all 2,000? Unless the compensation package allows for such possibilities the situation becomes out of control. Compensation limits should be agreed and the package flexible so that you can direct your fire power in whatever direction is necessary to maintain or increase profitable sales without such embarrassing pay situations arising.

## Stimulate selling efforts

No sales person starts work at nine every morning and continues with the same effort throughout the day until five o'clock, week after week throughout the year. This is not possible physically or psychologically. People work in waves of effort: a moderate, normal rate with occasional bursts of high activity.

Your compensation package should recognise this wave pattern and provide for the extra efforts needed from time to time to accomplish specific objectives. If you do not have a commission scheme, you should consider a system of bonuses to reward extra efforts. Relate such rewards to gross profit and not to sales volume or turnover, otherwise you may find that the stimulated effort produces higher turnover but lower profits.

## Ensure adequate customer servicing

Make it easy for customers to repeat their purchases from you. This means, link one sale with another by the standard of your service. To sell a product to a customer and receive payment is not enough. You must ensure that the customer receives what they paid for—satisfaction in using the product. No one buys a product for itself alone but for the satisfaction and service it provides.

Pay your sales force for keeping your customers happy. Include in the compensation scheme rewards for a sales person helping a customer, such as by making an urgent delivery to one of their customers; by holding a special training session for the customers' sales people; by setting up a special display at the customer's exhibition stand, and so on.

# Short-term objectives

To achieve the long-term objectives you need a two-part compensation package. The major portion is fixed and the other portion permits flexibility and enables you to redirect your sales efforts from time to time.

Although there is no limit to the number of short-term objectives that could be devised, if you have too many they will prove to be counter-productive. Keep your compensation package as simple as possible. As soon as you announce it, members of the sales organisation will automatically be calculating 'what's in it for me?'. This is a normal reaction.

Time your new compensation package to arrive at every sales person's home on a Saturday morning and you will make (or ruin) their weekend. Here are three fixed, and five variable suggestions you could include in your scheme.

## Sell the range

Most companies have hundreds of items in their product range. Profit percentages are obviously not the same on every item and some are purchased in greater quantities than others. To encourage sales of all products right across the range, the compensation packages should include some differential but fixed bonuses on certain products.

## Exceeding quota

Make sure that the sales quotas are fair, realistic and attainable with sustained effort. Reward sales in excess of quota with a controllable percentage commission or bonus. If you are worried about sales people earning more in commission than anyone else in the company, allow for the possibility of the quota being greatly exceeded, such as with an unexpectedly large order, by limiting commission to an upper figure. Another approach is to exclude large, one-off orders from this scheme and agree special commission terms for very large orders.

## Reducing expenses

Always reward sales people who work their territory and service customers at lower than budgeted expenses. But you cannot expect a sales person to reduce expenses every year and you must safeguard the quality of customer servicing. Don't introduce a scheme for rewarding lower sales expenses by creating a disinclination in your sales people to travel, and preference for phoning customers instead. Face-to-face sales presentations are vitally important.

Compare the travelling costs of sales people in comparable areas and try to establish an average cost per customer, cost per order, and so on. By doing this, you will have a guide to the average cost of servicing customers. You then agree an expenses level with individual sales people and pass on a proportion of the saving to them.

*Profitable accounts*

Some accounts will be highly profitable to your company. If the sales person increases sales to these or increases the actual number of strong accounts, he or she should receive extra bonus. Also, if you have a variety of products, it is possible that some of your sales people sell the least profitable but easiest to sell. Reward sales of products that improve gross profits.

*Unprofitable accounts*

From time to time, accounts become unprofitable because they order in too small a quantity, buy an inadequate amount per year, or even buy only those products with a small return to your company. Agree with the sales person concerned how to increase the profitability of these accounts or whether they should be dropped from the live list. Any reduction of such unprofitable accounts should win the sales person a reward.

*Opening new accounts*

The reward you give to sales people opening new accounts should be related to the average numbers of new accounts opened previously.

*Resurrecting accounts*

If an account has been dormant for a period of, say, a year, you should reward its resurrection.

*New products*

Introducing new products to customers takes more time and effort than selling products that customers know. Agree a percentage of sales volume or value to be achieved in the territory with new products and reward accordingly.

## Three basic compensation schemes

There are three basic ways to compensate sales people: salary, commission, or a combination of both. You also need to consider payment of expenses. This can be as incurred, or at a fixed rate, and can be in the form of a 'float', or paid in arrears. In addition to remuneration and expenses, peripheral benefits can be organised.

# Salary

A good basic salary is essential to obtain sales people who will adequately service your company's customers according to the job specification. It is easier to move salaried sales people from one area to another, and to grade salaries to reward long service. Your salaried sales people also have a better sense of security.

You must consider the nature of the job and the product before you decide on a salary-only system. If the product is highly competitive and is frequently purchased by customers, then salary-only will probably only work if your product is very heavily advertised. The task of the sales person then is not so much to achieve high sales as to service the customers: to ensure that they are making the most of the national advertising and promotional aids.

If the product is highly competitive but is such that it cannot be supported by heavy national advertising, then salary-only is unlikely to work. Similarly, if the product is unknown, then paying sales people a salary only is unlikely to stimulate sales.

You must balance the needs of the company with the needs of the sales people. If you want to employ and retain good people, you must pay them a wage that takes care of their main financial obligations—house, insurance, food, clothing, illness, etc. You must pay them to service the company's customers who are the only people who supply profit.

Nevertheless, it is important to agree with each sales person the amount of business that has to be obtained to justify the salary being paid. This should be on an annual basis and broken down into months or weeks. No one should be allowed to fail to achieve the expected results continuously; this creates severe morale problems and, ultimately, the person is discharged for not turning in the required sales. Selling is a partnership between you and your field sales people; if they fail, you are also failing.

This obviously requires you to allow for new people to build their sales gradually over the months during which they are not going to be profitable to the company. You can see the stupidity of engaging a succession of sales people and getting rid of them because they fail to achieve results. You would never achieve results this way and, before long, it would be you who was required to leave the company.

Generally, a salary-only scheme is best used when you have a well-balanced sales job and adequate daily or weekly supervision is possible. Some of the situations are:

- Newly recruited sales people in training, who cannot sell sufficient to be profitable to the company.
- A sale is an involved or complex operation over many months.

- Several sales people are required to negotiate the sale of a product over a long period.
- Orders are not usually achieved and the main activity is promotional or missionary.
- The job entails close working with middlemen whose staff may need to be trained, or displays have to be supervised.
- A new territory is being developed.
- New products are being introduced and demonstrated to possible dealers and customers.

In particular, all new sales people need to be treated like newly planted shrubs and trees. They must be put into good soil, supported with stakes, protected from the elements and pests, fertilised, and carried until they start to flower or bear fruit.

## Commission

There are three main factors: a base on which performance is measured and payment is made; a rate of payment for each unit of sale; a level of sales at which payment starts.

The base is either sales value or sales volume. The commission rate can be a regular payment for each unit of sale or a percentage of turnover. The level at which commission is paid is immediately sales are achieved if the scheme is commission-only, or at an agreed level if there is provision for advances against future earnings. Apart from these, there are no rules that govern the payment of commissions to sales people; each company establishes its own scheme and, generally, this reflects the policy of the industry in which the company is engaged. It is quite common for certain products offered to householders on a door-to-door basis to be sold for commission-only; the sales person only receives payment if a sale is made.

If you engage sales people and only pay commission on sales made, it is obvious that after a few weeks, if no sales are made, you are making no profit and the sales person probably has other lines which produce money.

Normally, a commission-only scheme requires that a much higher rate of commission is paid for sales and this can be as high as a third of the price or more. Some situations where you might consider a straight commission scheme are those where:

- part-time sales people are used
- commission-only is the norm in the industry
- adequate field supervision is not possible

- the company has insufficient finances to fund a sales force
- great incentives are needed to sell the product

## Commission base

Most bases relate to turnover or to number of units, but profits may also be used as a base. The main disadvantage of using profit as a base is that the company can change the rules and deflate the profits to the detriment of the sales person. Sometimes the net sales of a group of sales people is used as a base, or the number of sales of a limited product line, or to a certain class of customer.

If it is possible to agree gross margins for a product over a specific period, it is possible to use gross margin, or gross margin less sales expenses, as a base for paying commission. This encourages attention to expenses by the sales people.

## Commission rate

Base the rate of commission on such factors as profitability of the product, difficulty in selling, likely number of sales, classes of customers, location of customers, potential development of turnover.

Rates may be uniform over all levels of sales volume, or on a sliding scale going upwards or downwards as turnover increases. Some companies combine commission scales, having the rate increasing, or progressing, to a certain level of sales, then decreasing, or regressing, after that point. If they are uniform, the sales person is paid the same rate if 100 or 100,000 are sold. The scheme of commission rates is very important: you must calculate all possible 'what if' situations for products.

Generally, calculate commissions on a cumulative basis. If you have agreed a sales quota for the year with a sales person, this should be broken down into monthly or weekly figures that will conform with the seasonality of sales. Then, establish the cumulative sales to be achieved by each quarter, month or week and calculate the cumulative commission payable. Commission already paid is deducted from the cumulative figure, and the balance paid.

## Starting point for payment

This may be the first unit of sales or after a quota of sales has been achieved. Quotas are calculated annually and are often the cause of disagreement and creation of poor morale. It is not unknown for quotas to be increased by a fixed percentage every year, and I once worked for a very well-known company who also adjusted the annual quotas for increased costs. This meant that it was almost impossible to achieve sales figures that provided incentive commissions.

Whichever method you choose for your organisation, ensure that the commission terms are clearly written and understood; calculate various likely and unlikely sales figures to see the effect of your scheme.

To illustrate some of the difficulties, suppose that in two territories you had established sales quotas of £200,000 and £211,000 and 1 per cent commission was paid on sales over quota. The first territory achieves a turnover of £233,000 and the second, £212,000; commissions of £330 and £10 would be paid. If commission is paid as it is apparently earned, over-payments will result. The calculation for the first is shown in Table 6.2.

**Table 6.2** *Calculation of commission on sales over quota[1]*

|  | Monthly Quota (£) | Sales (£) | Commission payable on (£) | 1% Commission (£) |
|---|---|---|---|---|
| Jan | 10,000 | 12,000 | 2,000 | 20 |
| Feb | 12,000 | 14,000 | 2,000 | 20 |
| Mar | 14,000 | 15,000 | 1,000 | 10 |
| Apl | 18,000 | 19,000 | 1,000 | 10 |
| May | 20,000 | 21,000 | 1,000 | 10 |
| Jun | 21,000 | 22,000 | 1,000 | 10 |
| Jul | 22,000 | 24,000 | 2,000 | 20 |
| Aug | 20,000 | 22,000 | 2,000 | 20 |
| Sep | 20,000 | 24,000 | 4,000 | 40 |
| Oct | 18,000 | 22,000 | 4,000 | 40 |
| Nov | 15,000 | 20,000 | 5,000 | 50 |
| Dec | 10,000 | 18,000 | 8,000 | 80 |
| Totals | 200,000 | 233,000 |  | 330 |

Everything appears to be in order but you may be questioned by the board about the high commissions paid in the last three months of the year and why the quotas are apparently set low. The calculation for the second territory, illustrating over-payments is shown in Table 6.3. Over the year, sales have only been £1,000 over quota and £10 would have been payable. The monthly calculation ignores the months where sales were below quota. Commission should always be calculated on a cumulative basis as illustrated in Table 6.4. However, the problem has still not been overcome. Commission might be paid on the maximum exceeded during the first quarter—£2,000—and, in the second quarter, on a further £1,000 because cumulative sales have exceeded cumulative quota by a total of £3,000.

**Table 6.3** *Calculation of commission on sales over quota*[2]

|  | Monthly Quota (£) | Sales (£) | Commission payable on (£) | 1% Commission (£) |
|---|---|---|---|---|
| Jan | 10,000 | 12,000 | 2,000 | 20 |
| Feb | 12,000 | 11,000 | — |  |
| Mar | 14,000 | 15,000 | 1,000 | 10 |
| Apl | 18,000 | 17,000 | — |  |
| May | 20,000 | 21,000 | 1,000 | 10 |
| Jun | 22,000 | 23,000 | 1,000 | 10 |
| Jul | 24,000 | 22,000 | — |  |
| Aug | 23,000 | 21,000 | — |  |
| Sep | 22,000 | 21,000 | — |  |
| Oct | 20,000 | 21,000 | 1,000 | 10 |
| Nov | 15,000 | 16,000 | 1,000 | 10 |
| Dec | 11,000 | 12,000 | 1,000 | 10 |
| Totals | 211,000 | 212,000 |  | 80 |

The difficulty arises because cumulative sales never exceed cumulative quota by more than £1,000 in the last six months and you would have paid commission on a total excess of £3,000 instead of on £1,000.

The only simple way to avoid this problem is to pay commission on all

**Table 6.4** *Cumulative calculation of commission*

|  | Monthly quota (£) | Cumulative quota (£) | Sales (£) | Cumulative sales (£) | Cumulative sales exceed cumulative quota (£) |
|---|---|---|---|---|---|
| Jan | 10,000 | 10,000 | 12,000 | 12,000 | 2,000 |
| Feb | 12,000 | 22,000 | 11,000 | 23,000 | 1,000 |
| Mar | 14,000 | 36,000 | 15,000 | 38,000 | 2,000 |
| Apl | 18,000 | 54,000 | 17,000 | 55,000 | 1,000 |
| May | 20,000 | 74,000 | 21,000 | 76,000 | 2,000 |
| Jun | 22,000 | 96,000 | 23,000 | 99,000 | 3,000 |
| Jul | 24,000 | 120,000 | 22,000 | 121,000 | 1,000 |
| Aug | 23,000 | 143,000 | 21,000 | 142,000 | — |
| Sept | 22,000 | 165,000 | 21,000 | 163,000 | — |
| Oct | 20,000 | 185,000 | 21,000 | 184,000 | — |
| Nov | 15,000 | 200,000 | 16,000 | 200,000 | — |
| Dec | 11,000 | 211,000 | 12,000 | 212,000 | 1,000 |
| Totals | 211,000 |  | 212,000 |  |  |

sales from zero. If you operate on a sales quota system, or have sliding scales of commission, a downturn in sales during the year will upset your calculations. Furthermore, you cannot avoid a natural inclination of some sales people arranging for large orders to be processed to benefit their commission payments.

Some companies pay commission in arrears on sales over cumulative quota to even out the payments, but this tends to reduce the incentive to sell.

Perhaps the best way is to calculate a low percentage commission for each product according to its saleability and profitability, and reward all sales from zero. A bonus, or additional commission, could be paid if total sales for the financial year exceed a certain figure.

## Drawing account

If sales are likely to be erratic and commission calculations difficult, a drawing account could be established. This enables a sales person to draw any amount desired up to a predetermined limit related to the actual or estimated commission earnings. If the sales person does not earn enough in commissions to cover any advanced funds in one period, the balance of the debt is carried over to the next period.

Assume that a salesman, entitled to commission of 5 per cent on all sales, has drawn, say, £500 during the first period. If he achieved sales of £15,000 during the period, his commission would be £750, out of which the company would deduct the advance of £500. If he only achieved £8,000 during the first period, his commission would be £400 and his drawing account would be debited with £100. He would start the second period £100 in arrears. The company limits the amount that the drawing account may be in arrears.

The advantage of operating a drawing account system is that it offsets some of the difficulties of varying commission payments. However, if you operate such a scheme, estimate the maximum amount of money likely to be owed to the company by the sales people, for what period of time, and calculate a percentage interest on the sum. Thus, with 36 sales people all being able to draw up to £500, this could be £18,000 outstanding for most of the year. At 12 per cent, this will cost £2,160 and must be taken into consideration in your overall commission scheme.

## House accounts

Develop a clear policy for customers who will be considered as house accounts. These are customers who place large orders with your company and who are serviced by senior executives. The conflicts that can arise from the classification and treatment of such accounts has already been discussed in Chapter 2. Normally, no remuneration is made to sales persons when sales are made to these accounts. The key to a good policy is the servicing of the account; this must reflect the size of the business obtained from the customer.

You must ensure that these major accounts are adequately serviced and avoid paying commission without commensurate effort.

## Peripheral incentives

While money remains the main incentive in stimulating most people, other things are important. However, in recent years, non-cash rewards to employees have attracted the attention of the tax authorities—holidays, dinners and functions, hospital insurance, clothes, gift vouchers, even the annual Christmas celebration is not sacrosanct. If the reward can be translated into a cash value, then it is liable to come under the scrutiny of the tax inspector. Before embarking on any incentive scheme, take professional advice and, if necessary, have a meeting with your local tax authority.

Items that will not attract the interest of the tax people include status rewards such as special ties, scarves, car and personal badges, improved work equipment, sitting at top table during the annual conference, etc. Even personal letters to the person's home play their part in rewarding recognition. One company I know of permits the leading sales person to use the company Rolls Royce for a month. This not only interests the winning sales person but is an impressive talking point with customers when their 'local rep' turns up in a Rolls rather than the usual car.

Construct your incentive scheme to reward effort rather than results. That is, every person should be able to win from their increased effort and someone working a small territory should be able to compete on equal terms with an experienced person in a very lucrative area.

# 7

# Market Analysis

Before embarking on a sales campaign, it is desirable to know the disposition of customers and competitors. You are shown how to brief the investigators to obtain the information you need and, if you do it yourself, some of the principles to adopt and pitfalls to avoid.

## Analysis is essential

Before you start to sell your products, you must analyse the market. This chapter deals with the way analysis should be conducted or commissioned. Table 7.1 lists the percentages of nearly 300 companies reporting the analyses they normally conduct.

**Table 7.1** *Percentages of companies reporting various analyses*

|  | Industrial products (%) | Consumer products (%) |
|---|---|---|
| *General business* |  |  |
| Long-term forecasting (4 years upward) | 75 | 65 |
| Sales forecasting (1 year) | 65 | 65 |
| Business trends | 55 | 65 |
| Costs analysis | 40 | 45 |
| Location of distribution points | 25 | 45 |
| *Product research* |  |  |
| Present products versus competition | 70 | 75 |
| Research on competitors' products | 65 | 60 |
| Pack and packaging design and physical characteristics | 35 | 55 |
| Acceptability of new products | 30 | 90 |
| Product testing | 30 | 70 |

|  | Industrial products (%) | Consumer products (%) |
|---|---|---|
| *Market surveys* | | |
| Market share analysis | 78 | 78 |
| Market potential analysis | 75 | 65 |
| Studies of market changes | 60 | 62 |
| Determining characteristics of market segments | 55 | 78 |
| *Sales and distribution research* | | |
| Sales analysis | 78 | 76 |
| Establishment of sales quotas | 60 | 55 |
| Identifying sales territories | 35 | 45 |
| Distribution costs | 25 | 50 |
| Channel effectiveness | 15 | 60 |
| Incentives analysis | 20 | 38 |
| Distribution audits, test markets | 12 | 45 |
| Discounts, offers and deals | 5 | 28 |
| *Advertising research* | | |
| Media studies | 30 | 48 |
| Copy research | 20 | 52 |
| Motivation research | 18 | 58 |
| *Export markets* | | |
| Market research | 45 | 60 |
| Product research | 25 | 45 |
| Sales and distribution research | 40 | 40 |
| Advertising research | 12 | 35 |

Sales and market share analysis are considered to be important by all companies, as is the comparing of a company's products with those of competitors. The very high concern of consumer product companies for new product acceptability contrasts markedly with the low percentage for industrial companies.

## What marketing research will do

It will do nothing! It is what military intelligence is to the general; what a dictionary is to the writer. All the stories that have ever been written can be found in a dictionary—if you put the words in the right order!

Marketing research provides information: information vital to your selling. Three things you should think about before you conduct a research are: time, cost and facilities.

It takes *time* to conduct adequate research; for matters of great urgency you won't have time. It *costs* money; often several thousands of pounds; you cannot get it on the cheap. Use whatever *facilities* exist in the company; they might not be perfect but they'll be better than nothing. When you have the results of the research, you need the *facilities* in the company to be able to implement action.

## Who should do the analysis?

Information must be as accurate as possible and sought in a professional manner. Only large companies can afford a full-time market analysis department; small companies engage specialist organisations or instruct their advertising agency. Provided that you make allowances for the inevitable bias that will occur, you could use the sales organisation to determine some of the basic facts of the market.

## Main stages of a project

If you commission a research into the market, there are seven main stages:

(1) Briefing. Information is required on which to base sales and marketing plans. The problem is discussed with the people who are going to carry out the research.

(2) Terms of reference. A programme of research is agreed between the originator and the person who will be responsible for the research.

(3) Desk research. Published sources and researches previously carried out are searched to see if there is anything relevant.

(4) Internal research. Company records are scrutinised for data.

(5) Field research. Primary research is carried out in the market.

(6) Analysis of results. Conclusions are drawn from the research and used to comply with the terms of reference.

(7) Report writing. The results are presented to the originator of the research.

Briefing and terms of reference are critical and require an input from company management.

### The briefing

This is an exercise in communications. You have an information requirement which you explain to the researcher, who will convert it into research terminology. For example, you may need information about the people who could use your product, the best methods of distributing it, the competitive products available, the price ranges of similar products, and the possible reactions to a new product. A feasibility study is sometimes carried out in the company at this stage to ensure that the research terms are appropriate to the capabilities of the company: that the company would be able to implement the likely actions. An example of an actual research is given at the end of this chapter. It would not be prudent to undertake such an analysis if the company were unable to initiate and sustain distribution in the country in which it is interested.

The objectives of the briefing are to define in both management and marketing research terms the information required and the reasons why. You and the researcher must agree on what is needed, the scope and depth to which the investigation should be taken, any constraints concerning time and cost.

To avoid costly errors, after the initial discussion, prepare a written brief and have a detailed face-to-face discussion; subsequently, confirm this in writing.

## Terms of reference

The terms of reference are prepared by the researcher. It is a working document setting out what is to be done, when and how, with what expected results and at what cost. It is submitted to the company for approval and forms a contract between the two parties. While the contents will vary depending on the circumstances, notes on the various headings that could be included are given below:

- Introduction: date of briefing, personnel present, background of the proposed research.
- Objectives: main and subsidiary objectives of the research from the view of management; the scope of the research is defined.
- Questions to be answered in the research: these clarify what specific information is to be obtained, such as:
  (a) What is the estimated size in volume and value for 1988?
  (b) What has been the trend of sales since 1980 and is this trend expected to continue beyond 1988? Information is to be broken down into: volume, value, by region, type of end-user.
  (c) What is the range of prices paid for the product at each level in the distribution chain?
  (d) Who are the suppliers of at least 80 per cent of the market and where are they located?
  (e) What distribution and selling methods are used?
  (f) What degree of product servicing is provided and is this centrally organised by manufacturers?
  (g) What market shares are held by the main suppliers, how are these calculated and by whom?

(h)  How would end-users react to: a broader product range; a new manufacturer entering the market?

- Research methods to be used. List of the published sources to be consulted; size and composition of the samples for field work; internal company data to be used; forecasting methods to be employed; description of questionnaire if used; consultations with industry, authorities and discussion groups.

- Timing and cost. When research will be started; estimated time to complete the survey and report; cost and expenses detailed; invoicing arrangements and currency of payment, VAT, etc.

- Staff involved. Profiles of the supervisory and main staff who will organise and carry out the research: name; age; qualifications; brief record of career; other relevant surveys conducted.

## Desk research

You may have no budget for marketing research; it is still important that you have up-to-date knowledge on your product's performance, your market and your competitors. Desk research, and the next section, internal research, are low-cost ways of getting data. As the name implies, it can often be done from one's desk for the cost of a letter and postage stamp.

An invaluable source of information is your public library. Consult the reference librarian who is usually able to provide some data. Desk research costs very little and will save time and money. Even if you are going to conduct your own desk research, detail the relevant parts to keep your investigation on track.

Consult: government publications and statistics; industry and trade association handbooks and statistics; directories, yearbooks and buyers' guides; authoritative weeklies; periodicals and national press; multi-client studies from research agencies.

Desk research is 'secondary research' and is always out-of-date. This should not deter your search because all statistics are 'out-of-date': they freeze information at a point in time and are only a close approximation of the facts. Desk research accounts for up to about 75 per cent of a survey's total content.

## Internal research

Analyse data available in the company, such as: sales records; production records; production costs at various levels of activity; credit control records; packing, distribution and warehouse costs; advertising expenditure. Internal records are one of the first sources to be consulted in any analysis of the market; they will provide an authoritative and factual background. Internal research is usually between 10 and 20 per cent of a survey's costs.

## Field research

This expensive, primary research should be undertaken when you have questions that can only be answered by field surveys. It involves talking to end-users, buyers, middlemen in the distribution channel, competitors, trade associations, government offices and any other parties connected with the market being analysed. These surveys are normally done by personal meetings. Up to 50 per cent of the cost of the total research might be for primary research: it is vital to construct it with care.

The researcher will define the universe for investigation; decide on the method to be used; prepare a questionnaire; select a sample from the universe. Typical universes are: local authorities in the UK with their own road maintenance department; users of wooden crates in Kent for exporting products; owners of certain motor cars in the home counties; factories with more than 200 employees in the area of South Limburg; companies in north east England who have training officers.

Postal surveys have the lowest response rate—depending on the standing of the research organiser, between a low 3 per cent to around 25 per cent. If you use a postal survey, make it worth the effort of respondents by offering some small incentive such as a special ballpoint pen, diary, address book. If you survey the trade by post—factories, stores, dealers, etc—at least offer respondents a summary of the findings of the research in return for their participation.

Telephone research should be restricted to objective approaches such as specific industrial enquiries to named individuals, or for qualifying sales leads.

Personal interviewing is very flexible and offers the best response rate. The sample of respondents and the interview can be controlled; trained interviewers can usually detect exaggerated or suspect information; complicated enquiries can be made; checking is easy to supervise. Such interviews may be free ranging, semi-structured or, as is usual, with a questionnaire.

## Designing the questionnaire

Questionnaire design looks simple but it isn't: it is difficult. Suppose you have to decide in which morning newspaper it would be best to advertise a product and you want to find out which papers people read. The opening question could take many different forms:

- 'Which paper do you read?' (But how often? Every day? Sometimes?)
- 'Do you read a daily paper?' (But, regularly, every day?)
- 'What daily paper do you buy?' (Are you looking for buyers or readers?)
- 'How often do you see a daily paper?' (Every morning on the bookstall!)

The way this question is usually posed by professional researchers is with two postcards, A and B, with the same papers listed in different orders. Respondents are asked:

'Which of these newspapers (show card A) do you see regularly, that is, about three times a week?'

Card B is alternated with card A to avoid the order of the papers introducing bias. Follow-up questions seek to find out what paper they have read that day and the day previously.

Use a professional to prepare your questionnaire. If you really must do it yourself, here are some guidelines:

- Do not use questions which tax the memory: responses will be vague, or guesses will be given:

    'Where did you see this advertisement?'
    'When did you buy this product?'
    'When did you start using this product?'

- Questions should ask only what can be easily remembered by respondents:

    'Did you see this television programme yesterday?'
    'What papers did you happen to read last Sunday?'
    'What brand are you using now?'

- Do not ask for generalised answers or for responses that call for an 'average':

    'How often do you use your deep fryer?'
    'How many gaskets a week do you use on average?'
    'What is the average number of tubes of toothpaste you sell per month?'

- Ask for responses that focus on possible answers:

    'Did you shop at Marks & Spencer this week?'
    'What grade of lubricant are you using now?'
    'What type of bread, if any, did you buy today?'

- Make the meaning of every question clear to the least intelligent respondent likely to be met in a survey. Don't use complicated questions, technical jargon or vague terms:

'What kind of soup do you prefer?' (Hot, thick, packet, canned, tomato!)

'What is the best way to get your customers interested?' (Haven't any idea!)

'Do your sales people use "pulls" of your advertisements?' (Pulls?)

- Do not use 'leading' questions (the classic is, 'When did you stop beating your wife?') in an attempt to obtain favourable replies. A check-list often leads the respondent to check more than is strictly true. Indicating who is the sponsor of the survey will introduce bias in the answers:

  'Do you always take the Financial Times?'

  'I take it that you approve of Persil?'

- Do not use questions that raise personal bias, unless it is the object of the survey, because answers are mostly given inaccurately. Use questions that obtain facts. Opinion surveys are a special category. They are interpretive surveys and the respondent reports on motives. Questions invite free responses which the professional researcher has to summarise. These are not surveys for the amateur to attempt without appreciating the size of the error that might be introduced:

  'Why do you use this product?'

  'What do you think of the car's performance?'

  'Would you say that the company's service is adequate?'

- Eliminate questions with more than one element, that is, asking about one activity but with others below the surface. The following example ignores the fact that there is one reason for discontinuing a product and another reason for adopting the new:

  'Why did you change to this brand?'

- Provide for conditional responses. The most common violation in poor questionnaire construction is to ask the respondent to make a choice without allowing for 'I don't know', or 'I have no particular preference'. The percentage of respondents who are not sure is just as important as those with definite answers.

- The sequence of questions must be logical. Regard the questionnaire as similar to a tree: the main flow of thought is the main tree trunk and the branches are the subsidiary questions. After the subsidiary questions, use lead questions back to the main trunk of the questionnaire.

- Control questions are used to check on other answers: questions that ask for responses on advertisements that do not exist, or knowledge of products that are not on sale.

## How big a sample?

If you are working with a researcher you will be advised on the size of the sample. If you have to decide this yourself, use the following simple formula to indicate the number of respondents in the sample:

(1) Decide what percentage of error in the responses is acceptable; probably up to 5 per cent

(2) Halve this percentage

(3) Square the result

(4) Divide 0.25 by the figure obtained in (3) to give the size of the sample

Suppose you are willing to accept an error of, say, 4 per cent. Therefore:

(1) 4 per cent error is 0.04

(2) Halve this: $0.04/2 = 0.02$

(3) Square this: $(0.02)^2 = 0.0004$

(4) $0.25/0.0004 =$ sample size of 625

The effect on sample size, and costs, can be seen if a lower error were required, say, 2 per cent:

(1) 2 per cent error is 0.02

(2) Halve this: $0.02/2 = 0.01$

(3) Square this: $(0.01)^2 = 0.0001$

(4) $0.25/0.0001 =$ sample size of 2,500

## Industrial market sampling

For an industrial market survey, in general, consult all the largest companies and take a sample of the remainder. The assumption is that the largest companies will purchase the majority of a product, possibly around 80 per cent of total industry sales.

## Sampling terms

The following terms are used by researchers in sampling.

*Random sample.* Also known as a probability sample; each member of the universe has an equal or known chance of being selected in the sample.

*Stratified sample.* The universe is divided into mutually exclusive homogeneous groups of known size, and a random sample is taken from each group.

*Quota sample.* A type of stratified sample in which the selection from the groups is not random but according to known, or estimated, characteristics in the universe.

*Sampling frame.* A specification of the universe that permits the identification of individuals.

*Multi-stage sample.* A sample is drawn from the universe in several stages, usually after stratification by region, district, streets. When using the electoral registers for a sample, a three-stage drawing is common: constituencies, wards, electors.

## Analysis of results

Responses are analysed and presented so that they relate directly to the questions raised in the terms of reference. Interpretation and analysis are essential and require considerable work.

## Report

Answers to the questions posed in the terms of reference should form an early page in the report. Each question should be repeated and the general answers indicated by the survey. From these are derived the recommendations for action. All tabulations, statistical work and detailed comment should be at the back of the report. A copy of the questionnaire(s) used forms an appendix.

# Specimen proposal

The following specimen proposal can be used as a model. Names and figures have been changed where necessary to preserve confidences.

---

**Proposed Marketing Research**
**for**
**Some Company Ltd**

*Contents*
Your objectives
Recommendations
Stage 1 Feasibility study
Stage 2 Secondary research
Stage 3 Primary research
Stage 4 Attitudinal survey
Timing of the research
Personnel
Costs and contingencies

## Your objectives

Generally, to survey the West German market for (an industrial chemical product which has repeat purchases) with the intention of entering that market.

Specifically, to establish the current state, and estimate the trend, of the West German market for these products; to ascertain the names, locations, and distribution methods of the present suppliers and market price structures. To identify the current and potential customer base. To determine the sales and marketing effort and costs likely to be needed to enter and sustain operations in this market to secure a profitable share within a reasonable period of time.

## Recommendations

To direct the marketing research to those situations and activities specifically relevant to your company's intentions and capabilities, a pre-survey feasibility study is recommended. This is Stage 1 of a four-stage investigation. Stage 2 is a secondary research with some field research. Stage 3 is a factual field survey and Stage 4 is an attitudinal survey and also used to elaborate on any points that arise from Stage 3.

## Stage 1 Feasibility Study

This will take the form of an analysis of current company operations in the home and any export markets insofar as they are relevant to the proposed research. Some of the data to be established:

Range and types of products currently being marketed.
Technical characteristics of products and compliance with recognised standards.
Ability of company to expand production.
Similarities and differences between competing products.
Branding policy. Packaging policy.
Pricing strategy and structure. Recent price variations.
Transportation cost ratios. Discount policy.
Current main and subsidiary customer base.
Distribution methods and stocking points.
Delivery and stock control policy.
Market coverage and pentration.
Current selling practices.
Advertising appropriation and media policy.
Sales literature and direct mail activities.

Other specific questions will include:

Preferred entry in the W German market.
Own organisation or through intermediaries?
What current staff could cope with control of proposed marketing operation?
What language fluency exists in the company?
Desirability of having local stocks.
Initial, break-even sales estimate and profit aims.
Sufficient funds in company or is financial backing required?

At the conclusion of Stage 1, terms of reference will be agreed. These will include the main and subsidiary objectives from management's viewpoint and a definition of the scope of the market research report.

## Stage 2 Secondary Research

This will be conducted on official and privately published material to establish the situation currently existing in W Germany and to indicate areas where primary research should be undertaken. Some of the questions you requested to be answered are:

Total market for each type of product by category.
Market trend since 1982.
Expected growth to 1988 and beyond.
Prices of products at original equipment manufacturers, distributors and users.
Main competitors and suppliers.
Selling methods used in the W German market.
Estimated market shares of existing suppliers.
Distribution methods used by suppliers.

Some field research will be conducted to substantiate the data obtained from secondary sources, such as price structure, current promotional literature, advertising copy, selling methods, distribution, etc.

## Stage 3 Primary Research

Approximately 20 to 30 personal interviews will be conducted with distributors and end-users in Hamburg, Düsseldorf, Cologne, Frankfurt, Stuttgart and Munich, as these cover the vast majority of the W German market for such industrial products.

A semi-structured questionnaire technique will be used with guidelines for further discussions to allow for moderately free-ranging responses.

Respondents will be selected in proportion to their importance in the total industry sales and distribution of the products.

Data in this stage will be obtained from specific replies to the questions, analysis of the free-discussions and by observation.

## Stage 4 Attitudinal Survey

Approximately 20 to 30 interviews will be conducted with distributors and end-users (different from those interviewed in Stage 3).

Likely reactions and responses to the entry of a new supplier will be sought and any points that have arisen from the earlier stages will also be clarified.

## Timing of the research

| | | |
|---|---|---|
| (1) | Feasibility study and terms of reference: | 2 weeks |
| (2) | Secondary research, initial field research and Interim Report No. 1: | 4 weeks |
| (3) | Primary research to ascertain market structure, Interim Report No. 2: | 4 weeks |
| (4) | Attitudinal survey, Final Report and post-research discussions with company: | 4 weeks |
| | Total | 14 weeks |

## Personnel

The research will be conducted in the UK and in West Germany by Dr L A Rogers, Mr P T Harries, Mme C Paquet, and Dr B J von Klatt.

## Costs

Fees are payable after each stage on submission of the relevant invoice, and are stated with contingency allowances which are estimated may be necessary should the planned meetings, visits, interviews and travelling be altered due to circumstances beyond our control. This is particularly relevant in Stage 4 with attitudinal investigations.

| | Estimate (£) | Contingencies (£) | Minimum (£) | Maximum (£) |
|---|---|---|---|---|
| Stage 1 | 1,500 | | | |
| Trav & Accommodation | 475 | 125 | | |
| | 1,975 | 125 | | |
| Cost for stage 1 | | | 1,975 | 2,100 |
| Stage 2 | 5,000 | 1,000 | | |
| Trav & Accommodation | 600 | 150 | | |
| | 5,600 | 1,150 | | |
| | | | 5,600 | 6,750 |
| Cost for stages 1 and 2 | | | 7,575 | 8,850 |

| | Estimate (£) | Contingencies (£) | Minimum (£) | Maximum (£) |
|---|---|---|---|---|
| Stage 3 | 5,000 | 1,000 | | |
| Trav & Accommodation | 1,500 | 500 | | |
| | 6,500 | 1,500 | | |
| | | | 6,500 | 8,000 |
| Cost for stages 1, 2 and 3 | | | 14,075 | 16,850 |
| Stage 4 | 2,500 | 2,500 | | |
| Trav & Accommodation | 1,000 | 500 | | |
| | 3,500 | 3,000 | | |
| | | | 3,500 | 6,500 |
| Cost for all four stages | | | 17,575 | 23,350 |

# 8

# Distribution

**The nearer you get to the user, the more costly is distribution but the greater control you retain over the selling process. Seven factors are discussed to guide you in the construction of an optimum distribution system and decide on an overall policy.**

## Global activity

Viewed as an overall activity, physical distribution includes all movements of a product from its basic sources, through the factory, into finished stock and finally to its ultimate use. It is a global activity and what occurs in inward goods, the factory, despatch, warehouse, transportation, and delivery to the stockist or user, are parts of the total system. In this chapter, we concentrate on the main area of influence of the sales manager—stocking and distribution of finished goods.

Your task is to ensure that the company has an effective and efficient distribution system getting its products from the factory to the user. You can't do this if you only look at parts: you must consider all activities as a combined operation.

For example, if you are considering the methods used by the company to deliver products to customers, it is not sufficient to restrict your investigation to costs of delivery. You should look more widely and consider the advantages and costs of having stocks held at convenient local points, and of less transportation. If the company operates an in-stock service for customers, thus reducing the quantities that need to be kept at retail outlets, you should assess the influence this has on obtaining orders and whether the cost involved, and profits made, justify it.

Basically, you have to balance the needs of customers with the total cost of the company's distribution system.

Customer needs are for the right goods, in the right quantities, at the right time, at the lowest delivery charges. The total cost of distribution includes the production cost and stock costs of finished goods, local warehouse costs, transport and delivery charges.

## Distribution objectives

As with most business operations, the development of objectives helps to focus activities on the end results desired. Examples include: minimising of transport costs; maintaining certain service levels; adhering to specific delivery times; reduction of stock levels; increasing stock turnover.

Because you are in competition with other companies, you must maintain a degree of flexibility with the distribution element in your marketing mix. If a competitor decides to change distribution methods and supply a competitive product to cut-price stockists, or direct to the user, you may need to amend your previously agreed objectives.

To some extent you can insist that people pay the price you ask for a product but you cannot insist that they purchase that type of product through a given channel. If a competitive product is available at a more convenient outlet or at a lower price, you will lose sales if you are not prepared to compete in the distribution channel.

I know one company who refused to let cash-and-carry wholesalers handle its well known range of domestic products. They argued that to do so would damage the image of the company and its products; instead, they continued with their approved dealers. What happened was that customers, wishing to buy domestic products at the lowest price, bought the competitive products from the cash-and-carry wholesalers. The first company had to face the fact that, if they wished to retain their market share, they had to change their distribution policy or develop a completely different range of products for the cash-and-carry wholesalers. They adopted the former course of action and, to date, their image has not been damaged or altered in any way.

## Channels of distribution

There are three main channels of distribution: direct to the user, to a middleman, and to more than one middleman. The middlemen are factors, wholesalers, retailers or franchisees. You have to choose which channel is best suited to your company's products, and a lot will depend on the quality of the middlemen.

# Methods of distribution

In any one channel of distribution you can adopt different methods of getting your finished products to the ultimate user. Consider just one—selling direct to the user. You could operate a shop in the factory; acquire the company's own retail outlets; have sales people sell door-to-door; equip vans and sell from them in the streets; take space in exhibitions and sell from the stand; advertise in newspapers and periodicals and sell through the post. Six different physical methods in the one channel.

## Exclusive distribution

Consider a different channel—selling to retailers. You could adopt some of the six methods mentioned but you could restrict supplies to only one retailer in any area. Such distribution would be on an exclusive basis and the retailer would be given an assurance that all enquiries received from the area would be passed on. There is normally an agreement for a certain period of time and a minimum level of sales for the exclusive rights. Cars, expensive watches, and silverware, are often marketed in this way.

## Selective distribution

Not as restrictive as the exclusive method is selecting outlets as turnover increases in the market generally. You could appoint a stockist for your products and, as business developed, appoint others in the area. None is appointed on an exclusive basis and the number of stockists relates to the growth of sales.

## Intensive distribution

This is the most liberal method of distribution. Any outlet that is prepared to handle the product is supplied. You are not concerned if adjacent shops sell your goods. You have an intensive distribution policy: if they'll stock it, you'll sell it.

# Importance of distribution

When you develop a marketing mix for a product you consider the relative importance of the product, price structure, distribution method, promotional support and servicing required. This relative importance of the four Ps plus S (product, price, place, promotion, service) varies from product to product and from time to time.

The product is very important because, without a product, you have nothing to sell. Price is important and has to be set at a level that will attract customers. But, even with a superb product at a very attractive price, if you don't make it available to customers, that is, distribute it effectively, you won't sell it. Distribution is often the key to a successful sales and marketing policy. How often do we hear these words from consumer and industrialist alike: 'It wasn't what I really wanted, but it was all that was available at the time'.

If you are selling women's perfume, promotion will play a very important part in the mix. But place is also important; you can distribute through chemists, supermarkets, department stores, independent shops, airports, and so on. In fact, place is becoming more and more important in the marketing mix for women's perfume.

If you are selling an industrial product, such as sulphuric acid, you cannot do much with the product in marketing terms. You cannot differentiate it in the mind of the buyer; you can't put blue speckles in one month and offer it as the new, improved acid: sulphuric acid is sulphuric acid. Similarly, promotion is unlikely to play a very important role; you are not going to increase sales very greatly by your advertising. However, distribution *is* very important. How you pack your acid, what type of containers, where you hold local stocks, how quickly you can deliver, all contribute greatly to your success.

One of your early tasks is to decide on the relative importance of distribution for your products in the overall marketing mix. Then you must decide how near you need to get to the actual user.

## Distribution chain

The shorter the chain from manufacturer to user, the more effective is control over selling efforts. It is also the most costly: the closer you get to the user, the greater the cost. Highest distribution costs are involved when selling direct from maker to user.

The longer the chain, the least costly is distribution; but you have much less control over the selling effort.

## Seven factors

The following seven factors should be considered when constructing your distribution policy:

- the product
- size and value of each sale
- area of proposed operations
- prevailing methods of distribution

- strength of effort necessary
- cost of the effort
- servicing required

They must not be considered as separate, isolated factors but as different views of the same distribution operation. As each factor is considered, it will become apparent that it affects others: you cannot review the prevailing methods of distribution without considering the area of operations; you cannot assess the cost of the effort without considering the strength required, and so on.

## The product

A consideration of the product, to whom it will appeal, who will use it and who will buy it, will indicate the class of customer. If it is a consumer product, you must decide how important the product could be to different people and relate it to their hierarchy of needs. Some products are essential, or at least, extremely important, and are at the top of people's lists. Lower down the list are products not so important and, towards the bottom of the list, are products that might be obtained if, and when, finances are available and nothing more urgent is required.

The products foremost in people's minds are needs. Other products have different degrees of importance to different people and may be described as wants and desires.

Selling consumer needs is fairly straightforward. Everyone has to eat, be clothed and sheltered. After that, the lists of products are as varied as there are people. You should estimate the degree of importance of your product in terms of needs to indicate how best it might be distributed. A general consumer 'need' product has to be made widely available; a consumer 'desire' product does not require the same availability because consumers will tend to search and compare offers.

Selling industrial needs is, similarly, fairly straightforward. Wide availability is necessary with, perhaps, local stocks for quick delivery. An industrial 'desire' product may need considerable education of intending users and will certainly be the subject of much greater search by the professional buyer.

## Size and value of sale

A product of small size and low value requires a wide, intensive distribution operation. Because of its low price it can have wide appeal and therefore it has to be made as widely available as possible within the constraints of your sales budget.

Large size and high value products will appeal to a smaller number and class of customer, irrespective of whether they are consumer or industrial products. They also cost a lot more to distribute and therefore a more limited and controlled distribution system is needed.

## Area of operations

The size of your intended market will obviously affect the size and cost of your distribution operations. The larger the proposed area of your operations, the more extensive must be your distribution capabilities. Supplying your products to customers who are within, say, 50 kilometres of your factory is a different operation from supplying the whole country.

As you expand your area of operations you will find that different products are favoured in different areas; different strengths of competition are encountered, with some competitors very strong, others weak; different methods of distribution will be found; middlemen in some areas are well organised and efficient.

Construct your distribution plan with a definite area of operations in mind and not as a general plan for the whole country unless you intend to attack the total market from the start. If you do this, you will need a very deep faith and a very deep pocket.

## Prevailing methods of distribution

As you develop your plan, assessing the various areas in which you intend to operate, you will find differing distribution methods favoured by competitors. In the north you may find strong middlemen with their own well organised sales organisations; in the south you may find that competitors tend to sell with their own sales forces. Some areas may have a number of outlets from where the products, similar to yours, can be obtained; other areas may have few outlets. As you look at the area of your intended operations, carefully appraise the prevailing methods in the different regions of the country.

## Strength of effort

A product with potentially high appeal in a large area of operations will require a strong distribution effort. A product in a highly competitive market will also need powerful sales efforts.

To get your product onto the market may require a very strong initial sales thrust and continuing substantial efforts. Don't underestimate the strength necessary to get your product distributed.

Consider an everyday example. If you were trying to get your product distributed through chemists' shops, how easy or difficult do you think it would be to get the product distributed and displayed on chemists' counters? The next time you visit a chemist, look critically at the counter; there isn't much space available usually and your product would need to have tremendous back-up and appeal for the chemist to accept it for display.

In Chapter 15 you will read of the efforts of one of my competitors selling plastics bearings to steel mills. The effort and time necessary to sell some products can be very great, with little returns. At that time, I was with the Vickers Group and we had developed the first plastics-coated fabric under a research contract for the government. As part of the deal, we had to set up a garment factory to produce clothing for many different purposes. To offset the costs of the garment factory I was asked to investigate the possibilities of selling foul-weather clothing to the UK fishing industry.

The strength required to get that traditionally-minded market to accept a 'new-fangled plastic mac' was great indeed and it was nearly 18 months before we had an adequate distribution system. The fishermen suffered from sea-boils because of the irritation of the old-fashioned oil-skins. They wanted something different, but they didn't want anything new—especially plastic! When I eventually secured their interest and active co-operation, we couldn't supply sufficient quantities because our distribution system was not geared up for the sales I generated.

I altered the distribution arrangements by persuading a company in Wells, Somerset, to stock our garments on call against orders I would generate. This company also had a nation-wide sales force and started to generate their own orders and enquiries for other types of foul-weather and specialist garments.

The tiny garment-making factory at Vickers was unequal to the task and was soon overwhelmed with orders. I was faced with mounting demand and no distribution. I changed the system yet again and succeeded in getting a factory in Bristol to make up the garments from our raw materials and supply against orders from the Wells company. The Bristol company had been in the business of making rubber-proofed clothing for many years and were a little wary of taking on the new plastics; especially as this involved them in the purchase of electronic welding equipment from a company in Reading.

What started as a simple quest eventually became a long, involved series of negotiations and meetings. I had to convince my superiors at Vickers of the wisdom of changing distribution arrangements not once, but twice; I had to convince the company in Wells that if they stocked the goods, I could generate orders to justify it; I had to convince the Bristol company that they should change from rubber to plastics, and accompanied them to the electronics factory in Reading to buy the new equipment; I held a meeting of the directors of the Bristol and Wells companies to finalise matters.

Sometimes the strength of the sales effort required to get things properly distributed can be formidable.

## Cost of effort

Once you have estimated the strength of the effort required to get your product adequately distributed, you must cost it for the area of operations in which you intend to distribute. How much will the field sales people cost? How much advertising and promotion? How many middlemen? How often will they and customers have to be serviced? How many articulated lorries, low-loaders, tail-lift trucks, refrigerated transport, shipping containers, pick-up trucks and light vans of what sizes and cost will be required? How much stock will need to be kept centrally and, perhaps, at local points?

## The radio kit

Products have to be serviced; stockists and customers have to be serviced; your sales force needs servicing.

As an advertising agent, I once handled the advertising of a small mail-order company and every weekend we took spaces in various popular newspapers and weekly magazines. One incident in particular stands out in my mind as a classic example of overlooking the service required.

The mail-order company had a limited advertising budget so we kept to small spaces equivalent to about 6 cm single column. Various products were advertised but the most successful was a do-it-yourself radio kit. All you needed was a screwdriver and soldering iron and you could construct an effective little radio for £1.

One week, the mail-order company thought they would like to increase their publicity and it was agreed that we take a half-page in one of the Saturday tabloid papers. A second colour was used to liven up the ad but the message was still the same: send a £1 postal order or cheque for the kit and full instructions on assembling it.

We had considered the product, its price, the publication that was to carry the ad, and the treatment of the larger message. Nobody thought of the servicing required.

The following week, thousands of envelopes, each containing £1, started to flood the tiny premises of the mail-order company. There was so much mail, it was impossible to sit down. No one had thought of the greater servicing that might be required should the ad pull well. The company could not obtain sufficient supplies of the kit and had to write to everyone asking if they were prepared to wait or would they prefer their money returned. Many hundreds of pounds had to be returned.

This was some years ago, but the same mistake is still being made today.

A well known calculator was advertised by a mail-order company at a special, low price and the company was unable to cope with the response. Extra staff had to be employed and delays in sending out the calculators created considerable problems. Eventually, because new supplies were at a greatly increased price, it was not possible to supply all who had applied and their money had to be returned.

A company, marketing a weekly-parts encyclopaedia for cookery, offered a spice-rack at a very low price and couldn't supply the unexpected thousands who responded. They had to write explaining there would be a delay of many weeks and offered to return the money. Not only was there damage to the company's name, there was a considerable loss of profit because of the extra work involved. It is so easy to overlook the servicing required 'back at the ranch'.

## Stock control

The more extensive your distribution, the greater your servicing requirements, especially with regard to availability of stock. Apart from the needs of some products that have to season, age or mature and be kept in stock for certain minimum periods, the reason for holding stock is to provide a distribution service to customers equal to, or better than, that of competitors. One of your important distribution weapons is strategically sited stocks and stock levels. However, the final accounts of any company will show that a considerable amount of money is tied up in stocks — finished goods and work in progress. As sales manager, you can often exercise considerable control over the amount of stock carried, centrally and locally.

The quantity held in stock should relate to the time it takes to replenish it. If it takes two months to obtain a replenishment, then a minimum of two months' stock will mean you have zero stock when a new delivery is received. This does not take into account unexpected calls on stock or delivery taking longer than normal. Sufficient quantity should be held in case delivery is delayed or unusually large orders are received. A buffer or minimum stock should be held at a level just above the zero line. This is shown graphically in Figure 8.1. We have assumed that depletion of stock and delivery times are regular — the slopes are the same and the distances between uprights, representing deliveries, are identical.

To calculate the optimum stock level we need to know the average stock held. This is usually considered over the financial year of a company and, depending on the way in which it is calculated, either physically or arithmetically, the results vary slightly. The most simple formula is:

$$\frac{\text{Opening stock plus closing stock}}{2}$$

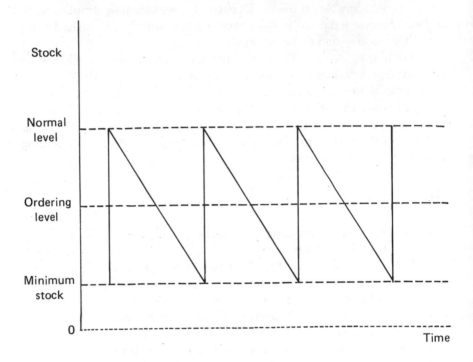

**Figure 8.1** *Stock levels*

It assumes that stock is depleted regularly but it is easy to see that, using this formula, if you start and finish with no stock, your average stock is zero. It would then be better to find out the highest levels of stocks held, add these amounts together and divide by the number of levels taken. In Figure 8.1, if the four highest levels were 8,000, 7,000, 8,000, and 7,000, then average stock would have been the sum of these divided by four, ie 7,500.

You should keep as little as possible in stock bearing in mind the usage rate and the cost of ordering. The less you have in stock, the more frequently you must order on the factory or with suppliers and arrange for delivery into central or dispersed warehouses. You can arrange to have fewer deliveries into stock but this means that higher stocks must be held.

The optimum number of orders to place with suppliers or on the factory per year is when:

total ordering costs = total carrying costs

Substituting letters for words:

$N$ = Optimum orders to be placed per year
$U$ = Total usage of the product per year
$V$ = Total value of items used per year
$C$ = Cost of ordering
$S$ = Cost of carrying stock expressed as a percentage of average stock

The formula expressed in letters is therefore:

$$N \times C = V/N \times \tfrac{1}{2} \times S$$

Note that $V/N$ is the value per order and, assuming that there is a regular usage of stock, average stock will be half of $V/N$. The formula is simplified:

$$NC = \frac{(V/N)}{2} \times S$$

$$NC = \frac{VS}{2N}$$

$$2N^2 C = VS$$

$$N = \sqrt{\frac{VS}{2C}}$$

Assume that we have the following information:

U = (total usage over one year) = 3,300
Cost of each item = £23

Therefore, $V$ (total value of items used per year) = £75,900 (ie 3,300 × £23)

$C$ (cost of ordering) = £200
Average stock held = 188 items
Value of average stock held = £4,324 (ie 188 × £23)
Cost of average stock (20 per cent interest on value) = £5,189
Cost of carrying the average stock held = £3,630

Therefore, $S$ (cost of carrying stock as a percentage of cost) = 70 per cent. We can now put the figures in the formula:

$$N = \sqrt{\frac{75,900 \times 0.7}{2 \times £200}}$$

12 (nearest whole number)

The optimum number of deliveries to arrange per year is therefore 12, each order for 275 items (3,300/12).

If it was possible to reduce the average stock level from 188 to 100 you would save by reducing the value of the average stock to £2,300 (100 × £23) and the interest on the value of the stock from £865 to £460, reducing the cost of carrying the average stock from £3,630 to £3,225. The cost of carrying the stock as a percentage of cost of stock is therefore 140 per cent. Inserting these new figures in the formula:

$$N = \sqrt{\frac{75,900 \times 1.4}{2 \times £200}}$$

$$= 16 \text{ (nearest whole number)}$$

This would mean around 16 orders per year, each of 206 items (3,300/16).

This is only a tool to be used in your decision-making for optimising stocks, and the answers derived are only as good as the data you feed into the formula. You will not need to analyse the stocks of every item you have and you must distinguish between items that account for a large part of your stock values and those of minor importance. The pattern in Table 8.1 is usual. Of the total stocks held, 25 per cent accounts for 85 per cent of the value and it would be product groups A and B that need to be carefully controlled.

Table 8.1 *Typical stock values*

| Product group | Importance | % of stock | % of annual value |
|---------------|------------|------------|-------------------|
| A | Extremely high | 10 | 75 |
| B | Very high | 15 | 10 |
| C | Medium | 35 | 8 |
| D | Low | 30 | 4 |
| E | Minor | 10 | 3 |

## Segmented distribution

After analysing the total market for your company's products, you will find that it is possible to divide it into separate, homogeneous segments. These may be simple geographical areas or distinguished by type of outlet, type of industry, or other identifiable characteristics. Your distribution policy may take three different forms.

## Undifferentiated distribution

Distribution will be to the whole market with one type of product or product range, using the same channels and pricing structure. Advertising and promotional strategy will be the same throughout the country and there will be no difference in types of packaging or containers.

## Differentiated distribution

A different policy is adopted for each segment of the market and this may mean different products for different channels. With a consumer product, this could be one type of product and packaging when sold through wholesalers, and a different type of packaging and perhaps even brand name, when sold through stockists. Obviously, different price structures would be needed, and different promotional messages.

With an industrial product, it is often more important to segment the market and distribute distinctly for highly defined industrial needs.

## Concentrated distribution

This form of distribution can be adopted when a company wishes to enter a market, especially a highly competitive one, but does not have the financial resources to tackle the total market from the start. By concentrating on one well-defined and contained segment, it is possible to compete with the biggest competitors. As profits grow, so can market expansion.

# Push-pull

You will appreciate that it is possible to push products or to pull them through a distribution channel. The former is selling in to the middlemen and gaining their support in selling on to the users; the latter is advertising and promoting heavily to users to persuade them to seek out and buy from your channel agents.

The most expensive form of distribution is getting near to the actual user and using long-term pull. This requires heavy inputs of advertising and selling over a long period. It should be restricted to products that can be easily identified and distinguished from competitive offers.

The least expensive form of distribution is by remaining at a distance from users and employing a push strategy. One company I know has developed the push-pull concept quite considerably. They have a firm belief that if one of their products has to stand on the floor, they push it through the channel; if it will sit on the shelf, they pull it. It is an oversimplification of distribution and promotional strategy but nevertheless an interesting view that you might consider for your products. Bulky and heavy products cannot easily be hidden in storerooms, and take up selling space in outlets. The sooner they can be demonstrated and sold, the sooner that space is available for new deliveries. Channel middlemen are therefore inclined to sell such products. Lightweight products that can be neatly arrayed in their packages on shelves can be left there for the customer to ask for them.

## Franchising

These are contractual licenses under which the franchisee is permitted to conduct business under a trade name and/or trade mark belonging to the franchisor. The franchisor controls the way in which the franchisee does business and provides on-going advice and assistance.

Franchising, which is normally associated with fast food—fried chicken, hamburgers, soft ice cream, etc—is developing into other areas. It has been applied to car tuning, dancing instruction, drain clearing, estate agencies, and hotels, among others. Many franchises do not deal with the public direct but supply industrial services.

To have a franchise operation, you must be able to provide a genuine service or product for users, and the distribution by franchisees must be a viable proposition to your company, the franchisee and customers. You will need to provide adequate protection for any money advanced by intending franchisees in anticipation of the provision of goods, services and support. In view of the nature of this form of distribution, if you are interested in considering such a method, you should contact the British Franchise Association, 75a Bell Street, Henley-on-Thames, Oxon RG9 2BD; 0491 578049.

# 9

# Sales Forecasting

The primary planning document in a company is the sales forecast but it is also advisable to have a market forecast so that an estimate of market share can be made. Errors in forecasting have to be paid for in a number of ways, and therefore the underlying importance of developing a sound sales forecast is explored.

## Primary planning document

If you are to manage the sales and sales organisation of your company professionally, you will need a sound plan. The basis of all company planning is the sales forecast: no one can do anything until someone, explicitly or implicitly, decides the sales and, therefore, the production level of each product. This should relate to market potential and the estimated share that the company aims to achieve.

Market potential is the total quantity of a product that a market could absorb within a reasonable period of time before the product is modified or replaced. This could be over a year or several years. Sales potential is the share of the market potential that the company considers it can obtain.

A sales forecast is an estimate of sales for a future period in terms of volume or value, guided by a proposed marketing plan, and under an assumed set of economic conditions likely to prevail during that period. This is usually for a year and often relates to the company's financial year.

The probable economic conditions are important yet sometimes overlooked. Failure to consider such things as the annual budget, cost of borrowing, interest rates, export climate, general price levels and similar factors may result in your forecast being wildly inaccurate.

All sales forecasts are inaccurate but they differ in the extent of their 'wrongness', that is, in the size of the discrepancies between the forecasts and actual results. We can never be sure that what we forecast will happen.

Some things we can be sure of. We can be sure that we will die: we can say with confidence that there is a 100 per cent probability of that event taking place. We can even say that there is a 100 per cent probability that the sun will rise tomorrow morning. Apart from such certainties, all future events have degrees of probability of occurring.

The more accurate your forecasts, the better the performance and morale of the organisation and, because errors in forecasts cost money, greater forecasting accuracy means higher profits.

## How to improve forecasts

Forecasting can be improved by acquiring more data, but this alone does not improve the accuracy of the forecast. With too much data there is a possibility of errors creeping in. Errors in sales forecasting have to be covered in a number of ways:

- holding more stocks
- idle production and other capacity
- requiring emergency sources of supply
- embarrassing explanations to customers

Each of these costs money or market share. Having to hold extra stock when sales are less than what was forecast has to be paid for in the cost of the goods in stock and the cost of storing them.

Idle production capacity means unit costs will be higher because of under-recovery of fixed overheads. Emergency sources of supply are usually at a higher than normal cost. When orders cannot be fulfilled, customers are frustrated and buy elsewhere; profits are lost because of sales not made and there is a loss of market share.

## The market forecast

Whenever you make a sales forecast, make a market forecast. An esti- mate of sales is also an estimates share of the market. If your particular market's sales are increasing each year, your sales should also be increas- ing at the same rate. Consider Table 9.1. This is a forecast for a year by a company marketing windows and doors and an estimate of industry sales so that estimated market shares of 3 per cent for windows and 1.5 per cent for doors are made. The actual sales achieved for the year were as

**Table 9.1** *Calculation of estimated market share*

|  | Windows | Doors |
|---|---|---|
| Sales forecast for year | 45,000 | 8,100 |
| Market forecast | 1,500,000 | 540,000 |
| Estimated market share | 3% | 1.5% |

shown in Table 9.2. Apparently, the company did a good selling job for windows—10 per cent more than forecast—but not so good with doors, which were 10 per cent below forecast.

**Table 9.2** *Calculation of percentage of forecast achieved*

|  | Windows | Doors |
|---|---|---|
| Actual company sales | 49,500 | 7,290 |
| Percentage of forecast | 110% | 90% |

This is where we see the value of having total industry estimates and market share forecasts. By obtaining estimates of total industry sales from various sources such as government statistics, published accounts, trade associations, etc, the results found were as shown in Table 9.3.

**Table 9.3** *Calculation of actual market share*

|  | Windows | Doors |
|---|---|---|
| Total industry sales | 1,980,000 | 364,500 |
| Actual company sales | 49,500 | 7,290 |
| Actual market share | 2.5% | 2% |
| Estimated market share | 3% | 1.5% |

Thus, what was thought to have been a good selling job for windows was not; market share was 2.5 per cent, not the estimated 3 per cent. What was thought to have been a poor effort on doors was actually a good effort; market share was 2 per cent compared with the estimated 1.5 per cent.

Although the company lost some market share for windows, it had to produce an extra 4,500 to satisfy demand (49,500 - 45,000). As far as doors were concerned, it had at least 810 extra doors in stock (8,100 -7,290).

## Accuracy of forecasts

Do not aim for the greatest accuracy in a sales forecast but for the greatest value from the time, effort and money you spend on it. Aim for the highest savings at lowest cost. A question often asked is: 'How much should be spent on forecasting?'. If only a modest error in the sales forecast would have a significant effect on profits, then more resources must be applied to the forecasting activity.

## Uses of the sales forecast

Company executives should agree that the sales estimate is used as a guide for production, sales, and finance and all three should be involved in the preparation of the forecast.

Production people advise on such things as levels of output, degree of production flexibility, availability of raw materials and components, feasibility of holding any extra stocks that might be needed, costs of production at different levels of activity.

Sales personnel will report on current trends of customers in the company's markets, likely new markets, distribution cost analysis, possibilities of securing new customers, indications of turnover at different prices.

Financial personnel calculate the optimum levels of company trading, cost of holding stocks, cost of increasing sales, the amount of credit that has to be allowed to customers, and so on.

## Costing the error in a forecast

The error in the forecast for doors in Table 9.1 was 810. If each door cost £200 to make, the company would have 810 × £200=£162,000 of extra stock to finance. (This means that the costs of production, ie £200 each, would have been paid for each of the 810 doors.) The company's available cash has been reduced by £162,000.

If the cost of borrowing money is, say, 12 per cent per year, these doors will cost the company £1,620 every month in interest just to keep them in stock. Even if the company is not borrowing money, it is deprived of the use of the £162,000.

## Types of trends

Trends exist everywhere in the environment. These are general tendencies for events to continue in recognisable patterns. Markets exhibit an expanding trend simply because population itself tends to increase; social conditions change over time; technology has a trend of advancement because of expanding knowledge and the acquisition of greater skills. Your business operations should be geared to these trends.

## Use of the trend

Table 9.4 is an example of the use of a trend. In the first five years, sales of a product increased from 500 to over four times this by the fifth year. What estimate can be made for year 6? First, the trend is obviously increasing. But how 'increasing' is defined requires the application of forecasting skills.

Table 9.4 *Example of a trend*

| Year | Sales |
|------|-------|
| 19x1 | 500 |
| 19x2 | 700 |
| 19x3 | 1,500 |
| 19x4 | 1,700 |
| 19x5 | 2,050 |

The increase from year 1 to year 5 was 1,550. This is an average annual increase of 387.5 (1,550/4). If this average increase is tabulated against the actual figures, as in Table 9.5, apart from year 4, there is not a good match. We might not feel so confident now to add 387 to 2,050 and estimate sales of 2,437 for year 6.

Table 9.5 *Tabulation of actual figures against average increase*

| Year | Sales | Average increase | Variation |
|------|-------|------------------|-----------|
| 1 | 500 | 500 | — |
| 2 | 700 | 888 | +188 |
| 3 | 1,500 | 1,275 | −225 |
| 4 | 1,700 | 1,663 | − 37 |
| 5 | 2,050 | 2,050 | — |

There was a much greater increase in the third year (800), a smaller increase in the fourth year (200), and an even smaller increase in the fifth year (350). It could be argued that the increase in year 6 might be around 250 and sales estimated at 2,300. This is only 138 different from the estimate using the annual average increases of 387 and might therefore renew our confidence in adopting a forecast of between 2,300 and 2,500 for year 6. If we wish to justify this estimate further we could obtain further information, perhaps quarterly or monthly sales figures.

There are no magic formulae you can apply to data to calculate accurate forecasts. Forecasting sales and setting targets require the application of fairly straightforward techniques, but modified by an intelligent application of sound common sense. Always, you should ask yourself: 'Does this result seem reasonable? Is this what I might have expected?'.

## Three components of a trend

In any series of data there are normally three types of variation about the average or general level: the basic trend, the seasonal pattern, and a random fluctuation. Sales of a product in an expanding market normally exhibit an increasing trend. There will be seasonal fluctuations about this trend and others which are random.

We are more concerned with short-term trends of a year or so than with long-term trends which are studied by economists looking at such things as total economies, or movements of population over many years. Long-term analyses of business are not of great or immediate assistance to the sales manager setting targets and for month-by-month control.

## Why use the trend?

When you construct a sales forecast you consider what has happened in the past, and conjecture what might occur in the future. The justification for using trends for forecasting sales is that the company has invested a considerable amount of effort in the market in advertising and general publicity, selling activities, distribution, perhaps local branches and factories, and there is the experience of owners, users and stockists of the company's products. All these things have a cumulative effect on the market generally and will have created a certain awareness and image of the company and its products. Once this general tendency or trend has been established it will continue if the company continues to be active. It is like a train that has been started and is moving along the track; provided it receives appropriate quantities of fuel it will continue to move along the track.

We relate the forecast to previous sales by using the trend which reflects this total market investment.

Trends are affected by different production standards, modifications of product range, product performance, change in publicity, varied distribution methods, different sales organisation, changes in company personnel and other internal influences, in addition to changes in the market.

Stable conditions are only stable up to a point. Everything is in a state of continual change. You judge how far an extension of the trend can be supported by examining the previous figures.

## Identifying trends

Statistically, the greater the number of figures, the more readily you can identify any trend. Figures for seven years are better than for five years; ten years' figures are even better. Trying to establish a trend from 18 months' figures may not be practicable. Much will depend on the nature of the figures.

The unit sales of a company for the past 11 years are given in Table 9.6: from 500 units in the first year to 1,120 in the eleventh year—a general trend of progress of about 8 per cent per year with the 'usual variations'. But look more closely. Although the 11-year trend has been increasing, the last four-year trend has been decreasing; in fact decreasing at nearly 3 per cent per year.

**Table 9.6** *Unit sales of a specimen company*

| Sales in 000s |
| --- |
| 500 |
| 550 |
| 660 |
| 835 |
| 955 |
| 1,030 |
| 1,100 |
| 1,220 |
| 1,185 |
| 1,148 |
| 1,120 |

While it is true that the more data you have, the better it is statistically to establish a trend, you must nevertheless determine whether what happened five, six or more years ago has any impact on today's sales. If you ignore this, you might estimate the sales trend for the above company for year 12 about 8 per cent higher—1,209,600 units. From an inspection of the data for the last four years, however, you could also estimate the sales trend at about 1,088,500, or around 3 per cent lower, for year 12. Something has been happening in the market and the trend of the last four years is more significant than the total trend. Of course, if you could ascertain the reasons for the declining trend and it were possible to change things, you might avert the decline and even achieve increased sales.

Trends are a valuable source on which to base forecasts, but do not allow the long-term trend of several years to cloud your judgement of the most recent results.

## Territory comparisons

If you have a product that can be related to population, whether people, factories, or some other factor in the market, then a useful method of forecasting is by comparing territory results. Table 9.7 lists four areas with sales and populations showing area D to be the best. First, we make an assumption that the areas are different only in size of population, and

**Table 9.7** *Calculation of sales from population*

| Area | Sales (£) | Population |
|------|-----------|------------|
| A | 50,000 | 80,000 |
| B | 30,000 | 50,000 |
| C | 15,000 | 20,000 |
| D | 84,000 | 120,000 |

other characteristics are similar. An index is calculated for each area: sales divided by population multiplied by 100. For example, area A is:

$$50/80 \times 100 = 62.5$$

The full list is given in Table 9.8.

**Table 9.8** *Calculation of area indices*

| Area | Index |
|------|-------|
| A | 62.5 |
| B | 60.0 |
| C | 75.0 |
| D | 70.0 |

Although D might be considered a good area because it has the highest turnover, C is the best area with the highest sales-to-population index. The turnover for each of the other areas is calculated, using the same index as area C, in Table 9.9.

**Table 9.9** *Calculation of turnover by area*

---

If a population of 20,000 produces 15,000, then:
Area A should produce   80,000(75/100) = 60,000
Area B should produce   50,000(75/100) = 37,500
Area D should produce 120,000(75/100) = 90,000

---

Naturally, we would need to look closely at Area C to determine whether there are any significant reasons why it produces such a good sales-to-population ratio. Another aspect is that we would be suggesting that the other areas produce (A) 20 per cent, (B) 25 per cent, (D) 7 per cent, greater sales. These are substantial increases and it is pointless simply to state an increased target figure for the areas. Obtaining sales is a partnership of managers and field sales people. There would need to be agreement on where and how the extra sales are to be achieved.

## Sales force composite forecast

Companies often make use of their sales force in the preparation of a forecast. This is particularly appropriate with industrial products. The total number of potential buyers is small compared with the large mass markets for consumer products and they are more easily considered on an individual basis. Also, it is not unusual for the bulk of a company's turnover to come from a relatively small percentage of total possible customers. There are a number of arguments for and against this:

*Advantages*

- It uses knowledge of the people who are closest to the market.
- It places the responsibility for forecasts in the hands of those who have to produce the results.
- The sales force has greater confidence in quotas that are developed from such forecasts.
- It tends to give forecasts greater accuracy and stability because of the size and spread of the sample.
- It lends itself to easy development of product, territory, and customer breakdowns.

*Disadvantages*

- Sales people are not always good estimators—they tend to be either too optimistic or too pessimistic.

- If forecasts are to be used for quota setting, sales people are likely to underestimate sales.

- Sales people are often unaware of the broad corporate plans that are shaping the future of the company, or of the economic forces affecting industry and business generally.

- The method requires extensive use of time by what is essentially a selling force.

## Market factor derivation

This method is based on the assumption that future sales depend on, or are related to, some factor or factors in the market. The task is to identify and isolate these factors and measure them to form a basis on which to estimate future demand for another product linked with them. Thus:

- The number of new houses is related to the number of new families.

- Purchases of car tyres are related to the number of cars in use and the new ones to be produced.

- Sales of foodstuffs are related to population.

- Sales of abrasive discs are related to engineering companies using cutting and grinding machines.

- Sales of welding equipment are related to the number of metal fabricators and metal repairs establishments.

The average motorist buys a set of tyres every 2 years. To estimate total market potential for car tyres in, say, 1988, we add up all cars registered in 1986, then two years previously, 1984, and back every two years to perhaps 1976 or 1974. This will provide an estimate for repeat purchases. This is added to the estimated UK car production and importation for 1988 to arrive at the total potential for car tyre sales in 1988. Some share of this will be company sales potential from which a sales forecast is calculated.

Great care is essential in adopting a market factor, because the relationship to a product's sales may not be supported factually. Sales of prams are considered related to babies and, if we obtained the numbers of births in any one year, we could calculate the potential pram sales for that year. The relationship is not as simple as this. New prams are often used by the second baby, and a more relative market factor would be, 'surviving first births'. This would then need to be modified to allow for at least the second child using the same pram.

Similarly, sales of central heating equipment are not directly proportionate to new houses and those being renovated. Many factors influence the purchase of domestic central heating systems and to use only new and existing houses as market factors would most likely result in unreliable forecasts.

While this method of forecasting is the most accurate to use, it requires relevant factors to be found. When you have decided on some factor or factors, you should compare the statistics of these with sales of your product for the same four or five years. Chapter 10, on statistical methods, shows you how to determine the degree of correlation between a proposed market factor and sales of a product. Obviously, without a high degree of correlation, the factor is unreliable.

## How to prepare a sales forecast

The following ten points summarise the general approach to the construction of a sales forecast.

(1) Determine the purpose or purposes for which the forecasts are to be used; for example: sales quotas, production scheduling, expenses, advertising appropriation, media plan, cash flow, etc.

(2) Divide the company products into homogeneous groups.

(3) Determine the factors affecting sales of each product group and their relative importance.

(4) Choose the methods best suited.

(5) Gather all available data.

(6) Analyse the data.

(7) Check the deductions made from the analyses.

(8) Make assumptions regarding the effects of factors that cannot be measured and, if possible, estimate the probability of the accuracy of the assumption.

(9) Convert the deductions, assumptions and probabilities into specific product and area forecasts.

(10) Apply to company operations and revise periodically.

# 10

# Statistical Sales Forecasting

Forecasting sales is predicting what the future might be; it has many traps for the unwary. The more extensive and firmer the base on which forecasts are made, the more confidence we can have in taking decisions based on the forecasts. A multi-method approach is illustrated with a number of examples to provide you with the tools to apply to your own company.

## A worked trend exercise

Table 10.1 gives the monthly sales of heating units made by a company for a year. Total sales for the year were 3,000 units: an average of 250 units per month. Using a similar method to that in Chapter 9, Table 9.5, we can make a tentative forecast of sales for the next six months of 6 × 250 = 1,500 units, and then look more closely for any discernible trend.

**Table 10.1** *Monthly sales of a specimen company*

| Month | Sales of heating units |
|-------|------------------------|
| Jan | 272 |
| Feb | 261 |
| Mar | 249 |
| Apl | 242 |
| May | 153 |
| Jun | 164 |
| Jul | 108 |
| Aug | 184 |
| Sep | 285 |
| Oct | 337 |
| Nov | 320 |
| Dec | 425 |

## Secular trends

A secular trend is the general increasing or decreasing movement of a set of data. It is a trend over several years and may be simple or complex. A simple trend is a linear trend: increasing or decreasing by a constant amount periodically. A complex trend is multiplicative, increasing or decreasing by a constant ratio. Population trends are examples of complex trends. Consider the sales for the first and second six months in Table 10.1:

| | |
|---|---|
| Sales in the 2nd six months | 1,659 units |
| Sales in the 1st six months | 1,341 |
| Difference | 318 |

This is an average increase of 318/6 = 53 units a month.

If the trend is simple, the forecast for the first six months in the next year is:

$$1,659 + 318 = 1,977 \text{ units}$$

If it is complex, the ratio for the two six-month periods must first be calculated. This is 1,659/1,341 = 1.237, and the forecast for the next six months is:

$$1,659 \times 1.237 = 2,052 \text{ units}$$

We have two different forecasts of sales for the six months, using different assumptions about the secular trend: 1,977 units and 2,052 units. This difference of 75 units, almost 4 per cent, may or may not be significant. We explore the figures further.

## Seasonal trends

The quarterly sales and monthly averages for each quarter indicate a degree of seasonal variation, as shown in Table 10.2. The seasonal trend is higher sales in the winter (4th and 1st quarters), lower sales in the summer (2nd and 3rd quarters).

**Table 10.2** *Seasonal variation of sales*

| Quarter | Sales | % of year | Monthly average |
|---|---|---|---|
| 1 Jan-Mar | 782 | 26.1 | 261 |
| 2 Apl-Jun | 559 | 18.6 | 186 |
| 3 Jul-Sep | 577 | 19.2 | 192 |
| 4 Oct-Dec | 1,082 | 36.1 | 361 |

Table 10.3 gives the annual sales pattern for the past 10 years with the average monthly sales as percentages of the year's total sales. The average quarterly percentage sales, 29 per cent, 18.5 per cent, 18.4 per cent, and 31.4 per cent conform closely to the quarterly averages for the recent

**Table 10.3** *Monthly sales as average of year's total*

| Month | 10 years' monthly sales as average of the year's total (%) | |
|---|---|---|
| Jan | 9.7 | |
| Feb | 9.8 | 29 |
| Mar | 9.5 | |
| Apl | 8.3 | |
| May | 4.9 | 18.5 |
| Jun | 5.3 | |
| Jul | 3.5 | |
| Aug | 6.0 | 18.4 |
| Sep | 8.9 | |
| Oct | 10.8 | |
| Nov | 9.8 | 34.1 |
| Dec | 13.5 | |

year in Table 10.2. If monthly sales for this most recent year in Table 10.1 had followed the 10-year seasonal pattern, they would have been as shown in Table 10.4. The monthly variations are also calculated.

**Table 10.4** *Sales forecast with monthly variations*

| Month | (1) Actual sales (Table 10.1) | (2) 10-yr average (%) (Table 10.3) | (3) Expected (2) × 3,000 | (4) Variation (1)−(3) |
|---|---|---|---|---|
| Jan | 272 | 9.7 | 291 | −19 |
| Feb | 261 | 9.8 | 294 | −33 |
| Mar | 249 | 9.5 | 285 | −36 |
| Apl | 242 | 8.3 | 249 | − 7 |
| May | 153 | 4.9 | 147 | + 6 |
| Jun | 164 | 5.3 | 159 | + 5 |
| Jul | 108 | 3.5 | 105 | + 3 |
| Aug | 184 | 6.0 | 180 | + 4 |
| Sep | 285 | 8.9 | 267 | +18 |
| Oct | 337 | 10.8 | 324 | +13 |
| Nov | 320 | 9.8 | 294 | +26 |
| Dec | 425 | 13.5 | 405 | +20 |
| Totals | 3,000 | 100.0 | 3,000 | 0 |

In column (3) are the monthly sales we would expect if the 10-year seasonal pattern continued. Sales for the first four months were 95 units below the 10-year average expectation, $(-19, -33, -36, -7 = -95)$, but are increasing over what would have been expected for the remainder of the year. Sales regularly decline from December to July, and then increase to December. Thus, for the first six months of the next year, sales are unlikely to increase in a simple extension of the annual trend, and a more sophisticated approach is required.

## Exponential smoothing

We try to 'smooth out' the peaks and troughs. One method is to devise a new series of smoothed figures for the trend by applying a smoothing device to the existing data. A percentage, call it $X$, of the first figure in the series is added to a percentage, say $Y$, of the second figure to give a new, smoothed figure. Percentage $X$ is taken of this new figure and added to percentage $Y$ of the third figure in the series, and so on until a new smoothed series has been obtained.

The percentages $X$ and $Y$ vary for monthly, quarterly and annual data. Statisticians generally agree that 70% and 30% are used with monthly data; 50% and 50% for quarterly data; 30% and 70% for annual data. The reasoning for the monthly percentages is that the months are relatively in the same time period and therefore 70% of the previous month's experience, marketing input, advertising effort and demand is still likely to have an effect in the following month. Similar reasoning is used for the smoothing percentages of quarterly and annual data.

The monthly sales figures from Table 10.1 are:

272   261   249   242   153   164   108   184   285   337   320   425

To smooth this series we take 70% of the first figure, 272, and 30% of the second figure, 261, to obtain a new second figure, 269. This is used to calculate the third smoothed figure, using the same percentages: 70% of the 269, 30% of 249, the next in the original series:

70% of 269 = 188; 30% of 249 = 75   Result = 263
The fourth term: $(0.7 \times 263) + (0.3 \times 242) = 257$
The fifth term: $(0.7 \times 257) + (0.3 \times 153) = 225$

The original series of monthly sales and the smoothed trend are:

*Original:*
272   261   249   242   153   164   108   184   285   337   320   425

*Smoothed trend:*
272   269   263   257   225   207   177   179   211   249   270   317

Variation of trend from original:

+8   +14   +15   +72   +43   +69   −5   −74   −88   −50   −108

While this method has smoothed the original series, it has not added a great deal to our knowledge. There is a fairly constant increase in each of the last five months of the year but the smoothed trend varies greatly from the original results over this period.

## Smoothing peaks and troughs

Another method of smoothing is to tabulate the data, add successively several terms together, and take the successive averages. The number of terms added together should include both high and low figures. With quarterly data, summing successively in fours will usually smooth out low and high quarters. With monthly figures you should sum successively in sixes or twelves. The number of terms to be added together successively to smooth out the peaks and troughs is determined by inspecting the data.

If you have monthly figures for, say, three years or more, you can establish a moving annual total (MAT), say, January to December, February to January, March to February, and so on. The 12 months' totals moving forward in monthly intervals establish the trend.

Because of the quarterly variations, the heating unit sales from Table 10.1 are smoothed in a slightly more sophisticated way. We add in moving totals of three months at a time, then divide each of these three-monthly totals by three to obtain the monthly moving averages in Table 10.5.

**Table 10.5** *Monthly moving averages[1]*

| (1) Original | (2) Summed in 3s | (3) Divided by 3 |
|---|---|---|
| 272 | | |
| 261 | 782 | 261 |
| 249 | 752 | 251 |
| 242 | 644 | 215 |
| 153 | 559 | 186 |
| 164 | 425 | 142 |
| 108 | 456 | 152 |
| 184 | 577 | 192 |
| 285 | 806 | 269 |
| 337 | 942 | 314 |
| 320 | 1,082 | 361 |
| 425 | | |

The third column is the trend of sales using this method. Notice that the totals in column 2 and the averages in column 3 are 'centred': the totals are placed at the mid-point of the number of data being added together. This is important when adding even numbers of data.

If you add in fours, the first sum of four would be placed between the second and third terms, the second between the third and fourth terms, and so on. The averages of these successive totals of fours would be placed on the same level and would not relate to specific months. To overcome this, we add the successive sums of fours, in pairs, and centre them; each pair of summed fours is added and centred, then divided by eight to establish a trend. Using this method on the same series, we get the results shown in Table 10.6.

**Table 10.6** *Monthly moving averages*[2]

| (1) Original | (2) Summed in 4s and centred | (3) Summed in 2s and centred | (4) Divided by 8 | (5) Deviations |
|---|---|---|---|---|
| 272 | | | | |
| 261 | | | | |
| | 1,024 | | | |
| 249 | | 1,929 | 241 | + 8 |
| | 905 | | | |
| 242 | | 1,713 | 214 | +28 |
| | 808 | | | |
| 153 | | 1,475 | 184 | −31 |
| | 667 | | | |
| 164 | | 1,276 | 160 | + 4 |
| | 609 | | | |
| 108 | | 1,350 | 169 | −61 |
| | 741 | | | |
| 184 | | 1,655 | 207 | −23 |
| | 914 | | | |
| 285 | | 2,040 | 255 | +30 |
| | 1,126 | | | |
| 337 | | 2,493 | 312 | +25 |
| | 1,367 | | | |
| 320 | | | | |
| 425 | | | | |

Column 4, if plotted on a graph, indicates the trend. By deducting the trend figures from actual figures, the deviations of sales from the trend for each period are obtained.

## Comparison of trends

We have established trends by the four methods shown in Table 10.7.
Four different trends, with the last two, obtained by moving totals, tend-
ing to match each other. Note that only one of these methods provides a
trend figure for all of the months.

### Table 10.7  *Calculation of trends*

| Month | Original sales | 10-yr pattern | 70%/30% | 3s | 4s & 2s |
|-------|-----------|-----------|---------|-----|---------|
| Jan | 272 | 291 | 272 | — | — |
| Feb | 261 | 294 | 269 | 261 | — |
| Mar | 249 | 285 | 263 | 251 | 241 |
| Apl | 242 | 249 | 257 | 215 | 214 |
| May | 153 | 147 | 225 | 186 | 184 |
| Jun | 164 | 159 | 207 | 142 | 160 |
| Jul | 108 | 105 | 177 | 152 | 169 |
| Aug | 184 | 180 | 179 | 192 | 207 |
| Sep | 285 | 267 | 211 | 269 | 255 |
| Oct | 337 | 324 | 249 | 314 | 312 |
| Nov | 320 | 294 | 270 | 361 | — |
| Dec | 425 | 405 | 317 | — | — |

Of these four methods, the most promising one for this set of data
appears to be the 10-year seasonal pattern, and we explore this further in
Table 10.8, concentrating on the increased actual monthly percentages
from May to December.

### Table 10.8  *Actual monthly percentages May-December*

| Month | 10-year average (Table 10.3) (%) | Actual % of year | Increase of actual over 10-year pattern (%) |
|-------|-----------|-----------|-----------|
| May | 4.9 | 5.1 | 0.2 |
| Jun | 5.3 | 5.5 | 0.2 |
| Jul | 3.5 | 3.6 | 0.1 |
| Aug | 6.0 | 6.1 | 0.1 |
| Sep | 8.9 | 9.5 | 0.6 |
| Oct | 10.8 | 11.2 | 0.4 |
| Nov | 9.8 | 10.7 | 0.9 |
| Dec | 13.5 | 14.2 | 0.7 |

The most recent sales—October, November, December—are all higher than previous average percentages. This increase, say 0.5% might be continued into the new year. The 10-year averages for January, February and March are 9.7%, 9.8% and 9.5%. Thus, when we have an estimate for the year, we could take 9.7% + 0.5% = 10.2% of that estimate as the January forecast; 9.8 + 0.5% = 10.3% for February; and 9.5% + 0.5% = 10% for March.

## Annual trends

Table 10.9 gives the company's annual sales by volume for the past seven years. From year one to seven, there has been an increase in sales of 2,130 units, which is 2,130/6 = 355 per year increase on average. A simple sales estimate for year 8 might be 3,000 + 355 = 3,355 units.

**Table 10.9** *Annual sales by volume*

| | |
|---|---|
| 1 | 870 |
| 2 | 1,020 |
| 3 | 1,295 |
| 4 | 1,620 |
| 5 | 1,990 |
| 6 | 2,505 |
| 7 | 3,000 |

The sales figures in Table 10.9 are plotted in Figure 10.1. A dotted line has been inserted that could 'best fit' all the data. But it might not be the most accurate fit, and several other straight lines with different slopes could be drawn.

## How to find the line that best fits data

The general algebraic formula for a straight line is $Y = a + bx$. Instead of $x$, we use $d$, to represent the deviations in time of each term from the middle. Provided we know $a$ and $b$, for any given $d$, $Y$ can be found. Where the line cuts the vertical axis is $a$; the slope of the line is $b$.

The method for finding the line of best fit is called 'The Method of Least Squares', and is simple to use. Here are the steps:

(1)  Tabulate the data in a column. This column is $Y$.

(2)  Decide which term is the mid-point of all the terms. With an odd number such as we have—7—the mid-point is 4. With an even

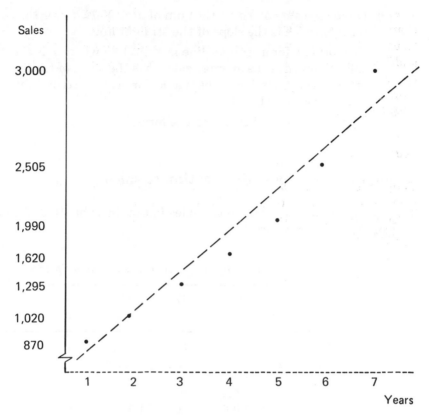

**Figure 10.1** *Sales figures plotted graphically*

number of terms, the mid-point would be mid-way between the two middle terms.

(3) Insert, for each of the data, the number of terms (years with this example) from the mid-term (year 4). Year 1 is -3 from the mid-year; year 2 is -2 from the mid-year; year 3 is -1; year 4 is obviously zero. Year 5 is +1; year 6 is +2; year 7 is +3. This column (the deviations) is $d$.

(4) Multiply each of these deviations by the sales for that year. This will give $Yd$.

(5) Square each deviation $d$, to remove the negative signs. This gives column $d^2$.

(6) Sum ( $\Sigma$ ) the first column and find the average. This gives the term $a$.

(7) Sum the $Yd$ column ( $\Sigma Yd$).

(8) Sum the $d^2$ column ( $\Sigma d^2$).

(9)  Divide the sum of $Yd$ by the sum of $d^2$ ($\Sigma Yd/\Sigma d^2$) for the term $b$, which is the slope of the straight line.

(10)  The formula for a straight line is $Y = a + bd$ where $Y$ is the sales figure, $a$ is the average sales, $b$ is the slope of the line, and $d$ is the deviation of the particular year (or term) from the mid-year (or mid-term).

(11)  Apply the terms obtained to the formula.

## Using the line of best fit to estimate sales

In Table 10.10 we apply this to the sales figures in Table 10.9; the numbers of the steps are in brackets.

**Table 10.10**  *Application of the best line to sales figures*

|  | | (1) | (3) | (4) | (5) |
|---|---|---|---|---|---|
|  | Year | Y | d | Yd | d |
|  | 1 | 870 | −3 | −2,610 | 9 |
|  | 2 | 1,020 | −2 | −2,040 | 4 |
|  | 3 | 1,295 | −1 | −1,295 | 1 |
| (2) → | 4 | 1,620 | −0 | 0 | 0 |
|  | 5 | 1,990 | +1 | 1,990 | 1 |
|  | 6 | 2,505 | +2 | 5,010 | 4 |
|  | 7 | 3,000 | +3 | 9,000 | 9 |

(6) $\begin{cases} \Sigma Y = 12,300 \\ \text{Average} = 12,300/7 = 1,757 = a \end{cases}$

(7)  $\Sigma Yd = 10,055$

(8)  $\Sigma d^2 = 28$

(9)  $b = 10,055/28 = 359.1$

(10)  $Y = a + bd$

(11)  $Y = 1,757 + 359.1 \times 4$  (4 is deviation of year 8)

$= 3,193$ sales estimated for year 8

## Exponential growth

Growth and decay do not normally follow straight lines. Sales can increase from present customers, prospects are converted into customers, and new customers enter the market. Similarly, population trends can be observed from studies of insects which reproduce more quickly than human beings; not only do couples have offspring, but as the offspring mature, they too have offspring, who mature and have offspring, who ...

Human populations have to be studied over long periods of several generations to observe population growth; microbes, rodents and rabbits can be studied for much shorter periods. The growth observed in such groups is called 'exponential', which means growth at a multiplicative rate.

A formula for calculating exponential growth is:

$$100\left\{\left(\sqrt[m]{\frac{Y_n}{Y_t}}\right)-1\right\} = \text{average percentage per period}$$

In the formula, $m$ is the number of periods *between* the first term, $Y_t$, and the final term, $Y_n$.

In our example, $m$ is 6 years; $Y_t$ is 870; $Y_n$ is 3,000, so the calculation is:

$$100\left\{\left(\sqrt[6]{\frac{3,000}{870}}\right)-1\right\} = 22.9\% \text{ per year}$$

This sixth root can be extracted directly with a scientific calculator or by logarithms. Starting with 870 and multiplying by the growth factor of 22.9%, the results are as shown in Table 10.11.

**Table 10.11** *Calculation of exponential growth*

| Year | Projection |
|------|------------|
| 1 | 870 |
| 2 | 1,069 |
| 3 | 1,314 |
| 4 | 1,616 |
| 5 | 1,986 |
| 6 | 2,441 |
| 7 | 3,000 |
| 8 | 3,687 |

## Comparing different trend projections

We have now obtained three possible estimates for year 8:

| | |
|---|---|
| Additive, average 355 increase per year: | 3,355 |
| Line of best fit: | 3,193 |
| Exponential: | 3,687 |

By comparing annual projections of each method with actual sales for the previous year in Table 10.12, we see a close fit for the exponential projection.

**Table 10.12** *Comparison of annual projections with actual sales*

| Year | Actual | Additive | Line of best fit | Exponential |
|---|---|---|---|---|
| 1 | 870 | 870 | 680 | 870 |
| 2 | 1,020 | 1,225 (−205) | 1,039 (− 19) | 1,069 (− 49) |
| 3 | 1,295 | 1,580 (−285) | 1,398 (−103) | 1,314 (− 19) |
| 4 | 1,620 | 1,935 (−315) | 1,757 (−137) | 1,616 (+ 4) |
| 5 | 1,990 | 2,290 (−300) | 2,116 (−126) | 1,986 (+ 4) |
| 6 | 2,505 | 2,645 (−140) | 2,475 (+ 30) | 2,441 (+ 64) |
| 7 | 3,000 | 3,000 | 2,834 (+166) | 3,000 |
| 8 | ? | 3,355 | 3,193 | 3,687 |

From these comparative projections we can feel confident to suggest a sales forecast of 3,500 for year 8.

## Seasonal effects and random variations

In any one year with spring, summer, autumn and winter, there are many influences: variations of temperature, hours of sunshine, periods of rain, winds, humidity, etc. There are also variations relating to the total social, political, economic, religious and commercial activities of a country, and all have 'seasonal' effects on sales.

Some products exhibit a readily understandable seasonality of sales: ice cream, umbrellas, holiday travel, electric lightbulbs, coal, central heating, building materials, and so on. Most other goods and services have a seasonality not always readily identifiable.

When establishing a trend, the seasonal effects must be isolated from the series. Table 10.13 is an example of a company's quarterly sales over five years. From inspection we notice a marked seasonality of a dip in the third quarter and, to smooth the peaks and troughs, we sum in 4s and 2s, and divide by 8 to establish the trend (4). The quarterly trend figures are

**Table 10.13** *Quarterly sales over five years of a specimen company*

| Year | Qtr | (1) | (2) | (3) | (4) | (5) | (6) | (7) | (8) (7) as % |
|------|-----|-----|-----|-----|-----|-----|-----|-----|--------------|
| 19x1 | 1 | 209 | | | | | | | |
| | 2 | 226 | | | | | | | |
| | | | 870 | | | | | | |
| | 3 | 174 | | 1,766 | 221 | −47 | −50 | + 3 | 1.7 |
| | | | 896 | | | | | | |
| | 4 | 261 | | 1,821 | 228 | +33 | +33 | 0 | — |
| | | | 925 | | | | | | |
| 19x2 | 1 | 235 | | 1,900 | 238 | − 3 | + 2 | − 5 | 2.1 |
| | | | 975 | | | | | | |
| | 2 | 255 | | 1,955 | 249 | + 6 | +14 | − 8 | 3.1 |
| | | | 1,020 | | | | | | |
| | 3 | 224 | | 2,103 | 263 | −39 | −50 | +11 | 4.9 |
| | | | 1,083 | | | | | | |
| | 4 | 306 | | 2,235 | 279 | +27 | +33 | − 6 | 2.0 |
| | | | 1,152 | | | | | | |
| 19x3 | 1 | 298 | | 2,365 | 296 | + 2 | + 2 | 0 | — |
| | | | 1,213 | | | | | | |
| | 2 | 324 | | 2,508 | 314 | +10 | +14 | − 4 | 1.2 |
| | | | 1,295 | | | | | | |
| | 3 | 285 | | 2,665 | 333 | −48 | −50 | + 2 | 0.7 |
| | | | 1,370 | | | | | | |
| | 4 | 388 | | 2,821 | 353 | +35 | +33 | + 2 | 0.5 |
| | | | 1,451 | | | | | | |
| 19x4 | 1 | 373 | | 2,973 | 372 | + 1 | + 2 | − 1 | 0.3 |
| | | | 1,522 | | | | | | |
| | 2 | 405 | | 3,142 | 393 | +12 | +14 | − 2 | 0.5 |
| | | | 1,620 | | | | | | |
| | 3 | 356 | | 3,345 | 418 | −62 | −50 | −12 | 3.4 |
| | | | 1,725 | | | | | | |
| | 4 | 486 | | 3,562 | 445 | +41 | +33 | + 8 | 1.6 |
| | | | 1,837 | | | | | | |
| 19x5 | 1 | 478 | | 3,716 | 465 | +13 | + 2 | +11 | 2.3 |
| | | | 1,879 | | | | | | |
| | 2 | 517 | | 3,869 | 484 | +33 | +14 | +19 | 3.7 |
| | | | 1,990 | | | | | | |
| | 3 | 398 | | | | | | | |
| | 4 | 597 | | | | | | | |

The columns are:
(1) Quarterly sales
(2) Column (1), the sales, summed successively in 4s
(3) Column (2), the summed 4s, summed successively in 2s
(4) Column (3) divided by 8
(5) Column (1) minus column (4); thus $174-221 = \text{-}47$ and $261-228 = 33$, and so on
(6) Derived from Table 10.14
(7) These figures are the random variations left after taking column (6) from column (5). Thus the first one is $(\text{-}47)-(\text{-}50) = \text{-}47+50 = +3$, a 1.7% variation.

deducted from the actual quarterly sales figures to obtain the quarterly deviations, column (5). These deviations are transferred to Table 10.14 to obtain average quarterly deviations, column (6). This average variation for each quarter is then deducted from the actual deviation for that quarter to determine the random variation, column (7).

**Table 10.14** *Average quarterly deviations*

| Year | Qtr: 1 | 2 | 3 | 4 |
|---|---|---|---|---|
| 19x1 | | | − 47 | + 33 |
| 19x2 | − 3 | + 6 | − 39 | + 27 |
| 19x3 | + 2 | +10 | − 48 | + 35 |
| 19x4 | + 1 | +12 | − 62 | + 41 |
| 19x5 | +13 | +33 | | |
| Totals | +13 | +61 | −196 | +136 |
| Average | +3.25 | +15.25 | − 49 | + 34 |

These averages, 3.25, 15.25, −49 and 34, sum to +3.5 but, as they are variations about the mean, they need to be adjusted to sum as near to zero as possible. Therefore we deduct from each one 3.5/4 = 0.875. The adjusted quarterly averages are then:

| Qtr 1 | Qtr 2 | Qtr 3 | Qtr 4 |
|---|---|---|---|
| +2.375 | +14.375 | −49.875 | +33.125 |

These are rounded:

| Qtr 1 | Qtr 2 | Qtr 3 | Qtr 4 |
|---|---|---|---|
| +2 | +14 | −50 | +33 |

and inserted for the appropriate quarters in Table 10.13 as column (6).

The random factors, which are residual in the series, are low for most quarters.

This analysis is used to estimate sales, by quarters, for the next year. From Table 10.13 we know that the trend has increased from 221 to 484. This is an average quarterly increase for the 16 quarters (15 increases) of 17.5, ie (484−221)/15, but, over the last year, the average increase was 22.7, ie (484−393)/4. Therefore the average increase per quarter for the sixth year is likely to be nearer to 23.

Let us assume an average increase of 23 per quarter and extend the figures to estimate the four quarters for year 6 as in Table 10.15. The figures for year 5 are first inserted, then the average quarterly variations, column (6), from Table 10.14. We add 23 successively to the trend figures, column (4). These are each multiplied by 8 for column (3), which are

successive additions of pairs from column (2). Column (2) can now be calculated and, as this column represents successive additions of 4s from
column (1), this column can now be completed.

Finally, starting with year 5 Qtr 3, the trend for this quarter, 507, is
deducted from the actual sales of 398 to obtain -109 for column (5). year 5
Qtr 4 has an expected trend of 530 and actual sales of 597 to give +67 for
(5). Year 6 Qtr 1 trend is 553 and estimates sales 554 to give +1 for (5).
When column (5) has been completed in this way, each quarterly variation has the appropriate quarterly variation, column (6), deducted to
obtain the random variations, column (7). These are calculated as
percentages of the quarterly sales figures for column (8).

**Table 10.15** *Forecast from average increase*

| Year | Qtr | (1) | (2) | (3) | (4) | (5) | (6) | (7) | (8) |
|------|-----|-----|-----|-----|-----|-----|-----|-----|-----|
| 19x5 | 1 | 478 | | 3,716 | 465 | + 13 | + 2 | +11 | 2.3% |
| | | | 1,879 | | | | | | |
| | 2 | 517 | | 3,869 | 484 | + 33 | +14 | +19 | 3.7% |
| | | | 1,990 | | | | | | |
| | 3 | 398 | | 4,056 | 507 | −109 | −50 | −59 | 14.8% |
| | | | 2,066 | | | | | | |
| | 4 | 597 | | 4,240 | 530 | + 67 | +33 | +34 | 5.7% |
| | | | 2,174 | | | | | | |
| 19x6 | 1 | 554 | | 4,424 | 553 | + 1 | + 2 | − 1 | 0.2% |
| | | | 2,250 | | | | | | |
| | 2 | 625 | | 4,608 | 576 | + 49 | +14 | +35 | 5.6% |
| | | | 2,358 | | | | | | |
| | 3 | 474 | | 4,792 | 599 | −125 | −50 | −75 | 15.8% |
| | | | 2,434 | | | | | | |
| | 4 | 705 | | 4,976 | 622 | + 83 | +33 | +50 | 7.1% |

The estimated random variations are slightly higher than previously but
the estimated total for the year, 2,358, seems reasonable and we can feel
confident in recommending a sales forecast of 2,400 for year 6.

If you look back at Table 10.12, you will see that actual sales for year 6
were 2,505 and the four quarters' sales were 588, 644, 524 and 749—all
higher than our adopted sales forecast.

It is normal practice to update statistical tables with the latest figures.
Therefore, Table 10.15 is modified by inserting the actual quarterly sales
for year 6, amending the average quarterly variations in Table 10.14 to
obtain a new column (6), and finally, recalculating the residual random
variations for a new column (7). This updating is set out in Tables 10.16
and 10.17.

**Table 10.16** *Table 10.14 amended, with additional data*

|                   | 1      | 2      | 3      | 4      |
|-------------------|--------|--------|--------|--------|
| Previous totals   | +13    | +61    | −196   | +136   |
| 19x5              |        |        | −113   | + 56   |
| 19x6              | +15    | +37    |        |        |
| New totals        | +28    | +98    | −309   | +192   |
| Average           | + 5.6  | +19.6  | − 61.8 | + 38.4 |

These sum to +1.8; therefore we deduct 1.8/4 = 0.45 from each to make them sum to zero:

|         | 1      | 2      | 3      | 4      |
|---------|--------|--------|--------|--------|
|         | +5.15  | +19.15 | −62.25 | +37.95 |
| Rounded | +5     | +19    | −62    | −38    |

These average seasonal variations are inserted in Table 10.17.

**Table 10.17** *Table 10.13 updated*

| Year | Qtr | (1) | (2) | (3) | (4) | (5) | (6) | (7) | (8) |
|------|-----|-----|-----|-----|-----|-----|-----|-----|-----|
| 19x1 | 1 | 209 | | | | | | | |
|      | 2 | 226 | | | | | | | |
|      |   |     | 870 | | | | | | |
|      | 3 | 174 | | 1,766 | 221 | −47 | −62 | +15 | 8.6% |
|      |   |     | 896 | | | | | | |
|      | 4 | 261 | | 1,821 | 228 | +33 | +38 | − 5 | 1.9% |
|      |   |     | 925 | | | | | | |
| 19x2 | 1 | 235 | | 1,900 | 238 | − 3 | + 5 | − 8 | 3.4% |
|      |   |     | 975 | | | | | | |
|      | 2 | 255 | | 1,955 | 249 | + 6 | +19 | −13 | 5.1% |
|      |   |     | 1,020 | | | | | | |
|      | 3 | 224 | | 2,103 | 263 | −39 | −62 | +23 | 10.3% |
|      |   |     | 1,083 | | | | | | |
|      | 4 | 306 | | 2,235 | 279 | +27 | +38 | −11 | 3.6% |
|      |   |     | 1,152 | | | | | | |
| 19x3 | 1 | 298 | | 2,365 | 296 | + 2 | + 5 | − 3 | 1.0% |
|      |   |     | 1,213 | | | | | | |
|      | 2 | 324 | | 2,508 | 314 | +10 | +19 | − 9 | 2.8% |
|      |   |     | 1,295 | | | | | | |
|      | 3 | 285 | | 2,665 | 333 | −48 | −62 | +14 | 4.9% |
|      |   |     | 1,370 | | | | | | |
|      | 4 | 388 | | 2,821 | 353 | +35 | +38 | − 3 | 0.8% |
|      |   |     | 1,451 | | | | | | |

**Table 10.17**  *Table 10.13 updated—continued*

| Year | Qtr | (1) | (2) | (3) | (4) | (5) | (6) | (7) | (8) |
|------|-----|-----|-----|-----|-----|-----|-----|-----|-----|
| 19x4 | 1 | 373 | | 2,973 | 372 | + 1 | + 5 | − 4 | 1.1% |
| | | | 1,522 | | | | | | |
| | 2 | 405 | | 3,142 | 393 | + 12 | +19 | − 7 | 1.7% |
| | | | 1,620 | | | | | | |
| | 3 | 356 | | 3,345 | 418 | − 62 | −62 | 0 | 0% |
| | | | 1,725 | | | | | | |
| | 4 | 486 | | 3,562 | 445 | + 41 | +38 | + 3 | 0.6% |
| | | | 1,837 | | | | | | |
| 19x5 | 1 | 478 | | 3,716 | 465 | + 13 | + 5 | + 8 | 1.7% |
| | | | 1,879 | | | | | | |
| | 2 | 517 | | 3,869 | 484 | + 33 | +19 | +14 | 2.7% |
| | | | 1,990 | | | | | | |
| | 3 | 398 | | 4,090 | 511 | −113 | −62 | −51 | 12.8% |
| | | | 2,100 | | | | | | |
| | 4 | 597 | | 4,327 | 541 | + 56 | +38 | +18 | 3.0% |
| | | | 2,227 | | | | | | |
| 19x6 | 1 | 588 | | 4,580 | 573 | + 15 | + 5 | +10 | 1.7% |
| | | | 2,353 | | | | | | |
| | 2 | 644 | | 4,858 | 607 | + 37 | +19 | +18 | 2.8% |
| | | | 2,505 | | | | | | |
| | 3 | 524 | | | | | | | |
| | 4 | 749 | | | | | | | |

## Trend projection—a worked example

We reconsider the problem we looked at in Chapter 9 in Table 9.4, which is reproduced again in Table 10.18.

**Table 10.18** *from Table 9.4*

| Year | Sales |
|------|-------|
| 1 | 500 |
| 2 | 700 |
| 3 | 1,500 |
| 4 | 1,700 |
| 5 | 2,050 |

Let us assume that we can obtain additional data as shown in Table 10.19.

**Table 10.19** *Table 10.18 amended, with additional data*

| Year | Qtr | Sales |
|------|-----|-------|
| 19x1 | 1 | 100 |
|      | 2 | 130 |
|      | 3 | 120 |
|      | 4 | 150 |
| 19x2 | 1 | 130 |
|      | 2 | 190 |
|      | 3 | 150 |
|      | 4 | 230 |
| 19x3 | 1 | 290 |
|      | 2 | 380 |
|      | 3 | 360 |
|      | 4 | 470 |
| 19x4 | 1 | 400 |
|      | 2 | 430 |
|      | 3 | 380 |
|      | 4 | 490 |
| 19x5 | 1 | 520 |
|      | 2 | 530 |
|      | 3 | 410 |
|      | 4 | 590 |

We find the line of best fit (method of least squares), as in Table 10.20.

**Table 10.20** *Line of best fit*

| Year | Y | d | Yd | $d^2$ |
|------|-----|-----|-------|-----|
| 19x1 | 500 | −2 | −2,000 | 4 |
| 19x2 | 700 | −1 | − 700 | 1 |
| 19x3 | 1,500 | 0 | 0 | 0 |
| 19x4 | 1,700 | +1 | 1,700 | 1 |
| 19x5 | 2,050 | +2 | 4,100 | 4 |

From the table, $\Sigma Y = 6{,}450$, $\Sigma Yd = 3{,}100$, $\Sigma d^2 = 10$, $a = \Sigma Y/5 = 1{,}290$, and $b = \Sigma Yd/\Sigma d^2 = 3{,}100/10 = 310$.
$Y = a + bd$ and therefore, $Y = 1{,}290 + (310 \times 3) = \underline{2{,}220}$.
(Note that $d$ for year 6 is +3.)

We can try to fit the exponential trend formula. The formula is:

$$\text{Rate} = \left\{ \left( \sqrt[m]{\frac{Y_n}{Y_t}} \right) - 1 \right\} 100$$

$$= \left\{ \left( \sqrt[4]{\frac{2,050}{500}} \right) - 1 \right\} 100$$

$$= 42.3\% \text{ per year}$$

We start with first year sales, 500, and increase this successively by 42.3% each year (multiply successively by 1.423), as in Table 10.21.

**Table 10.21** *Actual sales and exponential trend*

| Year | Actual sales | Exponential trend |
|------|------|------|
| 19x1 | 500 | 500 |
| 19x2 | 700 | 711 |
| 19x3 | 1,500 | 1,012 |
| 19x4 | 1,700 | 1,441 |
| 19x5 | 2,050 | 2,050 |
| 19x6 | ? | 2,916 (estimated) |

The exponential trend is not a good match with the original data, so we apply another analysis as already illustrated in this chapter in Table 10.13 (Table 10.22).

**Table 10.22** *Analysis of quarterly sales over five years*

| Year | Qtr | (1) | (2) | (3) | (4) | (5) | (6) | (7) | (8) |
|------|-----|-----|-----|-----|-----|-----|-----|-----|-----|
| 19x1 | 1 | 100 | | | | | | | |
| | 2 | 130 | | | | | | | |
| | | | 500 | | | | | | |
| | 3 | 120 | | 1,030 | 129 | − 9 | −38 | +29 | 24% |
| | | | 530 | | | | | | |
| | 4 | 150 | | 1,120 | 140 | +10 | +19 | − 9 | 6% |
| | | | 590 | | | | | | |

*Continued overleaf*

**Table 10.22** *Analysis of quarterly sales over five years—continued*

| Year | Qtr | (1) | (2) | (3) | (4) | (5) | (6) | (7) | (8) |
|------|-----|-----|-----|-----|-----|-----|-----|-----|-----|
| 19x2 | 1 | 130 | | 1,210 | 151 | −21 | − 3 | −18 | 14% |
| | | | 620 | | | | | | |
| | 2 | 190 | | 1,320 | 165 | +25 | +22 | + 3 | 2% |
| | | | 700 | | | | | | |
| | 3 | 150 | | 1,560 | 195 | −45 | −38 | − 7 | 5% |
| | | | 860 | | | | | | |
| | 4 | 230 | | 1,910 | 239 | − 9 | +19 | −28 | 12% |
| | | | 1,050 | | | | | | |
| 19x3 | 1 | 290 | | 2,310 | 289 | + 1 | − 3 | + 4 | 1% |
| | | | 1,260 | | | | | | |
| | 2 | 380 | | 2,760 | 345 | +35 | +22 | +13 | 3% |
| | | | 1,500 | | | | | | |
| | 3 | 360 | | 3,110 | 389 | −29 | −38 | + 9 | 3% |
| | | | 1,610 | | | | | | |
| | 4 | 470 | | 3,270 | 409 | +61 | +19 | +42 | 9% |
| | | | 1,660 | | | | | | |
| 19x4 | 1 | 400 | | 3,340 | 418 | −18 | − 3 | −15 | 4% |
| | | | 1,680 | | | | | | |
| | 2 | 430 | | 3,380 | 423 | + 7 | +22 | −15 | 3% |
| | | | 1,700 | | | | | | |
| | 3 | 380 | | 3,520 | 440 | −60 | −38 | −22 | 6% |
| | | | 1,820 | | | | | | |
| | 4 | 490 | | 3,740 | 468 | +22 | +19 | + 3 | 1% |
| | | | 1,920 | | | | | | |
| 19x5 | 1 | 520 | | 3,870 | 484 | +36 | − 3 | +39 | 8% |
| | | | 1,950 | | | | | | |
| | 2 | 530 | | 4,000 | 500 | +30 | +22 | + 8 | 2% |
| | | | 2,050 | | | | | | |
| | 3 | 410 | | | | | | | |
| | 4 | 590 | | | | | | | |

The deviations from column (5) are now set out in Table 10.23. These sum to 10. We adjust to sum to zero by subtracting $10/4 = 2.5$ from each and rounding to obtain the average seasonal variations which are inserted as column (6) in Table 10.22, ie:

$$-3 \quad +22 \quad -38 \quad +19$$

To project from the trend—column (4)—we look at the last seven trend figures: 409, 418, 423, 440, 468, 484, 500. The average quarterly increase is 15, $(9+5+17+28+16+16)/6$. We increase the trend by 15 for each of the four quarters for the sixth year (515, 530, 545 and 560) and project back to obtain the quarterly estimates of sales (Table 10.24). The estimate sales for year 6 by this method is 2,290 units.

**Table 10.23** *Average quarterly deviations*

| Year | Qtr: 1 | 2 | 3 | 4 |
|------|--------|-----|------|-----|
| 19x1 |        |     | − 9 | +10 |
| 19x2 | −21    | +25 | − 45 | − 9 |
| 19x3 | + 1    | +35 | − 29 | +61 |
| 19x4 | −18    | + 7 | − 60 | +22 |
| 19x5 | +36    | +30 |      |     |
| Totals | − 2  | +97 | −143 | +84 |
| Average | − 0.5 | +24.25 | − 35.75 | +21 |

**Table 10.24** *Forecast from average increase*

| Year | Qtr | (1) | (2) | (3) | (4) | (5) | (6) | (7) | (8) |
|------|-----|-----|-----|-----|-----|-----|-----|-----|-----|
| 19x5 | 1 | 520 |       | 3,870 | 484 | +36 | − 3 | +39 | 8% |
|      |   |     | 1,950 |       |     |     |     |     |    |
|      | 2 | 530 |       | 4,000 | 500 | +30 | +22 | + 8 | 2% |
|      |   |     | 2,050 |       |     |     |     |     |    |
|      | 3 | 410 |       | 4,120 | 515 |     |     |     |    |
|      |   |     | 2,070 |       |     |     |     |     |    |
|      | 4 | 590 |       | 4,240 | 530 |     |     |     |    |
|      |   |     | 2,170 |       |     |     |     |     |    |
| 19x6 | 1 | 540 |       | 4,360 | 545 |     |     |     |    |
|      |   |     | 2,190 |       |     |     |     |     |    |
|      | 2 | 630 |       | 4,480 | 560 |     |     |     |    |
|      |   |     | 2,290 |       |     |     |     |     |    |
|      | 3 | 430 |       |       |     |     |     |     |    |
|      | 4 | 690 |       |       |     |     |     |     |    |

## Comparing estimates by the different methods

The four figures obtained by the different methods are:

|                    |                       |
|--------------------|-----------------------|
| Simple additive    | 2,437 (Table 9.5)     |
| Line of best fit   | 2,220 (Table 10.20)   |
| Exponential        | 2,916 (Table 10.21)   |
| Trend projection   | 2,290 (Table 10.24)   |

Whichever figure we take is subjective but, if we exclude the highest and the lowest from the estimates, the average is about 2,350, which looks a reasonable target to set.

## Correlation

When using market factors to estimate sales there must be an acceptable statistical relationship between the market factors and the product being estimated. This relationship is called 'correlation'. Correlation is a statistical measurement of association but does not necessarily mean that one set of data is caused by another set. There is high correlation between hours of sunshine and sales of ice cream but neither causes the other; sales of sun-glasses correlate with sales of sun tan oil but they do not cause one another.

Correlation can be *positive*: as one set of data increases (or decreases), so another set also increases (or decreases) in harmony. It can be *negative*: an increase in one set of data is reflected by a decrease in another set. If two sets move in complete harmony, correlation is very high.

We would expect some positive correlation between data relating to rainfall and sales of raincoats. There is negative correlation between the price and the sales of strawberries—as price decreases, sales increase.

Two sets of data concerning the selling area in stores and their profits over a year are given in Table 10.25.

Table 10.25 *Specimen data—selling area and profit*

|   | Selling Area (000s ft) X | Profit (£ million) Y |
|---|---|---|
| A | 20 | 0.98 |
| B | 28 | 1.5 |
| C | 30 | 1.74 |
| D | 35 | 2.1 |
| E | 40 | 2.5 |
| F | 44 | 3.2 |
| G | 55 | 3.5 |
| H | 60 | 3.8 |

## Scattergram

A graphical solution is called a 'scattergraph' or 'scattergram'. Two axes are drawn, one for $X$ and one for $Y$; the axes need not extend to zero if not required. Each pair is plotted: 20 and 0.98; 28 and 1.5, and so on (Figure 10.2). If there is any degree of correlation, most of the points will tend to be in a straight line: if they are, it is worth calculating the coefficient of correlation statistically.

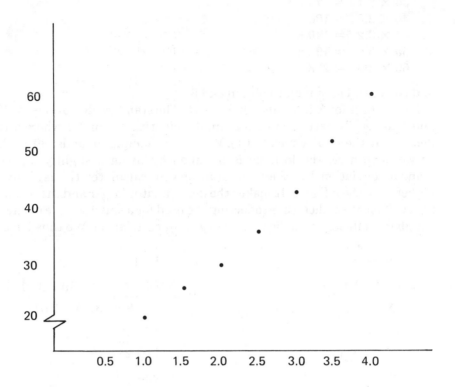

**Figure 10.2** *A scattergram*

## Coefficient of correlation

To calculate this, multiply each pair together, $XY$, and add to obtain the 'sum of $XY$'. Calculate the average of $X$, ($\bar{X}$), and the average of $Y$, ($\bar{Y}$). Find the standard deviation of $X$, and of $Y$. With $n$, the number of pairs, the formula for the coefficient of correlation is:

$$R = \frac{\Sigma XY - n\bar{X}\bar{Y}}{n\,\sigma_x\,\sigma_y}$$

$XY$ is obtained by multiplying the pairs in the table:

20 × 0.98 = 19.6
28 × 1.5  = 42
30 × 1.74 = 52.2

$$35 \times 2.1 = 73.5$$
$$40 \times 2.5 = 100$$
$$44 \times 3.2 = 140.8$$
$$55 \times 3.5 = 192.5$$
$$60 \times 3.8 = 228$$

and so on, and summing to obtain 848.6

The average for $X$ is 39, and for $Y$, 2.415. The standard deviations for $X$ and $Y$ are easily extracted with a simple scientific calculator where it is denoted by the small Greek 's' ($\sigma$). With small samples of under 30, such as we have here, the formula is modified by using a slightly higher standard deviation. Use the $\sigma$n-1 figure on your calculator; this is always higher than the $n$ figure. It makes the denominator larger and the resulting coefficient smaller, thus reflecting the need for a small sample to have a higher coefficient to indicate any degree of correlation. We thus have:

$$n = 8 \qquad\qquad \sigma_y = 1.01$$

$$\Sigma XY = 848.6$$
$$\bar{X} = 39 \qquad\qquad R = \frac{848.6 - (8 \times 39 \times 2.415)}{8 \times 13.64 \times 1.01}$$
$$\sigma_x = 13.64 \qquad\qquad = \frac{95.12}{110.21}$$
$$\bar{Y} = 2.415$$
$$= 0.86$$

## Significance of correlation

To determine whether a coefficient is significant, that is, whether it is large enough to indicate there is some relationship between sets of data, use the table of significance of coefficient of correlation, Table 10.26.

First determine the 'degrees of freedom' by deducting 2 from $n$, the number of data; with 8 pairs, there are 6 degrees of freedom. Read across the table at the appropriate number of degrees of freedom and look at the column for the level of confidence you want. The columns list three levels—5 chances in 100, 1 chance in 100, 1 chance in 1,000—that the coefficient could have occurred accidentally. The figure given is the minimum required to establish a degree of statistical correlation at that level of confidence and particular number of degrees of freedom. For marketing research and forecasting work, 5 chances in 100 (0.95 level) is normally used.

Suppose you are comparing two sets of, say, 12 data with a coefficient of correlation of 0.85. Degrees of freedom are $12 - 2 = 10$. On the 10-line, the minimum value for 0.05 (5 chances in 100) is 0.576. Therefore the figure of 0.85 is highly significant for the two sets of data.

**Table 10.26** *Significance of coefficient of correlation*

| Degrees of freedom | Coefficient of correlation | | |
|---|---|---|---|
| | 0.05 | 0.01 | 0.001 |
| 1 | 0.997 | 1.000 | 1.000 |
| 2 | 0.950 | 0.990 | 0.999 |
| 3 | 0.878 | 0.959 | 0.992 |
| 4 | 0.811 | 0.917 | 0.974 |
| 5 | 0.754 | 0.874 | 0.951 |
| 6 | 0.707 | 0.834 | 0.925 |
| 7 | 0.666 | 0.798 | 0.898 |
| 8 | 0.632 | 0.765 | 0.872 |
| 9 | 0.602 | 0.735 | 0.847 |
| 10 | 0.576 | 0.708 | 0.823 |
| 11 | 0.553 | 0.684 | 0.801 |
| 12 | 0.532 | 0.661 | 0.780 |
| 13 | 0.514 | 0.641 | 0.760 |
| 14 | 0.497 | 0.623 | 0.742 |
| 15 | 0.482 | 0.606 | 0.725 |
| 16 | 0.468 | 0.590 | 0.708 |
| 17 | 0.456 | 0.575 | 0.693 |
| 18 | 0.444 | 0.561 | 0.679 |
| 19 | 0.433 | 0.549 | 0.665 |
| 20 | 0.423 | 0.537 | 0.652 |

If there were two sets of 7 items with a coefficient of 0.72 and we wish to be sure of a high degree of significance of only 1 in 100 happening by chance, then looking across 5 degrees of freedom to the second column (0.01) we need a minimum value of 0.874. Unfortunately, there is no correlation with 0.72 and, even at the lower level of confidence of 5 in 100 (0.05), we would need a minimum of 0.754 before we could say there is some degree of correlation.

For the data in Table 10.25, with 6 degrees of freedom, at the 95% confidence level the minimum value is 0.707. Therefore, the coefficient of 0.86 is significant and we can have 95 per cent confidence that there is a relationship between the size of selling area of the stores and their profit.

## Coefficient of determination

You may not always have Table 10.26 to hand. A quick, approximate method of deciding whether or not a coefficient is significant is to square it to obtain the coefficient of determination. Thus, 0.86 squared is 0.74, which indicates that 74 per cent of the data are statistically associated. A correlation coefficient of 0.70 gives a coefficient of determination of 0.49.

Only 49 per cent of the data is statistically associated; 51 per cent could have happened by chance. This quick method does not take into account the number in the sample, so it must be used with care.

Two more sets of data are given in Table 10.27.

**Table 10.27** *Specimen data—selling area and sales*

|   | Selling Area (000 ft) | Sales (£ million) |
|---|---|---|
| A | 15 | 1.0 |
| B | 20 | 1.05 |
| C | 30 | 1.6 |
| D | 40 | 1.1 |
| E | 48 | 1.65 |
| F | 65 | 2.05 |
| G | 76 | 2.1 |
| H | 80 | 3.5 |

The scattergram is shown in Figure 10.3.

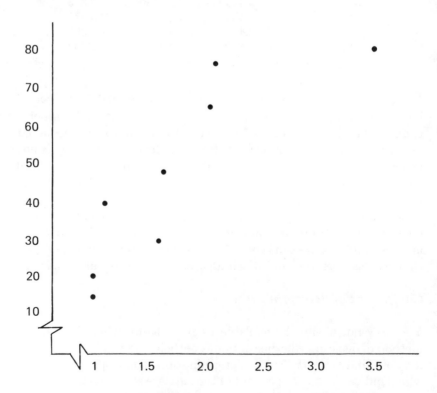

**Figure 10.3** *The scattergram of Table 10.27*

There may be some correlation, so we calculate the coefficient of correlation:

$$n = 8$$

$$\Sigma XY = 780.05$$

$$\bar{X} = 46.75$$

$$\bar{Y} = 1.756$$

$$\sigma_x = 24.92$$

$$\sigma_y = 0.83$$

$$R = \frac{\Sigma XY - n\bar{X}\bar{Y}}{n\sigma_x\sigma_y}$$

$$= \frac{780.05 - (8 \times 46.75 \times 1.756)}{8 \times 24.92 \times 0.83}$$

$$= 0.75$$

Reference to the significance table indicates that a figure greater than 0.707 is required for significant correlation at the 95% confidence level. Therefore, a small degree of correlation is evident between $X$ and $Y$.

## Market factor derivation

This is an accurate method of forecasting provided that relative factors can be isolated in the market. This takes time because the factors have to be extracted from whatever data is available, their reliability tested, and their relevance to the product verified.

Ken Roberts had recently been made responsible for forecasting in his company, which manufactures gas central heating systems for domestic use. They do not supply commercial buildings or factories. For the past 10 years, their sales had increased by about 10 per cent per year, from 5,900 units in 1974 to 13,400 in 1983. However, during the last three years, sales had been declining by about 3 per cent per year, although their market share had remained fairly constant at around 6 per cent. Table 10.28 displays this information.

**Table 10.28** *Sales of gas central heating*

| Year | Company | Industry | Market share (%) |
|------|---------|----------|------------------|
| 1974 | 5,904 | 191,000 | 3.09 |
| 1975 | 6,503 | 201,000 | 3.23 |
| 1976 | 7,768 | 251,000 | 3.10 |
| 1977 | 9,839 | 279,000 | 3.53 |
| 1978 | 11,230 | 277,000 | 4.05 |
| 1979 | 12,137 | 264,000 | 4.60 |
| 1980 | 12,952 | 224,000 | 5.78 |
| 1981 | 14,362 | 222,000 | 6.47 |
| 1982 | 13,953 | 232,000 | 6.01 |
| 1983 | 13,400 | 220,000 | 6.09 |

Mr Roberts appreciated that company sales of domestic heating is related to people's homes, and obtained figures for houses in existence and new houses and compared these with company sales, as in Table 10.29.

**Table 10.29** *Comparison of sales and housing*

| Year | Sales | Existing houses | New houses |
|------|-------|-----------------|------------|
| 1974 | 5,904 |            | 360,000 |
| 1975 | 6,503 |            | 310,000 |
| 1976 | 7,768 |            | 316,000 |
| 1977 | 9,839 | 15,800,000 | 325,000 |
| 1978 | 11,230 | 16,100,000 | 315,000 |
| 1979 | 12,137 | 16,300,000 | 290,000 |
| 1980 | 12,952 | 16,600,000 | 245,000 |
| 1981 | 14,362 | 16,900,000 | 235,000 |
| 1982 | 13,953 | 17,600,000 | 240,000 |
| 1983 | 13,400 | 17,900,000 | 280,000 |

From his enquiries he found that, in most years, up to 5 per cent of existing homes installed some form of central heating, but this depended on economic conditions. On the other hand, all new houses had some form of heating installed. He was told by the gas supply industry that approximately 41 per cent of new house construction opted for gas heating but that 1983 had been a poor year. Other forms of heating had gained ground and the gas industry had lost about 10 per cent of their market. In the existing houses market, although it is more difficult to run pipes through the walls, their share had remained constant at around 15 per cent.

He applied these percentages: 5 per cent of existing houses and 100 per cent of new houses installing heating; gas installed in 15 per cent of existing houses and in 41 per cent of new (31 per cent in 1983), to data for the past four years. The variations of estimated sales from the actual total industry sales were under 1 per cent. This is shown in Table 10.30.

He then took 3 per cent of the estimated sales to existing houses, and 10 per cent of new house estimated sales and compared the totals with actual company sales. This is given in Table 10.31.

This gave him confidence in applying similar percentages to the forecast for 1984. He decided to recommend a sales forecast of 13,500 units for that year and justified this as in Table 10.32.

**Table 10.30** *Variation of estimated sales from total industry sales[1]*

| Year | Existing houses | New houses | Estimated total sales | Actual sales | Variation |
|---|---|---|---|---|---|
| 1980 | 16,600,000 0.05 | 245,000 1.0 | | | |
| | 830,000 0.15 | 245,000 0.41 | | | |
| | 124,500 | 100,450 | = 224,950 | 224,000 | 900 |
| 1981 | 16,900,000 0.05 | 235,000 1.0 | | | |
| | 845,000 0.15 | 235,000 0.41 | | | |
| | 126,750 | 96,350 | = 223,100 | 222,000 | 1,100 |
| 1982 | 17,600,000 0.05 | 240,000 1.0 | | | |
| | 880,000 0.15 | 240,000 0.41 | | | |
| | 132,000 | 98,400 | = 230,400 | 232,000 | 1,600 |
| 1983 | 17,900,000 0.05 | 280,000 1.0 | | | |
| | 895,000 0.15 | 280,000 0.31 | | | |
| | 134,250 | 86,800 | = 221,050 | 220,000 | 1,050 |

**Table 10.31** *Variation of estimated sales from total industry sales[2]*

| Year | Estimated total sales Existing houses | New houses | Company sales Estimated | Actual | Variation |
|---|---|---|---|---|---|
| 1980 | 124,500 0.03 | 100,450 0.10 | | | |
| | 3,735 | 10,045 | = 13,780 | 12,952 | 828  (6.0%) |
| 1981 | 126,750 0.03 | 96,350 0.10 | | | |
| | 3,802 | 9,635 | = 13,437 | 14,362 | 925  (6.9%) |
| 1982 | 132,000 0.03 | 98,400 0.10 | | | |
| | 3,960 | 9,840 | = 13,800 | 13,953 | 153  (1.1%) |
| 1983 | 134,250 0.03 | 86,800 0.10 | | | |
| | 4,027 | 8,680 | = 12,707 | 13,400 | 693  (5.5%) |

**Table 10.32** *Calculation of sales forecast*

| Existing houses | New houses |
|---|---|
| 18,000,000 (Ministry estimate) | 290,000   (Ministry forecast) |
| 0.05 | 1.0 |
| 900,000 | 290,000 |
| 0.15 | 0.35   (Gas Industry forecast) |
| 135,000 | 101,500 |
| 0.03 | 0.10   (Mr Roberts' forecast) |
| 4,050 | 10,150 |

These totals added to 14,200 units and, as previous estimates contained an error of up to approximately 5 per cent, he decided to take 95 per cent of this calculation (14,200 × 0.95 = 13,490), as in Table 10.33.

**Table 10.33** *Correlation analysis of market factors*

|      | X1 | X2 | X3 | X4 | X5 | X6 | X7 |
|------|-----|-----|-----|-----|-----|-----|-----|
| 1974 | 590   | 191 | —   | 360 | 171 | 134 | 119 |
| 1975 | 650   | 201 | —   | 310 | 169 | 134 | 116 |
| 1976 | 777   | 251 | —   | 316 | 168 | 132 | 115 |
| 1977 | 984   | 279 | 158 | 325 | 174 | 131 | 116 |
| 1978 | 1,123 | 277 | 161 | 315 | 176 | 129 | 115 |
| 1979 | 1,214 | 264 | 163 | 290 | 182 | 140 | 122 |
| 1980 | 1,295 | 224 | 166 | 245 | 183 | 148 | 127 |
| 1981 | 1,436 | 222 | 169 | 235 | 180 | 151 | 128 |
| 1982 | 1,395 | 232 | 176 | 240 | —   | —   | —   |
| 1983 | 1,340 | 220 | 179 | 280 | —   | —   | —   |

(Zeros are removed and data rounded to three or four significant figures)

X1 = Company sales       X5 = Gross domestic product
X2 = Industry sales       X6 = Personal disposable income
X3 = Existing houses       X7 = Consumers' expenditure
X4 = New houses

Table 10.34 gives the coefficients of correlation using $\sigma$ n-1 in the formula because the samples are 7, 8 and 10.

Mr Roberts had based his forecast on percentages of existing and new houses because it is 'common sense' that central heating is related to houses. Unfortunately, common sense is not supported by statistical analysis. There is no correlation between company sales and existing

**Table 10.34** *Coefficients of correlation*

|  | Deg. of F | Coeff. required | Correlation |
|---|---|---|---|
| X1X2 R =  0.22 | 8 | 0.632 | None |
| X1X3 R =  0.69 | 5 | 0.754 | None |
| X1X4 R = −0.77 | 8 | 0.632 | Negative |
| X1X5 R =  0.78 | 6 | 0.707 | Slight |
| X1X6 R =  0.61 | 6 | 0.707 | None |
| X1X7 R =  0.63 | 6 | 0.707 | None |

houses (0.69) and there is negative correlation between company sales and new houses.

There are no simple ways of forecasting sales. While the market factor derivation method is the most reliable, it is not always easy to find relevant factors. What appears to be an obviously related factor sometimes fails when put to the correlation test.

# 11

# Product Policy

**The development of a company's product range must be related to its current and future markets; hence a product/market plan is necessary. There are possibilities but dangers in using too general a life cycle approach in planning, but considerable advantages in positioning your company's products. You must avoid the problems of a unilateral adoption of a product portfolio theory; the situation should always be subjected to analyses from several viewpoints.**

## Importance of the product

Without a product (or service) a company has nothing to sell to potential customers. The crucial importance of the product has inevitably led some companies to become product-oriented or production-oriented and to ignore the needs of the market. Although the product may hold this vitally important role it does not follow that production people are the best judges of what products should be included in a company's range.

## Who decides which products?

If the product is so important, who decides whether or not a product should be in a company's range? This is really two questions: who decides which products stay in the range, and who decides which products are added to the range.

Marketing is identifying what customers need and then deciding how to satisfy those needs. Customers do not decide what products are to be added to the range but they influence what products stay in the range by their purchases of the products. If those purchases are not great enough to make adequate profit for the company, management may decide to remove them. In Chapter 15 we look at some of the reasons why unprofitable products are sometimes retained.

Some products possess a high technology. They are developed by research scientists and engineers; their nature, function and use have to be explained to potential buyers. Other products are very simple and readily understood by customers. The more complex the product the more likely its introduction to the company's range is production-motivated; the more simple the product the more likely its inclusion is market-motivated.

The process of building a company's product range is not always formalised, is sometimes fortuitous and occasionally quite vague. If you are responsible for the management of a company's sales you have a vested interest in the product range.

## Developing a product policy

One of your early tasks on joining a new organisation as sales manager is to find out all you can about the product range and production methods. Visit the factory and make friends with the key production people. Understand their problems, what they like making, what they have found difficult to make, what new ideas have been developed in the past. Note especially any machinery that appears not to be used, and ask why. While you must not become production-oriented and suggest only those products that will make use of available or unused machinery, if you can introduce new products into the range that require no new investment in plant and equipment you will quickly gain the support of your colleagues—especially the financial ones.

Introducing products that customers will not buy soon achieves financial losses. But introducing products that the market will only buy in small amounts may also incur financial losses if your profit margin is too low. Customers sometimes value products less than their cost of production and distribution. Decisions on a company's product range are complex, difficult, and always a risk area.

## Pressures to remain silent

A manager in a large multi-national company was convinced that the product his company intended to market would be a failure and that to introduce the product would waste time and resources. He presented an impressive array of supporting evidence at the many meetings, but his attempts to get the project dropped were of no avail. Despite his strenuous efforts to prevent his company making what he considered to be a disastrous error, the product was launched. It proved to be moderately successful and is still selling in small quantities.

The pressures on people in a large company to stay silent in the face of considerable opposition are very great. No one becomes a hero by stopping a product that, if continued, might have become a failure—no one can prove that it would have been. The proposer recedes into the background of the company. This gives rise to what I call 'establishment' decisions. Managers are wary of being 'the odd one out', and genuine entrepreneurs in large organisations are rare.

## Product/market policy

Never consider product policy in isolation: always consider it in relation to a market. In the main you have two types of customers: current and potential. Similarly, you have two main types of products: current and new. Therefore, from your present base of selling your current range of products to current customers, your product/market policy can take three directions:

- new customers with current products
- new products to current customers
- new customers with new products

While all three are concerned with both products and the market, it is much easier, and less costly, to review products than to review market situations. On joining a new company, you should avoid initiating market surveys until you are thoroughly conversant with the products and the potentials of the company production facilities. The product range can be reviewed and developed in three main ways:

- individual products
- product lines
- the total range or mix

Ideally, you should plan company product policy on the total range. Sometimes, product lines have developed in a company for reasons of production convenience, and this is not always best for selling and marketing. Developing product policy on individual products can also result in a disjointed and unrelated range.

## Avoiding product policy dangers

Developing a product/market policy is a time-consuming task that requires many inputs and probably considerable research and development. The particular danger for the newly-appointed manager is that the impact on sales is not felt in the short-term.

Whenever you embark on long-term activities of this kind, ensure that you have something else going on at the same time that shows 'you are doing your job'. I know of a number of new sales and marketing appointments made in companies where the manager spends a large part of his or her time investigating the company's marketing organisation, products and markets. After a year or 18 months, there has been little tangible difference in turnover, profit or performance. Frequently, the only difference is that costs have increased because of the activities of the newly appointed manager.

Many years ago I was appointed to a senior position with a group and had responsibilities for 11 subsidiaries and divisions. Nine days after I joined, I attended my first board meeting and gave my report. This was an outline based on my week's discussions with the numerous executives on how I saw the group might best develop in the future.

The chairman's comments will remain seared in my memory for ever.

'I'm not interested in what you think,' he said, 'I want to know what you've done for the company since you've been with us!'

'But I've only been here for nine days,' I gasped.

'Nine days—nine weeks—nine months. Doesn't make any difference. What have you actually done since you've arrived?'

Unjust? Unprovoked? Certainly unforgettable. The lesson was clear to me then as it is today, perhaps even more today: it isn't what you know or what you are thinking of doing, it's what you do about what you know...

To be a successful anything, you have to work on two levels: while you are thinking about tomorrow, you must be doing things for today. Don't become so engrossed in company product/market planning that you spend the majority of your time thinking about tomorrow and failing to do things for today. Planning is essential to success; but don't immerse yourself so much in it that you fail to do something about what you know.

## Product/market analysis

There are two aspects you should look at when analysing your company's marketing capabilities:

- the various markets and market segments in which you operate
- the position of your products relative to competition in those markets

Along the top of a sheet of paper, insert the markets you know the company supplies; down the left hand side, list the main production activities of the company. An example is given in Figure 11.1.

Insert ticks for each of the pairs in which the company is active. Markets and segments should be homogeneous and not too general. For example,

|            | Electronics | Engineering | Furniture | Cars | Etc |
|------------|-------------|-------------|-----------|------|-----|
| Electrical |             |             |           |      |     |
| Metalwork  |             |             |           |      |     |
| Presswork  |             |             |           |      |     |
| Diestamping|             |             |           |      |     |
| Extrusions |             |             |           |      |     |

**Figure 11.1** *Product/market analysis*

'television sets' is too broad a definition of the TV market. You may need to identify portable sets, colour sets, monochrome sets, large sitting-room sets, projection sets, sets up to 20-inch, sets over 20-inch, and so on. The furniture trade would need to be broken down into, say, lounge furniture, dining-room furniture, bedroom furniture, kitchen furniture, garden furniture, institutional furniture, and so on. For the production facilities, obviously the production department will be able to advise.

After analysing your company's product/market situation in this way, you should be able to identify what opportunities there are for the future.

## Product life cycles

The only constant thing in nature is change. All things change. Humans change, products change, tastes change. As you are reading this now, you are changing; you are a different person from what you were a few minutes ago. You are getting older. No matter how small the change, it is occurring all the time. All humans are born, grow, mature, decline and die.

This concept can also be applied to products. They are born and introduced to the market; they grow, mature, and are eventually replaced by other products. Some products and product groups tend to continue for ever; salt is likely to be needed for as long as we inhabit the earth. Whisky, as a product group, continues its growth each year and is unlikely to decline although, in the late 1980s, there is an increasing demand for single malt whiskies at the expense of sales of blended whiskies.

A graph of this general tendency of a product's life cycle is an S-shaped curve (Figure 11.2).

Researches conducted during the last 25 years have demonstrated that motor cars, foodstuffs, non-food grocery items, cosmetics, refrigerators, chemicals, general engineering products, tyres, and many consumer durables all tend to follow the general pattern of an S-shaped product life cycle (PLC). In the high technology field, this typical PLC is observed but it is usually very short, lasting for about three years.

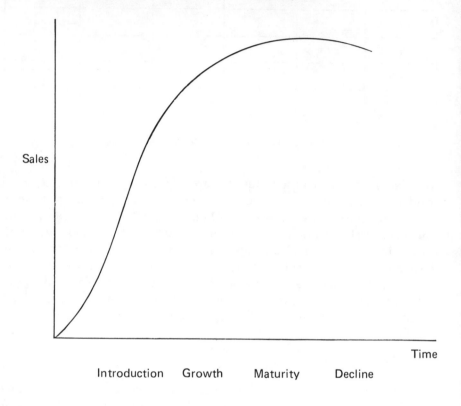

**Figure 11.2** *Product life cycle[1]*

## *Profit curve*

The graph of the profit line associated with this PLC is illustrated in Figure 11.3. The important point is that profits do not accrue until after the product has been launched and sales have started to increase. Accumulated losses may have to be carried for some time.

## *Planning with the product life cycle*

The main difficulty of using the PLC as a basis in planning is the discontinuity of the curve. We know where we are when in the introductory stage because we've just put the product on the market; we know where we are in the growth stage because of increasing sales, and when in the decline stage, because of declining sales. What we do not know is where

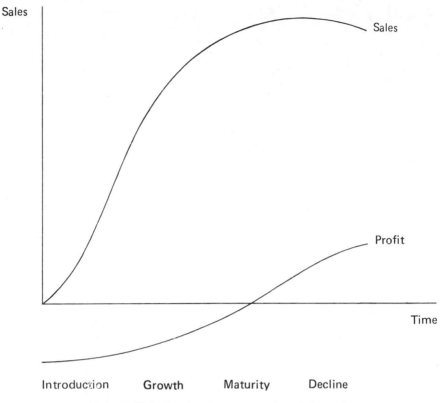

**Figure 11.3** *Profit during product life cycle*

the product is in the mature stage because its extent is unknown; it could extend for years or be cut short by changed processes or new products. The S-shaped curve is better drawn with breaks in the time base line and curve as in Figure 11.4.

When planning product/market policy a number of constraints have to be considered.

*Life cycle pattern*

The most common PLC is the S-shaped curve but several other patterns have been identified by researchers. Apart from products that quickly die, or remain with steady demand neither growing nor declining, all PLCs tend to have a slow growth stage early in their life, then a rapid growth stage, and finally, a second slow period late in life. If you are not sure of the shape of the PLC of your particular product, assume that it has these basic characteristics — slow early growth, rapid growth, slow late growth.

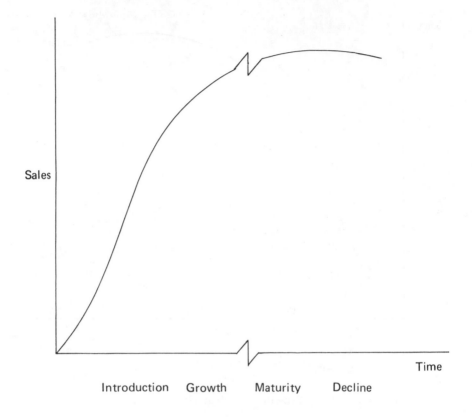

**Figure 11.4** *Product life cycle[2]*

If your product is in the same life cycle stage as similar competitive products, you have a more or less equal chance of succeeding. One of the main reasons for new product failure is the introduction of a new product onto the market when it is new only to the company and all competitive products are in their late, slow growth stage. It is vital to establish whether any observed slow growth is at the beginning or end of the PLC.

## Definition

How do you define the product? As an individual product marketed by your company or as marketed by all competitors? By product line or class? The PLC of your company's products are likely to be substantially different from the PLC of similar products of all suppliers. The product should be defined in relation to its market. For example, if you are marketing TV receivers, you should distinguish between sales of colour sets and monochrome sets. Sets with different screen sizes are in different market segments. Home produced sets should be separated from imported models.

Carefully define the unit of measurement so that your statistics relate to a specific product in a specific market.

## Measurement

Normally, the PLC curve is based on sales volume but it could equally well be based on sales value. Actual sales volume might be better adjusted to per capita sales. To what extent do economic conditions such as strikes affect the calculations? What allowances should be made for varying taxes imposed on sales?

## Market

Defining the relevant market is difficult. It is not homogeneous and is likely to fall into one of the following four categories:

- Type 1. A single, dominant product with well over 80 per cent of the market.
- Type 2. A leader with over 50 per cent of the market, and a dominant runner-up with approximately half of the market share of the leader.
- Type 3. More than three dominant products which, together, account for approximately 80 per cent of the market with the remaining 20 per cent highly fragmented.
- Type 4. More than three dominant products which account for about 50 per cent of the market but an actively competitive other half of the market.

The highest number of successful new entries into the market have been observed in a Type 2 market. The next most successful is a Type 4. The greatest failure rate for new entries has been observed in a Type 3 market.

## Time

Mostly, PLCs are considered in terms of annual data. But with many products, especially high technology products, the life cycle is very short and it may be necessary to use shorter units of measurement than the traditional annual data base.

### Gap analysis

If we start with the assumption that products do not last for ever then, irrespective of the shape of the PLC, we can illustrate a typical company's product range over time as in Figure 11.5.

There should not be periods with gaps, as arrowed in the figure. If you

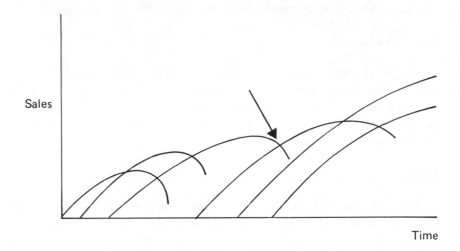

**Figure 11.5** *A typical company's product range*

consider the profit curve associated with each life cycle curve, with too many gaps, a company will have financial problems. With the decline in sales, profits will be declining at the very time when more funds are needed to develop and market new products. As old products approach their maturity, new ones should be increasing sales. If the introduction of new products is delayed until current products are in decline, gaps will be generated.

## Product positioning

Product positioning is an image in the mind of people and refers to the particular place a product (or brand) occupies in 'the market' relative to all similar or alternative products. This 'position' embraces all the more common meanings of the word: how it compares with competitive products; where it can be purchased; type of customer who normally uses it; its comparison in size, weight, shape, appearance, cost, with competitive products; what customers think about the product and its performance.

A product's position is determined by measuring the strength of people's perceptions and preferences for the product compared with those of competitive products. Perception is reasonably stable but preference will vary under different conditions. Products $X$ and $Y$ may have two different perceptions, with product $X$ preferred by a user under normal conditions; however, given abnormal conditions, the preference might be for $Y$ rather than for $X$.

If you wish to direct your selling firepower where it is most likely to be successful, you must identify preferences. Perception of a product occurs before preference for a product can be formed. Non-users as well as users have perceptions of products. Such perceptions are built up through publicity in all its forms, the types of people who use the product, the conditions under which it is sold.

You may be a non-smoker but you will have different perceptions of different brands; you may not have driven every make of car but you will have perceptions of most makes; you may not have visited every holiday resort in a brochure, but you will have a perception of the towns, regions and countries. You may be about to install a new system of heating in your factory and will have perceptions of different methods. Until you investigate and compare the different systems, your preference is conditioned by your perception.

## Quick way to position your product

The simplest way to position your product is to list all competitive products, the most expensive at the top, the cheapest at the bottom. The list should be scaled, that is, each product should be given a ranking that corresponds with its quality and prices. Obviously, this requires some subjective judgement. A product that is much more costly than a competitor will have a much higher ranking than the competitor. This ranked tabulation is a positioning and not just a simple list.

After this tabulation you could attempt a horizontal scaling based on what you consider is the most important customer benefit of the product. Frank discussions with good customers and editorial journalists of trade and technical papers will give you an insight into your product's position in relation to its main competitors.

## Formal positioning

In a formal market survey to establish positioning, respondents are asked to consider successive pairs of products with regard to a series of characteristics such as cost, convenience, versatility, etc. These are then combined statistically to give a spacial representation of the positions of different products, as in Figure 11.6.

This perceptual map illustrates the relationships between various products as perceived by the market, and indicates how near or how far apart the products are relative to each other. Products F, G and H are perceived by the market to be most unlike one another. Products C and D are regarded as very close to each other and, if you marketed one of them, you might wish to distinguish your product by changing the pack or by advertising and promotion.

From an inspection of the map it appears that there is room in the market for a new product to be positioned in the area of 'X'.

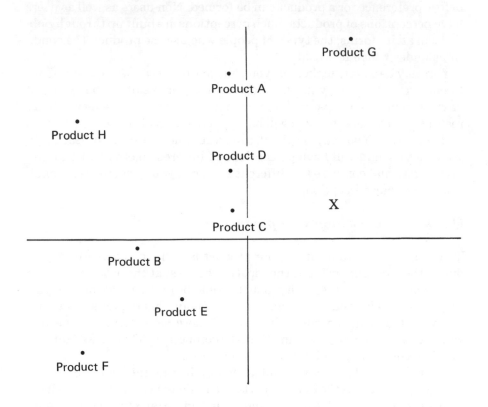

**Figure 11.6** *A Perceptual Map of Products*

## Basis for product positioning

The basis for positioning a product will depend on a number of criteria. You should consider the positioning strategy used by competitors; the company's market position; the capability of innovating as distinct from copying; relevance of the proposed positioning to the total product range; how different the marketing and selling might be for the newly positioned product; the ability of personnel to implement and exploit the proposed positioning; the resources available for the proposed positioning.

Product positioning is a useful framework for designing and assessing sales and marketing strategies. The closer the positioning of two products, the more likely they are to compete with each other. The more isolated a product is from competition, the more unique it is likely to be perceived as.

You can estimate where a particular product is positioned now and where it will be if changes are made in company strategies or if competitors initiate changes. This means you must continually monitor your competitors' advertising and promotion and estimate the position of their products relative to yours. This will often present you with ideas for product modifications, new products and different selling activities.

If you do not possess the time or resources to obtain all the data necessary for accurate positioning, a quick method is to analyse the appropriate benefits of your product compared with those of competitors. This can be done by physical product inspection and a survey of competitive advertising. An example is given in Figure 11.7. This is a quick method, but do not base your selling and marketing decisions solely on this analysis because it represents your views and not the market's perceptions of the product.

| Industrial cleaner | Easy to use | Cleaning efficiency | Fast action | Removes grease | Single application |
|---|---|---|---|---|---|
| Own product | ✓ | ✓ | ✓ | ✓ | |
| Product B | ✓ | ✓ | ✓ | ✓ | ✓ |
| Product C | | | ✓ | ✓ | |
| Product D | | ✓ | | ✓ | ✓ |

**Figure 11.7** *Analysis of Benefits*

## Product portfolio

There are many ways of classifying your company's product portfolio. If it is to be of real value, keep it simple; don't over-classify products, especially those not yet in the range. If you use a system that includes future products classified as 'tomorrow's breadwinners', you must be reasonably sure that those products will produce profits tomorrow: avoid committing resources to doubtful causes.

The simplest approach is to categorise your products into:

(1) today's profit earners
(2) potential earners
(3) has-beens

The first category must obviously be expanded in terms of actual profit earned. Sales efforts should be concentrated on those products that provide the greatest actual profit, not necessarily the greatest percentage profit.

What you do not know is when these current profit earners will start to decline. Continually monitor their progress and compare them with competitive products in the various market segments to get an early warning of changes that require actions by your company.

The second category is essential for a company's continued existence. Some of these products will make it, others will not. Your task is to maintain a close control over the development of the potential earners and assess the cost of every action proposed and its likely outcome.

The third category should include all those products that do not contribute adequate profit. Further investigation might reveal that some could be modified or improved to make them more attractive in the market; some may benefit from a different advertising approach; some may have to be retained to round out a line. In general, 'has-beens' are candidates for elimination from the range. However, time spent analysing these products can be expensive; it doesn't necessarily make money. By all means do it, but be aware of what you are doing, how much it is costing and what benefits might ensue.

## Portfolio analysis

Have clear guidelines for your product portfolio analysis. These could be market share, market growth, degree of attraction of the product, profitability, potential future demand, risk. Consider both current and potential products when preparing your target portfolio.

Do not restrict your analysis to individual products. Consider product lines and total product mix. Some products which might, individually, appear to be candidates for early retirement may be essential as accessories, or complementary products to others. Product analysis must always be considered in relation to markets. Therefore, your product portfolio should be prepared for different market segments and the distribution channels in these market segments.

A refrigerator manufacturer will certainly distinguish domestic from commercial models and may also distinguish small capacity from large capacity, auto-defrost from non-defrosting models, and distinguish between different distribution channels, appointed dealers, cash and carry stores, rental chains, independent retailers, and hotels. A book publisher will probably distinguish fiction from non-fiction, adult from children's books, hardback from paperback, and distribute through multiples, departmental stores, independent bookshops, bookstalls, airports and railway stations, book clubs, etc.

A market share for a product of, say, 10 per cent, will consist of several shares of sub-markets of the total market. You should be more interested in the sub-market share of a product rather than the share of the total market because it more accurately depicts the position of that product and is much more useful in your planning.

## Define the product

Define the product carefully and make sure you are comparing similar products. What exactly is a washing powder, a beer, a book, a machine tool, an integrated circuit? Does the description of your product also apply to its competitors? If not, you will be calculating faulty market share estimates.

Defining the market or market segment is even more difficult and depending on how you define it, a product can have widely differing market shares. A manufacturer of small electric cookers will have a tiny share of the total cooker market, a larger share of the market for electric cookers and a very large share of the 'baby' cooker market.

Define the *market served by a particular product* as precisely as you can. You are not necessarily competing in the total market; only in that specific segment that can be served by your product and its strictly competitive similar products.

## Boston box analysis

The Boston Consulting Group based their product portfolio analysis on observations of behaviour of unit costs of production with cumulative output. In all of the companies observed they found that every time a company reached a doubling of its cumulative output, unit cost fell by a regular percentage. Thus, if unit cost was, say, £400 when cumulative output was 20,000, then, when the cumulative output reached 40,000, unit cost had fallen by approximately 20 per cent. When cumulative output was 80,000, unit cost had fallen by a further 20 per cent. When cumulative output reached 160,000, unit cost had fallen yet again by about 20 per cent. With each cumulative doubling of output, unit cost was approximately 80 per cent of what it was previously and could be illustrated graphically as a downward-sloping 80 per cent curve. If logarithms of the reduction curve are plotted, the curve becomes a downward sloping straight line called the 'experience curve'.

These observations supported the hypothesis that a company with the highest cumulative output of a product would enjoy the lowest unit cost. And since a company doesn't go on producing if it's not selling, the company with the highest cumulative production would have the highest market share. The company with the highest market share is likely to be selling a product with the lowest unit cost and thus, the greatest unit profit.

You will recall the general shape of the product life cycle: slow growth, rapid growth and subsequently slow growth and decline. The market obviously reflects this slow or rapid growth and has products with a high or low market share. Figure 11.8 combines these two characteristics.

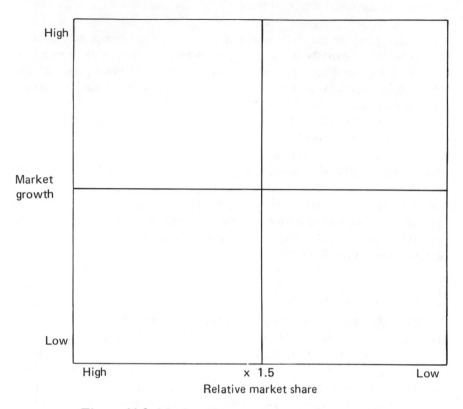

**Figure 11.8** *Market share against market growth*

Market growth depends on the industry and on the buoyancy of the economy. It could be low, perhaps 2 or 3 per cent, equal to the growth of the national product, or very much higher. Relative market share is calculated as a product's sales ratio compared with its largest competitor. A product with a market share twice that of its nearest competitor would be well to the left of the × 1.5 dividing line.

Companies can influence movement of their products across the vertical line; only total economy and industry can affect movement above or below the horizontal line.

A product in a high growth market requires a lot of attention (and resources) to maintain its market position. A product in a low growth, stable or even declining market does not require such a large investment of resources to maintain its market position.

Products in the four cells have been given names by the Boston Group:

(1) High market share, low growth market—cash cows.

(2) High market share, high growth market—stars.

(3) Low market share, high growth—problem children.

(4) Low market share, low growth—dogs.

From the previous observations made, a product with the highest market share probably has the lowest unit cost and therefore the highest margin; cow products are cash generators. They are not good products in which to invest further cash. They have a high market share and to obtain an even greater share is costly. Cash generated by cows should be invested in stars and problem children.

Stars require continuing investment to maintain market share and are therefore users of cash. Like the Hollywood stars of old, they have to be kept in orbit and this costs money.

Problem children need cash if they are not to stay with low market share for ever. If they remain problem children and market growth slows, they become dogs. The only logical marketing strategy for a problem child product is to go for market share and aim to turn it into a star.

Dogs use far more cash and management time than they are worth. They are low profit earners and greater market share can only be obtained from cow products. This would mean fighting highly profitable products in a stable market; it is not a recipe for success. It is often suggested that a company should divest itself of its dog products but this ignores the possibility that a dog might be complementary to another product or might round out a line. Such products might be considered as essential dogs—perhaps, 'kennel products'.

## Dangers to avoid

This analysis should not be adopted without considering other factors, because attempting to change a problem child into a star can be very costly. The amount of effort and money required to obtain a higher market share for a problem child in the face of opposition from star products can be so great that the expenditure in selling and marketing far outweighs the profits from the increased share.

I know of two companies who have seriously damaged their business and depleted their finances by attempting to go for growth in this way. By diverting resources to a problem child product, both companies made themselves vulnerable with other products. Although both acquired small increases in market shares, they were unable to cope with the attacks made by competitors on other products—for one company it was a strong attack on one of their cow products. The profits from the cow had been poured into a problem child without prudent stewardship. The company made very little headway with the problem child and lost considerable market share for its cash cow.

The second company spent considerable sums on its problem child, trying to promote greater sales with increased advertising and promotion. While there was a modest increase in their share of the market, the subsequent low profitability of the product was a prime factor in their deciding to close one of their factories that had been making the product.

Market share is undoubtedly important as a marketing objective but it remains but one of a number of objectives. The fundamental questions to be answered have always been: What are the basic objectives of the company and how does the company seek to achieve these? Increasing a product's market share is not always easy; sometimes it can only be achieved at a cost which is greater than the increased profit from the extra sales.

# 12

# Service

Service should not be confined to after-sales product service. A lot of service has to be carried out before any sales are made, and the sales organisation needs to be serviced, especially during the selling process. The basis of good servicing of the sales organisation is in a comprehensive sales manual.

## Scope of service

In its broadest sense, service means all activities that make the handling of products profitable for middlemen and help the ultimate user to obtain the maximum satisfaction from the product. Using this definition, activities such as product development, credit, leasing, training middlemen's employees, and promotion, are part of service. In a narrower sense, servicing refers solely to the repair and maintenance of the product.

In this chapter, service is considered from the viewpoint of the sales manager: service before sales, during sales and after sales. This is customer servicing, sales people servicing, and product servicing.

## Before-sales service

The majority of sales require a lot of work before the actual order is placed. Even the sale of locally bottled lemonade to the owner of the village shop requires some pre-sales service, if only the consideration of the type of flavours that will sell in that part of the world. At the other end of the scale, the amount of pre-sales service provided by a company that intends to tender for a large construction contract is enormous and costly.

The salesman from the department store in the nearby town is usually willing to call with his range of carpet samples, measure the room to be carpeted, advise on quality and design, and estimate the cost, all before a sale is made. And, if the sale is not made, the cost of the before-sales service has to be carried by the department store.

An engineering workshop that provides a wide range of metal fabrications will need to allocate considerable resources to the preparation of quotations for jobs. If too much time and money is spent on this pre-sales service, the profits of the workshop are seriously eroded. While the costs of the 'free' quotations and proposals cannot be passed on to the enquirer, they have to be covered in the prices charged to other customers. Thus, too much, or the wrong type, of pre-sales service will damage the company.

As sales manager, one of your important tasks is to monitor the amount of pre-sales service your company provides, calculate its cost and determine whether it is possible to make better use of the service. If it is appropriate for your company, establish the number of quotations and proposals as a percentage of orders obtained from the activity. Establish the cost of making a proposal or quotation; look at the type of jobs that are quoted for and see if any redirection of effort is needed.

## Proposals and quotations

If your company operations include the submitting of quotations to potential customers, with a little more thought and organisation you can transform these quotations into selling instruments.

A quotation is a traditional document used to specify the product, price, delivery and terms of payment. Often, printed on the reverse are the 'terms and conditions', which state practically every reason why the customer should *not* buy from you.

A proposal is a selling tool which contains the same data as a quotation, but also the reasons why the prospective customer *should* buy from you. You may have to supply the company's official quotation but this should be appended to the main proposal. There are five main sections in a proposal:

(1)  the customer's objectives

(2)  your recommendations

(3)  additional benefits

(4)  financial justification

(5)  guarantee and service

### Customer's objectives

Before preparing the quotation, establish exactly what it is that the customer wishes to achieve by obtaining a product or service from you. List these desired achievements as objectives in order of importance from the customer's viewpoint. Succinct statements of what the enquirer wishes to achieve should ensure that the proposal is read.

## Recommendations

State clearly how each objective will be met by your recommendations. If the proposal is for complex equipment, append a detailed specification to each section, keyed so that it is clear which recommendation relates to which objective.

## Additional benefits

The main recommendations you make in the proposal will relate to the main objectives and indicate the main benefits. In the light of your company's experience with equipment supplied to other users, try to include the additional benefits that the customer could experience.

## Financial justification

Set out the financial justification of acquiring your product or service in the first few sentences. If this is complicated, use a separate appendix and key to the appropriate sections. If the purchase of your product or service 'pays for itself', illustrate in the appendix a modest calculation that does not rely on maximum usage of your product to pay for itself.

Work on the assumption that the customer will not investigate the proposal in detail and attempt to justify the acquisition although, in fact, this will most likely to be done. By setting out the financial justification, you demonstrate that you have prepared the proposal from the prospective customer's point of view. If it is possible to calculate and illustrate the financial justification in more than one way, use them.

## Guarantee and service

Do not rely on the pale print on the back of your official quotations for your guarantee, warranty and after-sales service. State what you are prepared to do. The fact that this is stated as a major part of the proposal can sometimes secure the business. To underwrite what you offer in your guarantee and service, use third party references (with their permission).

*Specimen proposal*

---

Dear Mr Smith

As promised in my letter of 4 April following Miss Eley's call, I am now able to quote you for sales training.

You require a programme for 30 sales persons that will:

- enable them to open more sales successfully to new accounts
- analyse their current territories to find more customers
- optimise the working of their territories
- prepare a frequency call plan for new potential accounts

We recommend:

(1) The training is spread over one year in view of the fact that none of your sales people has received any training in recent years.

(2) An initial four-day course with all sales staff to introduce them to some of the modern methods of territory management, including the development of a customer database for use on your microcomputers.

(3) Starting two weeks after the end of the initial course, five separate two-day courses held in each of the regions with up to six people, to apply the general principles studied on the initial course to their own territories.

(4) A second four-day course about three months after the initial course to develop their selling techniques, and look at some of the specific ways of working their territories.

(5) Approximately six months after the start of the training, a second series of five two-day regional courses to monitor the implementation of the training and develop individual improvement plans.

(6) Approximately one year after the start of the training, territory sales results are compared with current achievements.

Additional benefits that will accrue will be: a greater understanding of the company's product and sales policy; a knowledge of the application of microcomputers to sales and marketing; raising of morale because there is at present a feeling of isolation among many of the field sales staff; development of presentation skills; identification of potential future management people.

The fee for this training programme is £30,000 plus travel and accommodation expenses, exclusive of VAT. This covers all training materials, loose-leaf binders, notes, use of video equipment, telephone charges, etc. There are no extras.

Each sales person will receive 12 days of training and development in addition to the coaching materials used between the courses. This represents an outlay of £83 per training day per delegate.

We guarantee that satisfaction with our training will be achieved. At the conclusion of each course, an appraisal questionnaire will be completed by the delegates and returned directly to you.

Appended are some of the clients with whom we have worked in the last 12 months and who have agreed to provide a confidential reference on our methods and achievements.

---

## During-sales service

The service with which you must provide your sales people for use when processing sales with potential customers is an adequate sales kit and training to do the job. A sales person who cannot deal with the vast majority of customers' enquiries as they are raised is not being serviced properly.

All of your sales people will need to be adequately trained in product knowledge. They should all represent the company in the same manner so that the image of the company is universal throughout the market, and products are presented and demonstrated similarly. Apart from the need to train your sales people on a continuous basis, giving them regular sessions to 'recharge their batteries', you should provide each one with a sales manual.

### The sales manual

The sales manual is one of the most widely used sales aids because it is also a training aid. It contains data on products and procedures that the sales person is expected to know and adopt, and on subjects which might only arise occasionally. The manual should be carefully prepared, clearly organised, interestingly presented and conveniently housed in a loose-leaf binder so that additional or substitute sheets can be issued. The general content of the sales manual is:

- historical background of the industry, the company, its products and general policies
- definition of the sales position, main duties and responsibilities
- sales organisation and field supervision
- technical data about the products
- data about competitive offerings

- specific information about the market—classes of buyers, types of problems, buying motives
- instructions for making effective sales presentations
- guidance for territory management
- non-selling tasks
- administration requirements
- suggestions on dress and personal deportment

While these are usually the minimum contents, they are by no means exhaustive and some manuals contain many topics and convey to sales people in varying degrees those things that should be known and those that must be done. The manual provides standards of behaviour and procedure. All of this information might be contained in one volume but, because of the bulk, it is often divided into separate sections, such as:

- *Sales manual:* outlining the marketing policy and presenting basic information for all sales people on the selling process, the pre-approach, approach, opening the sale, progressing the sale, dealing with objections, handling negotiations, closing the sale. Statement of advertising aims, the current campaign, display materials, pulls of current ads.

- *Product manual:* describes the company's products and the technical processes by which they are produced. Where appropriate, full details are given on how the products work, and examples of various product usages. Any specific arguments for the use of the product, and answers to usual questions or objections raised.

- *Stockists' manual:* guidance on getting the most out of the help available from the company. Hints on display, demonstration, product presentation. Details of training available for stockists' staff.

- *Service manual:* full information on installation of the product, its operation and maintenance. Exploded drawings illustrate the parts of the product and their reference numbers.

- *Company manual:* full information on the company, its background and personalities. Organisation charts showing how the various departments operate and are co-ordinated. The information is presented in a way that creates a feeling of belonging in the sales person.

- *Price book:* up-to-date prices of all products, discounts that may be given, terms of payment, credit granting procedure and suggestions on credit risks.

## Specimen sales manual

The index and first page of the sales manual which follows is from a company in the food trade. It is given to field sales supervisors.

---

### Index

1. Sales training manual—objectives
2. Your job—managing men
3. Two-way communications
4. Recruitment and selection of field staff
5. Evaluation of candidates at the interview
6. Selection guide
7. Personal history form
8. Job description—divisional manager
9. Job description—sales supervisor
10. Job description—representative
11. Job description—merchandiser
12. Man profile—salesman
13. Initial training—outline of selling principles
14. Initial training course—notes
15. Initial sales training for new personnel
16. Evaluating sales people's performance
17. Developing the trained sales person
18. How sales people should use advertising and public relations to build extra sales
19. Conducting sales meetings
20. Training—what it is and what it does
21. Motivating sales people
22. How to use market research statistics

### The Objective

The aim of this manual is quite simple:
*It is to help you, as a field manager, to do your job more effectively, more efficiently and more profitably.*
In order to achieve this aim this manual has been produced to:

1. Help you *select* the right sales person.
2. Help you *train* your sales people by using a basic plan which

aims to mobilise their full potential and abilities as quickly as possible.

3. Help you to *motivate* and *develop* your team so that it achieves and maintains full efficiency.

4. Set the right standards and help you to *assess* your people correctly against these standards.

5. Help you to fully understand and utilise the marketing facilities of the company.

This manual can only *help* to achieve these objectives, it cannot do the job for you. *You* have to use it intelligently and, if you do, you can become a more efficient and professional manager, an asset to yourself and to the company. Above all, this manual is intended to complement and not replace your natural skills as a manager.

## After-sales service

Components and materials, manufacturing techniques and workmanship, design and delivery are all unimportant if the user of the product fails to obtain satisfaction from its use. After-sales service helps to keep the product 'sold'. It builds goodwill and helps to promote repeat sales, if not to the same buyer, to others who learn of the satisfaction the product and the company provide.

The type of product will indicate the kind and amount of service necessary to ensure that buyers and users have continuous satisfactory use of it. New products, especially complex technical products, when first marketed, may need more service than later on: users become familiar with the product and experienced in operating it, and some service is not required; improvements in the product make it easier to use and keep in good condition so that less service is required.

The four main forms of service are:

- education
- installation
- routine maintenance
- repair

## Consumer products

The majority of low-priced, repetitively purchased consumer products require little or no service. Products which are comparatively new require some educational service. This can usually be provided on the packaging.

Often, such instructions are not clear to the user, particularly if the products are manufactured in another country where English is less than perfect. Even home-produced products sometimes have bewildering instructions. It is seldom easy to write educational instructions and this small, but important, service to customers should have your attention.

If your product requires educational service, try out the instructions on the least intelligent person you can find. Often, it is necessary to use illustrations because it is not possible to write the instructions unambiguously.

Installation of consumer products is mainly for domestic equipment and machines to heat, cool, cook, wash and dry things. Similarly, routine maintenance can be provided under contract.

The service that requires most thought is repairs. These can be centrally organised, decentralised or even franchised to approved service people. The type of product will influence the service method because large bulky products will have to be repaired *in situ* or at local points; it would not be sensible to return all such bulk equipment to a central point for repair.

## Using local facilities

If you use selected stockists or appointed service engineers to carry out the servicing and repair of your products, help them in the following ways:

- training in the product
- holding stocks of parts at local points
- supplying detailed instructions on repair techniques
- having service centres for major repair problems

## Industrial products

The four kinds of service—education, installation, maintenance and repair—are more important with industrial products than with consumer goods. Industrial plant and equipment is used to produce other goods, and their maintenance in prime condition is vital if production is to be kept at a satisfactory level. Educational service is often crucial with many industrial products, especially complex electronic, electrical, and mechanical plant and equipment. The war room described in Chapter 1 is part of a company that supplies considerable educational service to potential customers before, during, and after the equipment has been sold and installed.

Educational service is sometimes the basis for routine, or programmed, preventive maintenance of complex machinery and equipment and requires the preparation of maintenance manuals. These tell the customer what to inspect, how often, and when to adjust or replace. Such service, when properly carried out, reduces the amount of repair service necessary.

Installation service is obviously essential for a lot of plant and equipment and, with some products such as highly complex machinery, it can take several weeks for the equipment to 'settle down' and operate adequately.

Maintenance and repair service are often guaranteed for a definite period of time and provided without further payment by the customer. There must be an adequate spares service available and, during the routine inspection service immediately after the product has been installed, there is a splendid opportunity for additional educational service: how to get the most use out of the equipment.

Never forget that people buy products for the satisfaction and service they provide. The more service they can get out of the product, the greater the satisfaction. Any 'hiccups' in the product's operation that arise during the early days must be eliminated quickly. Initial satisfaction of the buyer is very important and can create a lasting impression. It is normal for products to falter and fail after much use; they should work well when they are new. You should ensure that your service arrangements are adequate to meet this task.

## Changing face of service

With the development of advanced quality control and quality assurance techniques, the reliability of products is now used as a sales weapon. For many years, manufacturers have been marketing products that have required after-sales service facilities. As product reliability has improved, company service departments have had less work.

With the slackening of turnover growth, service has also declined and, with the new electronic technologies applied to products, much additional training of service engineers and technicians has been necessary. These newly acquired skills have turned many into specialists who are less interchangeable in the workshop and must have a sufficient workload to be profitable. The future of product servicing is not clear.

## Service at a profit

Service departments have to be run at a profit rather than at a break-even level otherwise they erode company profits. As general service figures decline to non-viable levels, if these continue over a period of time, some service branches have to be closed. Often, such closures do not cut costs and improve the service but have the opposite effect: turnover falls, costs keep rising and stockists and users in the areas where branches have been closed complain of the decrease in service support.

Fewer calls on the service department because of improved product liability also mean fewer paid repairs (products out of guarantee period) which provide profit, and the closing of service branches reduces the opportunity of selling profitable maintenance contracts for equipment. Consequently, there is an under-recovery of fixed overheads.

## Service overheads

This problem affects all companies in the same industry and there has been increased competition between organisations offering service. Sometimes, the service branch to be closed is sold to former service engineers who, working for themselves, work longer hours with lower costs and attract other servicing business away from their former employers.

If the fixed overheads of the company are allocated on a pro rata basis to all departments, unless they are recalculated to allow for service branch closures, service costs, as a percentage, will increase. This often leads to other executives calling for the closure of more 'unprofitable' branches and leaving the work to independent servicing companies.

Good servicing facilities are usually an important element in the marketing mix, although stressing this in publicity can imply that the product is not entirely reliable.

Table 12.1 illustrates the servicing problem for one company for a period of six years. The repair frequency is the number of repaired products divided by the number guaranteed during the year. Although their total sales have increased each year, the increase has been less each year. Warranty work and repairs have fallen significantly over the period; the costs per product sold underline the increasing reliability of the product.

**Table 12.1** *Service profile over six years*

| Year | Repairs during guarantee | Repair frequency | Net price (£) | Cost per product sold (£) |
|------|------------------------|------------------|---------------|---------------------------|
| 1 | 1,938 | 0.42 | 385 | 10.93 |
| 2 | 2,168 | 0.32 | 395 | 10.76 |
| 3 | 2,472 | 0.26 | 380 | 7.95 |
| 4 | 2,640 | 0.21 | 332 | 6.74 |
| 5 | 2,788 | 0.17 | 322 | 4.50 |
| 6 | 2,925 | 0.14 | 320 | 4.65 |

## Cost of ownership

Perhaps the answer to the product servicing problem lies in the concept of 'cost-of-ownership'. It is not sufficient simply to purchase a product and expect it to operate continuously at peak efficiency until, one day, many years later, it fails. It deteriorates from the moment it is first used; customers must be educated in this.

If the product is pulled through the channel, it will be more costly to educate customers in the cost-of-ownership concept than if it is pushed through the channel, where you can influence the sales staff of the various agents in the channel.

Products which require regular servicing and are sold through middlemen should be marketed on a cost-of-ownership basis. Middlemen, who advise potential customers, should be schooled, and even trained, in the service element necessary and available with your product, to maintain it in first-class operational condition.

# 13
# Advertising

It is easy to spend money on publicity, so you have to get the most out of your appropriation when advertising in newspapers, commercial television, outdoor publicity, radio, and the cinema. Suggestions must be related to marketing and creative strategy if they are to transmit the right messages, and be critically assessed before you commit yourself. Knowing what works best in print, on posters, and on TV, will help you to develop sound advertising plans.

## Professional advertising

Advertising is a tough, professional business with many pitfalls, yet it is the sales manager's fire power that is employed in sales campaigns. Unless you develop your knowledge of some of the techniques and are reasonably well prepared, the first advertisement representative who calls on you and makes out a case for why you should 'take space' in his/her publication can easily lead you into unwise expenditure.

Successful advertising is like successful military operations. You must know your market (the terrain), the competition (the enemy), competing products (their weapons), and competitive publicity (their communications), all of which can be estimated from an assessment of market (or military) intelligence.

## Marketing strategy

Before you construct the advertising plan you must have a marketing plan: what type of products, at what prices, to what target market, with what estimated results.

A product is not purchased for itself alone but for the benefits it provides;

emphasise these in your advertising. First, make a list of the benefits of the product *from the customer's viewpoint*. Make sure that what you are selling is what the customer is buying; your advertising message should be developed from this harmonious relationship. Some years ago, I was invited to lecture to nearly 100 executives of the Ethiopian Airlines in Asmara and, before I started, I asked them all to write down what business they thought they were engaged in. With one exception, all wrote 'transportation'. The one exception, with which I agreed, was 'convenient or delightful destinations'. If you think about it, there are better ways of being transported than some six miles up in a pressurised canister! When you advertise, stress the benefits that the customer will receive.

## What attracts readers to ads?

Prospective customers read ads that inform them: 'How ABC Company cut costs in their plating shop', 'How RST increased profits using the XYZ system', 'A new glue to fix all sticky problems', 'Investment in an XYZ system reduces labour problems'. Sell the sizzle, not the steak!

## Advertising objectives

The primary objective of advertising is to transmit information about a product or service. It is a communications activity: messages are transmitted with the expectation that there will be responses from the target market.

To achieve an advertising objective, a minimum of two flows are essential:

- transmission from the advertiser to the customer
- acknowledgement by the customer that the right message has been received

The advertiser controls the first flow. The second flow is determined by advertising research or by customers' actions, such as purchasing the product. When you approve an advertisement, your selection may be influenced by the professional opinions of an advertising agent. But the real test of an ad is the reception by targeted customers. For this reason, if you have funds available, you should always pre-test advertisements. This should be done in a way that does not introduce bias. Respondents should not know the identity of the advertiser. Several different fictitious and real product names and companies should be used so that respondents can give objective opinions. If your company and product is the only real one, respondents will tend to give opinions biased toward your advertisement.

# The media

There are five main media:

(1) all forms of press—newspapers, magazines, trade, technical and professional journals
(2) commercial television
(3) outdoor hoardings, posters, transport, etc
(4) commercial radio
(5) cinema

These are listed in order of advertiser's expenditure in the UK but the ranking hides the overwhelming importance of press and TV advertising, which together account for about 95 per cent of total expenditure of the five.

Of the remaining three, five times as much is spent on outdoor advertising as on radio and cinema. Average total expenditures in the UK in the 1980s were:

| | |
|---|---|
| Press | 63.0% to 68.0% |
| Commercial television | 26.0% to 29.0% |
| Outdoor advertising | 3.6% to  4.2% |
| Radio | 1.7% to  2.2% |
| Cinema | under  1.0% |

Advertising agents, who place orders for space and time, normally receive a discount of 15 per cent on all bookings. This remunerates them for some of the work involved in preparing media schedules. Only these main five media operate a discount scheme, which is accorded only to 'approved agents'. Such approval requires submission of evidence to media owners that the agency is professionally and financially sound.

Below-the-line media are everything else, and are considered in Chapter 14.

# Building creative strategy

Creative strategy is developed from marketing strategy. This means, telling prospective customers in your target market how they can obtain the benefits of your product or service. There are two main considerations: what do we wish to say and, to whom do we wish to say it? For practical purposes we cover five points:

- What is the advertising intended to achieve?
- What is the target audience?

- Why should the prospect buy our product? Are there unique buying points (UBPs)? (Unique selling points—USPs—are not marketing-oriented because they emphasise selling rather than buying.)
- Reasons to support belief in the benefits offered.
- An identifying statement, slogan, headline, or other device that provides the product with its own image and personality to distinguish it from competitive products.

Products must never be considered in isolation; they must always be considered in relation to their likely market. Develop the creative strategy related to your product/market strategy. Get to know all about the market. Find out the likely users, how many, and where they are located. What competitive products are currently being offered, how are they distributed and promoted?

## How to check your creative strategy

(1) Understand your audience; find out who is likely to want or need your product. Don't concentrate too much on the attributes of the product but concentrate on what the customers are actually buying. Prepare a profile of a typical customer and direct your appeal to that person.

(2) Understand the competition. Unless you have a completely unique product your sales will come from your competitors because you will be taking a part of all your competitors' sales. Your creative strategy must recognise this by offering better use, better quality, better value, and so on.

(3) Stress what is important to the buyer, not what is obvious. If it's easy to see that the product is small, don't say so but talk of the benefits of using a compact product. If it's obviously a new way of doing something, don't say so but talk about the benefits that accrue from using the new method. Too many ads waste money stressing obvious product attributes; talk about the benefits that are not so obvious.

(4) Creative strategy must complement the marketing plan. When I was publicity manager of Moss Bros, one autumn I noticed that one of the branches had very low sales of suits. We were advertising riding wear nationally and, when I looked at the local papers in the branch's area, I found that they were advertising overcoats. The shop's window and store displays were mainly for evening wear and the branch's stock of suits was limited. I increased the number of suits, changed the window

displays to suits, supported this with a two-shot direct mail campaign and local advertising for suits. 'And', said Harry Moss to me, 'have one or two brown suits in the rack. Men don't wear brown suits, they wear dark blue or grey, but they like to see them so they can reject them!' I now call this 'the brown suit syndrome'. You often need to have some 'brown suits' for prospective customers to reject in favour of the products you really want to sell.

Don't let marketing, selling and creative strategy go in different directions. Dissipation of effort is a sure way to fail. If your marketing plan requires demonstrations of the product in use, it's no good having ads that show how fine it looks static and lifeless in the showroom or factory.

(5)  Keep your strategy up-to-date. The total market is in a constant state of change; so is your target market. Don't condemn out-of-hand what appears to be 'modern' or 'too advanced'. I once commissioned some fashion drawings for women's wear from a well-known artists' agency. They were drawn on blotting paper with the vital shapes outlined in tiny ink dots joined with vague lines. My initial reaction was to reject them: they looked child-like and 'different'. However, I suppressed my dislike and accepted these modern fashion plates and, when they appeared in print, they received wide approval. Likewise, don't readily accept what is obviously comfortable, understandable, traditional, old-fashioned; it will probably be lost and recede into the background. The key benefits of your strategy should be stable and not subject to frequent changes. When the 'copy platform' and image have been established for your product, keep them up-to-date with contemporary designs and descriptions but retain the basic framework and message.

(6)  It is not so important to be first in the market; it is much more important to be first, last! In other words, it isn't the supplier who is first in the market with the product who necessarily wins, it's the supplier who is the market leader when all other competitors have tried to displace him and failed, and the market has become fairly stable. If you can be first with something that competitors will find difficult or time-consuming to copy you have a great advantage.

(7)  Give your product a distinctive image. This can be achieved with the actual product design, its name, linking it with the inventor, the slogan or any number of creative devices. Extend the image beyond the product itself and aim to contribute to the long-term personality of the product. Case histories of the

product in use, especially with well-known companies or famous personalities, will help to develop the image.

(8) In your advertising give a definite promise to the user. As Robert Louis Stevenson wrote, 'To travel hopefully is a better thing than to arrive'. And, according to Dr Johnson, 'Promise, large promise, is the soul of an advertisement'. This does not mean that you have to 'con' prospective customers. It means that you have to ensure that your advertising stresses the satisfactions of ownership and use. It has been estimated by an American advertising agency chief that over a thousand million dollars have been spent promoting the six adjectives: cool, new, power, relief, refreshing, and white. Promises must be supported with facts and, if necessary, a statement that satisfaction is guaranteed or the purchase price is refunded.

(9) Commit your strategy to writing. Don't rely on memory or word of mouth. Put it on paper and circulate it to everyone connected with the marketing of your product. The first thing to ask of any proposed advert is: Is it compatible with the creative strategy?

(10) Make your objectives attainable: this means, make them reasonable. Don't overreach yourself. Over-ambitious objectives are the pitfalls of most strategies—they try to do too much by transmitting messages to too large an audience instead of to potential buyers of the product. Don't try to change people's deeply ingrained habits with your advertising—it's often easier to change the product! Of course, if your product *does* require people to change their habits and ways of doing things, your task will be that much harder and more costly.

## Advertising and sales results

Apart from direct advertising of, say, a product for sale in the mail-order columns of a newspaper, or a room to let, it is not possible to measure the effect of advertising. Sales are seldom, if ever, in proportion to advertising expenditure. Advertising does not work like this; it is only part of one component of the marketing mix. Your product or service must be in the right place (that is, accessible by potential buyers) at the right price (what people are prepared to pay) at the right time.

## Importance of the medium

Media are the various means by which people can see or hear advertising messages. No matter how interesting and persuasive the advertising messages, unless they are transmitted to the right people at the right time, those messages will be wasted.

A mediocre but well-timed advertisement to the right target audience will have a greater effect than a brilliantly conceived, clever and compelling message transmitted to the wrong market. The 'right' media are far more important than 'stunning' advertisements. Occasionally, you will meet professional advertising people who are more concerned with the actual advertisement, its layout and artistic impact, than with the medium in which it is to be used. When you next receive advertising proposals, pay particular attention to the presentation. Is there a tendency for a greater emphasis on the message, at the expense of the medium?

## The UK Audit Bureau of Circulations Ltd (ABC)

The ABC was founded in 1931 and was based on the American Audit Bureau of Circulations, founded nearly 20 years earlier. It exists to supply circulation data on almost 2,000 publications. Before it came into existence there was no reliable way of finding out whether an ad in a newspaper or magazine appeared in 1,000, 10,000, or how many number of copies.

An ABC figure is an audited net sale figure based on the average number of copies of a publication sold each issue (day, week, month, etc) over the preceding six-month period (calculated to 30 June and 31 December).

The audit is conducted by the publishers' own accountants on special ABC audit forms. An ABC certificate is issued after scrutiny of the returns. Net sales are copies of the publication bought by individuals. Copies which are bought in bulk by organisations and then distributed free are excluded from the computation. Special regulations apply to 'controlled circulation' publications. Publishers of these have to declare the number of copies requested and non-requested. An ABC figure is issued only if these requirements are satisfied. No circulation figure for a publication may be claimed as ABC until a signed certificate from the bureau has been received by the publishers covering the audit period concerned. Occasionally you will see a publication's circulation figure with the letters 'PS', after it. This is not an ABC figure but the 'publishers' statement'.

## Readership profile

All publications have a hard core of regular readers; others read it less frequently or by chance. The make-up of all readers, their age range, jobs,
where they live, how they usually spend their free time, is the publication's readership profile and can usually be obtained from the publishers.
It will help you to decide whether the publication is read by people in your
target market.

## National press

Britain is the only country in the world with such a dominant national
press, and can therefore be used as a basis against which to compare
media in other countries. The main newspapers are divided into national
and regional papers.

The national daily morning newspapers cover the whole of the country
and, in addition to the main general papers, there are sporting, shipping,
commerce papers and a unique daily or licensed victuallers (public houses,
hotels and licensed restaurants, etc).

The national Sunday newspapers enjoy full coverage throughout Britain and some include colour supplements which are magazines issued free
in the price of the paper. The advertising in these colour supplements
pays for the supplement's production and distribution costs.

Regional daily newspapers suffer from the double impact of rising
costs and the national dailies. Less than half a dozen have circulations in
excess of 200,000 and they are at a disadvantage compared with the
giants, *The Sun*, *Daily Mirror*, *Daily Express*, *Daily Mail*, *Daily Telegraph* and *The Star*, each with a circulation of well over one million, two
with well in excess of three million per day. The first four-colour daily,
*Today*, was launched in 1985 and, in 1986, *The Independent*, a new
quality-paper was published.

## Regional papers

The regional evening newspaper is nominally a paper appearing in the
evening but some have a morning edition, a lunch-time edition and even
two evening editions. There are about 50 or more such regional papers
which are popular local reading for the family. This is distinct from the
one-edition regional daily newspaper which is largely devoted to business
readership. Morning regional dailies are bought by business people,
taken to work and then disposed of. The evening regional tends to be
bought on the way home and is read by other members of the family.

There are a great many weekly regional papers, a large proportion of them truly regional, and some very local, containing news of small communities and individuals. It is quite common to find a 'series' of weekly papers circulating in a large county, each with its own title. The bulk of the news relates to the county and is the same in all papers in the series, but there are variations of news items of a secondary nature, usually on the inside pages, together with news items about communities as small as hamlets. Such series are useful for advertising in very restricted geographical areas.

## General magazines

It is difficult to place all magazines into specific categories because what might be considered a 'special interest' magazine by one group of people may well be regarded as 'general interest' by another group.

An example is *The Economist*, which has a wide general readership of business, commercial and political following, 50 per cent overseas, yet could well be considered as a 'special interest' magazine.

The primary classification for advertising might best be weeklies and monthlies; the description 'general interest' used for all magazines except those specifically devoted to a trade or profession.

## Women's magazines

In the UK, because women constitute a major influence in the purchase of consumer goods, there are a great many magazines devoted to their interests.

## Trade, technical and professional journals

There are hundreds of these, not only in the UK but throughout the world. A professional journal is one that is normally circulated to members of a 'recognised' profession. Trade and technical journals are a little more difficult to separate. You might agree that *The Engineer* is a technical journal, but how would you classify *The Director*, or *Farmers Weekly*?

In general, 'trade' magazines are read by distributors, factors, wholesalers, mail-order operators, retailers, agents, importers and exporters. Examples are *Business Equipment Digest*, *Retail Confectioner & Tobacconist*, *The Grocer*, *Car & Accessory Trader*. Technical journals are for those people engaged in manufacturing and service industries such as insurance, heating, lighting, air conditioning, etc.

There is a high mortality rate of publications generally and, if you intend to use any of these, you must obtain up-to-date information. Full details and costs of all publications can be found in British Rate & Data (BRAD).

## What works best in print

Look at a printed advertisement as a whole and try to view it placed in the intended publication. Don't read bits and pieces but obtain an overall impression of the ad. Glance at it quickly. Is it bold? Does the product appear strongly? Does the ad command attention? What is transmitted to you in that brief glance?

Having done that, look more closely. What is the essence of the headline? If there is an illustration, does the headline link with it? Is the copy clear and does it relate to the illustration? Does the whole ad describe the benefits that the product will provide? Check with these points:

(1) Headline. The headline should project the essence of the product, eg 'How XYZ Co cut costs in their planning department'. If a reader gets no further than the headline, your message must be understood. Only 20 per cent of readers continue after the headline. If you depend on body copy to put your story over, you are wasting 80 per cent of your advertising money.

(2) Signpost your ad. Use the headline to signal your audience. If you are appealing to chemists, indicate this in the headline. If you are talking to fathers, single them out in the headline: 'Good news for fathers who have to change the baby's nappies tonight!'.

(3) News is powerful when put in a headline. There is no word like 'new' and, if you have news about your product, hammer it out in the headline: 'New, turbo-charged sink disposal unit eats all kitchen waste in 30 seconds!'.

(4) Don't be afraid to use a long headline. Provided it punches out a fact-filled message about the product to the target audience, it will be read. Long, informative headlines tend to be read more than short ones, and help to get more sales. Several successful direct marketing organisations (mail-order companies) such as Littlewoods, Sears Roebuck, W H Smith, signal their ads with lengthy, data-backed headlines. In particular, Reader's Digest often uses long, powerful headlines. They have three guidelines for headlines: present a benefit to the reader; make the benefit quickly apparent; make the benefit easy to get.

(5) Use positive headlines. Only occasionally does a negative headline achieve high attention value. If appropriate, use the

words that have been proven to pull: cool, new, power, relief, refreshing, white (see para. 8 page 188).

(6) Use an illustration that attracts interest and links with the headline. The illustration should intrigue and stop the casual reader and make him/her read on. Consider the Benson & Hedges illustrations for cigarettes: they interest even non-smokers.

For preference, use a photograph. Far more readers can recall an ad using a photograph than one using a drawing. But don't sell the product, sell the product benefits. Use a photograph showing the product in use. If your product improves something, or offers superiority over existing methods, use 'before' and 'after' photographs. One picture is worth a thousand words; before-and-after photographs are worth a lot more. Even if the body copy explains everything, always have captions with photographs. Picture captions have a very high readership.

(7) Keep it simple. The message must project quickly, easily. The layout should be clean and uncluttered. The ad should be easy to read, easy to understand. A bold headline linked with one big illustration, or a composite before-and-after photo, is ideal and, if the whole ad matches the publication's editorial layout, it will be well-read.

(8) Decide whether your ad is looking for readers, or your product is for readers looking for ads. The thickest magazines, packed with adverts, have the highest circulation because their readers are interested in the products advertised. If your product is for readers looking for ads, don't be afraid of using long copy. Long copy is for those products with a lot of benefit facts for prospective buyers.

(9) Use 'trade-set' matter; that is, have your headline and body matter prepared by a specialist composing company. If your ad is 'paper-set', that is, the publication composes the type and uses whatever typeface is nearest to your instructions, the result will disappoint you. When you use a typesetting house to prepare your advert, use a typographer to 'mark up' the layout; this will specify the exact typefaces and size to be used. The resulting ad printed in the publication will be what you expected from the original idea. Trade-set ads cost more money than paper-set ads which incur no extra cost beyond the cost of space. But you get what you pay for!

If you do not use a typographer but specify the typefaces yourself, be guided by the typesetting house. Don't mix different typefaces; keep them all in the same 'family'. Don't have a lot of text 'reversed out'. This means that black (or colour) is printed with the words cut out in white, or the colour, of the paper. Reversed-out copy is much less read than the normal black on white.

If you are organising the advertisement yourself, paste a photostat of the proposed ad in a copy of the publication in which it is to appear; you will get a much better impression of it. If you look at a proposed ad on high grade paper, pasted onto a stiff board and the whole enclosed in an attractive folder, it will give you an entirely different impression.

(10) Don't be afraid of ads that are 'big, bold, black and bloody'! You are trying to get sales by telling people what you have to offer. Don't go for ads that will win advertising awards. Use ads that will be read, that tell the reader about the benefits and how to get hold of the product.

When I was handling the advertising for a large TV rental organisation, I kept all the ads lively. Competition from the other rental companies was fierce and all used well designed ads usually showing an elegant TV set, sometimes in a sitting room, with explanatory copy around the illustration.

I decided to 'sell' the client on a 'b, b, b and b' ad. Much to the disgust of my art director, I insisted on a large illustration of a TV screen on which was superimposed,

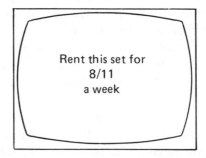

Rent this set for
8/11
a week

(the £ s d indicates the age of the incident). The figures were very large and 'hit' the reader when the newspaper was being read. The ad appeared in major local papers throughout the UK on Thursdays and Fridays. Enquiries in the shops on the Saturdays and Mondays increased beyond all expectations. As might be expected, other advertisers started to copy this layout and a few weeks later competitive ads were appearing with the headline, 'Rent this set for *only* 8/6 a week'.

## Commercial television

Commercial television is transmitted independently of the advertiser; sponsored television transmits programmes paid for by the advertiser, who can insert commercials. Non-commercial BBC television is paid for by annual grant from public funds and all TV owners pay an annual licence fee to operate their sets.

Commercial television was introduced into Britain in 1955. There are 14 areas in which programmes are transmitted by 15 contractors. There is no sponsored television and all TV ads in the UK are strictly controlled by the Independent Television Companies Association. Other countries have similar types of controls. In the UK, 140 minutes of advertising time is allowed during a 24-hour period. The permitted minutes of advertising per 24 hours in other western European countries in 1983 were:

| | |
|---|---|
| Austria | 20 min |
| Belgium | 68 min |
| France | 54 min |
| Germany FR | 40 min |
| Ireland | 83 min |
| Italy | 72 min |
| Netherlands | 30 min |
| Spain | 85 min |
| Switzerland | 60 min |
| Denmark | — |
| Norway | — |
| Sweden | — |

All TV commercials in the UK have to be approved at an early stage. These are usually written scripts with the proposed visual pictures drawn in TV screen shapes above the relevant script. Other inspections are made at various stages before and after recording so that the final commercial announcement which is viewed by the authorities prior to transmission is fully approved.

TV advertising costs are high. In 1986, one minute nation-wide—that is, all 14 regions, at peak time—cost nearly £200,000.

Long television commercials are boring unless they are carefully produced with a lot of interest, movement, and music, which is costly. The usual length is 15 or 30 seconds.

### How to get good TV commercials

Television has vision, sound, colour and movement. If you use TV advertising, make full use of the medium. When you next have the opportunity, make these tests: close your eyes and listen to the commercials. How quickly does the message come across in sound only about the product and the benefits offered? Do you recognise the product quickly by sound only? Does the commercial fail to project the product in sound, and rely on vision?

Turn the sound off and view only. How quickly does the product come across visually? How soon are you shown what the product does for the viewer? Does the commercial work without sound?

## How to judge a commercial

The proposed television commercial will usually be in the form of a story-board. A storyboard is the theme, action and sequence in a set of TV screen shapes like a strip cartoon. Under each of the 'TV screens' will be a description of what the viewer will see and hear. There may be technical terms on the storyboard to indicate the type of illustration, such as 'long shot' to show the whole picture; 'CU' (close up) showing a part of the whole; 'ECU' (extreme close up) showing a very small feature. A 'cut to' means one picture is changed to another, such as changing from a shot of a man's eyes to his hands holding the product. A 'dissolve' is fading out a picture to indicate passage of time and dissolving from one picture to another to indicate a change of location.

Various other camera devices and laboratory processes are called 'opticals': superimposing a new picture over another that gradually fades; various 'wipes' removing one picture and revealing another; 'matte' effects to combine pictures taken in different locations, such as to super-impose a CU of the product over the general scene in the commercial. A 'super' is lettering superimposed over the picture. 'Pop ons' are used to flash on and off the product, price or slogan during other pictures.

## How to judge a storyboard

When judging a storyboard, look briefly at the pictures. In 15 seconds your product benefit has to be put across in pictures and words. Do the pictures play their part? Do they tell the story? Don't spend minutes looking at them, but run your eye quickly over the sequence to see what is transmitted. Only then look at the words and read them aloud at conver-sational speed. Check against these points:

(1)  The pictures must tell the story. TV is a visual medium. This is why you should watch TV commercials occasionally without the sound so that you can appreciate the visual impact. Ask for the storyboard in two parts: one with the TV frames and illustrations only; the other with the illustrations and accompanying words. But look at the pictures first.

(2)  Is there a main picture or key illustration? One storyboard frame should contain the key of the whole commercial. This should relate to the creative theme. It is not possible to put across more than one main proposition in the commercial. If it has a number of different scenes it may be over-complicated and too long. Don't be afraid if the storyboard appears to be too simple. Simple ideas communicate.

(3)  Get your message in early. If you don't get the viewers' attention in the first few seconds they won't receive the rest of the transmission. Viewers' attention to commercials does not build, it recedes. The level of attention achieved in the first few seconds will be the highest for the commercial. Does a quick glance over the pictures of the storyboard grab your attention? Is there a certain 'something' that captures your interest? It has to be visual because viewers remember what they see, not what they hear. An advertising 'jingle' has to be repeated many times before it is remembered.

(4)  How long is the commercial? Average lengths are 30-second spots and you should plan around this time. If you go for a 15-second spot you can only project the product and promise a benefit. The 30-second makes the benefit more explicit; the 7-second spot is for reminder advertising in which you can only put over the name. If your campaign is to use both 30-second and 15-second spots, look at the 15-second commercial first. The key message should be punched out in 15 seconds. The same argument applies if you are using 60-second and 30-second spots. Look at the shorter first because, if the message cannot be put over in the shorter period, the suggestion lacks punch. The 60-second commercial should tell the same story as the 30-second spot. Longer commercials should not add more selling points. It is better to have two 30-seconds repeating the message than one 60-second.

(5)  Does the name of the product come over quickly, visually and in sound? Don't worry if the commercial irritates you because the name of the product and its benefit are repeated too often.

(6)  Show people using the product. Products shown only in their unopened or unused state lack interest. Show your product being used but, if appropriate, also show it at the end of the commercial as the viewer will see it for sale.

(7)  Suggest action. Show people, or animals, in action actually using the product. Illustrate that it does what you say it will: a woman admiring the clean, white clothes; the little dog unrolling the long toilet roll out of the house and down the garden; the

group of men drinking and obviously enjoying the lager; the woman stroking her man's clean-shaven cheek, and so on.

(8) Compatibility. Make sure that the total presentation of the commercial reflects your product's image. That is, the 'personality' of your product must be projected in your commercial. A machine tool has a different image, feel, and personality from a woman's perfume. Do not approve commercials that you consider conflict with the personality of the product.

(9) Involve people. No matter what your product, involve people and their problems that can be solved or avoided with your product. Concentrate on one or two benefits and, if you use a key person in the commercial, use that person as a continuing character. But the character must be someone with whom the viewers can identify.

(10) Demonstrate. If you can show the product doing something to advantage, show it in every commercial. Consider making the demonstration and variations of it a feature of every commercial, and follow it up with complementary advertising in the press.

(11) Identifiable references. Testimonials from users, especially well known celebrities, are powerful for consumer products, but take care when using testimonials from industrial references: the testimonial must be universally acceptable. Endorsements by so-called 'experts' are not very persuasive because viewers do not readily identify with the experts. In the USA, Shell petrol used testimonials in a new way. It disguised a professional interviewer as a garage attendant who tried to talk car drivers out of buying Super Shell. The different reasons argued by ordinary people as to why they wanted Super Shell had considerable impact on the viewers.

(12) Concentrate on the use of the product. Don't sell the steak, sell the sizzle. Show the product being used. Focus on facial expressions that indicate satisfaction with the product. Viewers are not interested in the product itself—only what it will do for them.

## Outdoor advertising

Outdoor advertising includes posters, hoardings, billboards, display signs and cabinets, illuminated and non-illuminated signs and displays, coach and railway station sites, poster sites and panels on transport. Outdoor advertising is an extensive medium including everything from an animated electric sign in London's Piccadilly Circus to the backs of municipal deckchairs at seaside resorts; from a panel inside a taxicab to a large poster on a hoarding by the roadside. Outdoor advertising may be static, displayed at one site, or attached to some transportation and moving.

Outdoor advertising needs special consideration of the message to be displayed and the circumstances in which it can be seen. A poster on the outside of moving transport must have short, easily seen messages. A poster on the inside of transport, such as bus cards, underground cards, taxi cab cards, can contain more information. Posters on hoardings near to shopping centres can be explanatory; posters at the side of trunk roads need shorter, easy-to-view messages.

Posters are based on 'sheet' size, the old printing size of 'double-crown', which is 30 inches by 20 inches. A double-crown size poster is called a single-sheet. A 4-sheet poster is 4 double-crowns in size; 8-sheet is 8 double-crowns; 16-sheet, 16 double-crowns. A 16-sheet poster measures $4 \times 30$ in deep (10 ft) by $4 \times 20$ in wide (6 ft 8 in).

There are approximately 5,000 poster sites in the UK, the majority 16-and 4-sheet size. All may be rented on a monthly rate basis.

## Getting the best from outdoor advertising

Irrespective of the type of outdoor advertising, it appeals to an audience 'in motion': either the viewer is moving past the ad or the ad is travelling past the viewer.

Consider poster messages where there will only be a few seconds of potential readership, as you would a five- or ten-second TV commercial. Basically it is reminder advertising, reminding the reader of the product benefits. Check poster suggestions against the following points:

(1) Relate the sites you choose to the distribution potential of your product. If your product is available from specific outlets, use posters near to the outlets. Outdoor advertising is the most localised of all media, you can select your target audience and limit the campaign geographically.

(2) If appropriate, show the product big and in full colour. Register the image of the product strongly and quickly with viewers.

(3) Crystallise the main product benefit in a short slogan or message; make it big, bold, colourful and easy to read in a couple of seconds. Even if you use posters and cards inside tubes, trains, buses, etc, still show the main product benefit strongly but back it up with easy-to-read reasons why. The average journey in public transport is approximately 20 minutes; don't bore travellers. Don't offer them things to drink; make them thirsty!

(4)  For static outdoor sites with passing traffic, concentrate on the essentials. Use one illustration, preferably 'cut out', that is, all the background removed and just the silhouette of the product or a person used. Keep words to a minimum—about six. Use bold lettering large enough to be read from 100 metres or so. As soon as your poster comes into view, your product should be identifiable. If the viewer has to travel within 30 metres of the poster before recognising what it is, it is not bold enough. Keep the colours to those which are easiest to distinguish. Yellow letters on a black background are strongest visually but, in general, use the stronger colour on the weaker. Make use of the primary colours, red, blue, and yellow. Good effects can be achieved with combinations: red and blue, from a distance, is purple; blue and yellow become green; red and yellow, orange. When viewing poster suggestions, place them upright several metres away from you, even in the next room, and look at them from a distance. If you must view them at your desk use a 'dimi-glass' (diminishing glass, which is the opposite of a magnifying glass) which reduces the image the further you hold the glass away from the visual. You will get an idea of what your poster will look like when on site. If you cannot get hold of a dimi-glass, have reduced photostats about 10 cm high of all poster visuals.

(5)  Look for the dramatic presentation. Emotion works well in posters—especially humour. Posters for, say, fire prevention, can use dramatic, colourful illustrations.

Beware of presentations based on psychological appeals; you are trying to sell products. Some years ago, a cigarette manufacturer used 48-sheet posters depicting a single cigarette, which stretched nearly the whole width of the poster, about to be lit from the flame of a single match. The virgin cigarette was about to meet the phallic flame! It was said that it would create an unconscious desire in the male smoker! It was dramatic; it was easy to see; it might even have won an award for a good poster design, but it didn't do much for cigarette sales. Unconscious desires may have been stimulated in the travelling male but he wasn't stimulated into buying more of the brand— and neither was there any increase in reported cases of rape. The brand did not link with the illustration; there was no direct message; it could have been for any cigarette. Avoid dramatic posters that don't sell your product.

(6)  Have a unified theme. Concentrate your advertising message into a main theme and do not dissipate the promotion thrust by using many different messages.

With a small metal 100-gram hammer, you could eventually knock a nail into a piece of wood. If the hammer was made of foam plastic, you could knock the nail for ever and not even dent the surface of the wood: the effort would be dissipated. The same is true of many kinds of effort: concentrate, don't dissipate the fire power of your advertising.

Posters must be part of a total publicity campaign. What you say on your posters must complement all your other advertising and promotion. The main idea in the poster must be repeated in press ads which can illustrate further; ads in journals can explain a lot more; direct mail shots can really punch home your message, support your argument, make your offer persuasively and suggest action.

Sales presentations must also be complementary to the publicity. Brief the sales force thoroughly in advance of the campaign.

## Determine the appropriation

This means deciding how much to allocate to the total advertising budget for corporate and product advertising, promotion, merchandising, and all the ancillary efforts that will accompany it. Some organisations include salaries and expenses of the staff employed in the advertising department, because they are part of the total publicity cost.

There are several methods of setting the appropriation. For FMCG such as cigarettes, the percentage of sales used for advertising is low. For slow moving products such as furniture, jewellery, the percentage is high.

For an ongoing campaign there will be records of promotion and sales for previous years and less money will be required than for a new venture that needs an initial thrust.

Experience in various industries has indicated that the percentages of sales for advertising of ongoing campaigns are as illustrated in Table 13.1.

Keep your eye on competition and the market position of your product. Compare your product with both competing and competitive products— that is, products which are similar and those that are different but which provide similar satisfactions.

Your product may be in a leading position, or second or third most favoured product, or one of the 'other brands'. Estimate the age of the product in terms of its product life cycle (PLC). Is it a new product generally or only for your organisation? Is it a recently modified product, with several competing products, and early in its PLC? A product with a lot of

**Table 13.1** *Percentages of sales for advertising*

|  | Percentage of sales |
|---|---|
| Clothing | 0.35 |
| Industrial | 0.47 |
| Retail | 0.49 |
| Financial/Savings | 0.63 |
| Motor cars | 0.69 |
| Tourism/Entertainment | 0.75 |
| Food | 0.95 |
| Drink/Tobacco | 1.12 |
| Household/Leisure | 1.61 |
| Publishing | 2.05 |
| Medical/Toiletries | 5.96 |

competition has to be publicised more than a product that has only light competition. Some reported percentages of sales are shown in Table 13.2.

**Table 13.2** *Advertising as a percentage of sales*

| Market position | Advertising as a percentage of sales |
|---|---|
| No competition | 0 − 0.1 |
| Light competition | 0.1 − 3.0 |
| Medium competition | 3.0 − 8.0 |
| Heavy competition | 8.0 − 15.0 |

The PLC stage of the product influences the weight of advertising required. If the product is in the decline stage, little advertising is needed — you should 'milk' the product. If the product is in the early growth stage, especially with competition, a great deal of advertising is necessary.

The costs of production of advertisements are considerable if you have frequent changes of copy, illustrations, or other body matter. A large supermarket, or a furniture store, advertising in local papers with weekly changes of illustrations and copy, or with regular special offers, will have high production costs; as high as 30 per cent of the cost of space. A national advertiser repeating the same copy will have very low production costs as a percentage of space costs.

If you use an agency or outside professional assistance, ask for estimates of costs for the preparation of the visuals, artwork and material for the publications. If you fail to do this, you may receive unexpectedly high invoices for production. It is better to set a budget and require the work to be done within that figure.

In one major survey, 90 per cent of companies reported that they had an arbitrary approach to setting the appropriation; 8 per cent stated that they considered the market situation; only 2 per cent really cared and tried to set their advertising appropriation accurately.

Here are some of the more usual methods of setting the appropriation:

(1)  Percentage of last year's sales turnover. This is a safe, conservative method; known data is used. There is obvious logic in the method, but it does tend to stultify growth.

(2)  Percentage of sales estimate. A more realistic approach, based on expected demand and the capacity of the factory to produce the quantity. If the sales figure is lower than forecast, then advertising will be a higher percentage than desirable. One advantage of this method: it increases pressure on the sales forecasters to be as realistic and as accurate as possible.

(3)  Competitive method. Useful method for new advertisers who have little knowledge of what to spend. It may be assumed that competitors know a reasonable figure to spend on advertising compared with their sales figures.

(4)  Task method. The most realistic and yet the most difficult method to use. It requires research to establish the level of advertising needed to achieve a given purpose, such as to sell a certain quantity of goods. Another task approach is the cost of exposure: the cost of reaching, say, 75 per cent of all households or farmers, or engineering works. Media statistics are the basis for estimating degree and cost of exposure.

(5)  Composite method. This takes into account all factors that influence the sales of a product. Some of these are:

- production capacity
- previous sales of the product over the past few years
- forecast sales for the next year
- effectiveness of the field sales organisation
- effectiveness of the distributor network or intermediaries
- likely attractiveness of the product
- seasonality of sales
- political, economic, social and climatic conditions

# 14

# Below-The-Line Advertising

An annual consideration is how much of the publicity budget should be allocated to the five main media and how much to 'below-the-line' media. You are given practical advice on the use of exhibitions, direct mail, and several others. The real value of public relations as the most cost-effective promotion, and an outline of the main 'publics' and how they should be approached, are discussed.

## The dividing line in advertising

On a media schedule a line is usually drawn after the five main media. Below this line are any media being recommended by the agency but on which they do not receive the normal 15 per cent commission granted by the main five. They charge clients a percentage oncost handling charge. Hence the name of these media — 'below-the-line'. They include all media other than the main five, such as direct mail, exhibitions, contests and competitions, point-of-sale, sales promotion, merchandising and sales literature.

## Direct mail

Direct mail is widely used all over the world, especially in the USA where more is spent on it than on the whole of advertising in the UK. Do not send one 'shot'. At least two and, preferably, a series of shots should be employed as a direct mail campaign. Plan what each shot is to achieve; whether they should be continued, changed or stopped to a recipient if a particular shot achieves a response.

As with other forms of advertising, the medium (the list) is more important than the message. Superbly produced shots sent to a poor list will be a waste of money.

With the aid of laser printing, computerised writing, addressing and mailing, direct mail shots can be sent to individuals with the name and address 'matched in' and, where required, the name of the individual included in the body of the letter and other literature.

Mass mailings should be produced in full colour, to a high standard. Smaller mailings need not be so lavishly produced but must be 'professional' in their presentation.

Keep your list as 'clean' as possible: update with correct names and addresses, appropriate titles; remove companies and persons who have moved elsewhere, and so on.

Unless you have direct mail publicity experience, do not write the letter yourself. What you may think is important may not be what the potential customer regards as important. Employ the services of a professional letter-writer. It appears easy to do but this conceals the skill of the art and marketing experience needed to produce letters that achieve results. A one- or two-page letter will cost between £50 and £500, depending on the nature of the project. When commissioning a letter, ask for two or three versions and test each one on a sample mailing of, say, 25 to 50 recipients.

## How to get better letters

Use the following ten points and notes to check your proposed letter. Award a mark between zero and ten for each criterion. A letter with a score of 75 per cent or over is likely to be satisfactory.

| Criterion | Maximum score |
|---|---|
| 1. Envelope and letter-heading | 10 |
| 2. Folding of contents | 10 |
| 3. Targeting | 10 |
| 4. Interest | 10 |
| 5. Proposition | 10 |
| 6. Credibility | 10 |
| 7. Desire | 10 |
| 8. Reference and guarantee | 10 |
| 9. Action | 10 |
| 10. Enclosures | 10 |

### 1. Envelope and letter-heading

The envelope must create a good impression. Brown envelopes should only be used for samples; use strong white envelopes. Machine stamping often announces a circular letter. If your mailing is small enough, an attractive stamp will give your letter a better chance of being opened and read. Consider having mail posted from overseas; it will often create added interest. Have only name and address and postal code on the envelope. Don't necessarily indicate the sender; it may go straight into the waste-paper basket unopened.

Letter-headings are very important. Use a high grade of paper and good printing. Avoid cluttered letter-headings with a mass of details. The positioning of a typed letter so that it lines up with the heading and other matter is also important. When designing a new letter-heading, select it with a typed letter temporarily fixed to it. Do not choose a letter-heading design prepared on art paper and enclosed in a fancy folder. That is not how they are received! For special mailings, it is worth considering a letter-heading and letter separately designed for that mailing. When I was with Moss Bros, I frequently designed special letter-headings with the letter printed to fit the design. One, in particular, for ski-wear, had a child in ski clothes standing against a snow-covered mountain background. All this was printed in pale blue and the letter black. The letter not only achieved a very high response, it won me a Dartnell Gold Medal in the States!

## 2. Folding of contents

Letter and contents should emerge the right way up when removed from the envelope. Don't allow the letter to be folded one way and the enclosures another; when they are removed from the envelope they have to be shuffled around so that they can be read. Have them folded so that it is easy for the whole of the contents to be removed and read in the order necessary to create the best impression.

## 3. Targeting

Write as you would talk to someone. Use simple but telling words. Avoid long words. Make it easy to understand what you mean. Carefully consider your target readers and then write your letter as you would talk to them. If you are writing to technical people—engineers, electricians, farmers, dentists—use the everyday technical language that they would use. If you use an appeal—ownership, pride, love, duty, gain, profit, self-indulgence, even fear—set it out in a logical, easy-to-understand sequence. Reason seldom sells anything. Man is not a reasoning animal; he is an emotional animal. Provide adequate data in the envelope. The letter and enclosures should supply complete information for the recipient to be able to decide.

## 4. Interest

Capture the interest of the reader as soon as the envelope is opened and the contents extracted. If you fail to capture this interest at the start, it is unlikely that your letter will be read.

## 5. Proposition
Present your proposition on a sound basis. Offer the reader something that can be used to advantage at a reasonable, fair price.

## 6. Credibility
Be convincing. Letter and enclosure must be convincing. You may have an excellent, low-priced product or service, but it must be offered under conditions that are believable.

## 7. Desire
Do not simply describe the product. No one buys a product for itself alone, but for the satisfactions it will provide. Your letter must create desire in the reader.

## 8. Reference and guarantee
A third-party reference is a powerful aid to selling. Have you used a reference or a testimonial? The testimonials or references must be: True; Relevant to the readers; Understandable; and Evoke interest. The capital letters, TRUE, are a convenient mnemonic to guide you. If the shot is seeking an order, include the words 'satisfaction guaranteed or money refunded'. This will make your proposition more effective and believable. If you are only inviting enquiries, still use the guarantee of satisfaction offer. Impress on readers that they have nothing to lose. Some will buy at this stage.

## 9. Action
If you read the good mail-order ads in the weekend newspapers, they tell you exactly what you have to do to obtain the merchandise. Use this method in your letter. Tell the reader what has to be done. Don't leave the reader 'in the air'. Invite her or him to take a definite action by sending in an order, or request for a sample, further information, or whatever. Make it easy to take action. Enclose postage paid envelopes or use 'Freepost'. Use simple instructions:

> 'If you wish to order this, insert your name here...'
>
> 'Write in your chest size here...'
>
> 'Cross out the model you do not require.'
>
> 'Send cheque, postal order or stamps to the value of...'.

## 10. Enclosures
If possible, use the maximum weight allowed by the postage you are pay-ing. Include attractive support literature such as a descriptive folder, or explanatory leaflet showing the product being used. If appropriate, enclose a folder, booklet or similar piece of publicity that can be used independently of the letter.

Read the letter aloud to a colleague or fearless friend, invite criticism and put the whole thing on one side for at least 24 hours before re-reading and taking action. If you do this, give the shot 5 bonus points!

## Exhibition check-list

Exhibitions can be a convincing and economic way of getting your message across and demonstrating your products. Always check on the organisers of an exhibition to establish their reputation and experience. Mistakes can be costly. The following check-list of activities should be modified to comply with company and industry practice and any special requirements of the exhibition organisers. Some items may need to be progressed earlier than indicated.

*One year in advance*
   (1)  Select the exhibition.
   (2)  Write for literature and reports on previous shows.
   (3)  Make a market analysis:
      ● Write to known contacts.
      ● Compare what other opportunities exist for exhibiting the company's products around the same time.
   (4)  Agree on size of stand, book space, order telephone line for stand if needed, and send deposit.
   (5)  Reserve hotel accommodation and ensure confirmation received.

*Nine months in advance*
   (6)  Check site and adjacent facilities through local contacts.
   (7)  With appropriate executives, determine likely products and new products to be exhibited.
   (8)  Start stand design.
   (9)  Prepare model of stand and any other working drawings.
   (10)  Check on size of doors and lifts at exhibition hall.

*Six months in advance*
   (11)  Check available literature; prepare new literature.
   (12)  Check availability of free samples and give-aways.
   (13)  Check exhibit schedule with designer and/or builder.
   (14)  Prepare shipping plan in accordance with exhibition rules.
   (15)  Check with advertising, PR, to ensure they are fully aware.
   (16)  Plan manning of stand.

(17)  Check on press releases.

(18)  Check on stand equipment order.

(19)  Order exhibition supplies.

(20)  Check stand is being constructed.

*Four months in advance*

(21)  Contact transportation, customs, freight forwarders, etc.

(22)  Check on all required documents and forms.

(23)  Send requisition for carpenters, electricians, plumbers, painters, sign writers, etc, at site.

(24)  Re-check on literature and translations.

(25)  Check on exhibit construction.

(26)  Advise stand personnel on tentative arrangements.

*Three months in advance*

(27)  Prepare manning schedule for exhibition.

(28)  Alert overseas personnel as necessary.

(29)  Re-check on supplies and equipment.

(30)  Make final approval on local and national publicity.

*Two months in advance*

(31)  Send list of stand personnel to exhibition organisers.

(32)  Send to hotel list of personnel who will be staying there.

(33)  Arrange to ship literature, samples, equipment, displays.

(34)  Order furniture, floor coverings, lighting, special equipment, gas, water, chairs and other items for stand if not already done, and all stationery required.

(35)  Order badges for exhibition personnel.

(36)  Check news releases and photographs.

(37)  Send out invitations to customers and potentials.

(38)  Arrange for photographer to take exhibition pictures.

(39)  Contact model agency for models if required.

(40)  Check transportation arrangements, reservations.

(41)  Circulate internal memo on all arrangements.

*One month in advance*

(42)  Insure the exhibit.

(43)  Check on delivery of stand, equipment and supplies.

(44)  Arrange for stand repacking and return.

(45)  Arrange for cleaning of stand and any security needed.

*One week before the exhibition*

(46)  Check with hotel.

(47)  Check with personnel who are manning the stand.

(48)  Check on hospitality arrangements, drinks, flowers, etc.

(49)  Arrange first meeting with stand personnel on site.

(50)  Check arrival and clearance of exhibit and equipment.

(51)  Prepare emergency tool kit for repairs of display units and equipment.

(52)  Check photographer—date and time of appearance.

(53)  Check exhibition forms, order books, scrap pads, visiting cards.

*Day before the exhibition*

(54)  Meet with exhibition organisers.

(55)  Check stand, furniture, equipment, all services, especially security for night before opening.

(56)  Check on layout of stand.

(57)  Check that all items are on stand and in good condition.

(58)  Note where crates are stored for speedy dismantling of stand and return of exhibits.

(59)  Check if telephone connected and notify HQ, hotel, and others as necessary, of stand phone number.

(60)  Ensure all important phone numbers—exhibition organisers, decorators, freight handler, doctor, local press, etc—are recorded and can be easily seen by stand personnel.

(61)  Advise stand personnel of hours on duty on stand.

(62)  Survey the entire exhibition.

(63)  Arrange for transport to exhibition next morning.

*Day of exhibition*

(64)  Have an early breakfast meeting and brief personnel.

(65)  Organise collection of all competitive literature.

*One week after the exhibition*

(66)  Check on return of exhibit.

(67)  Check all invoices.

(68)  Check service charges.

(69)  Send letters of thanks to all concerned.

(70)  Send sales leads and information to all personnel.

*One month after the exhibition*

(71)  Obtain statistics on total exhibition from organisers.

(72)  Meet with HQ personnel as necessary and assess the
      exhibition.

## Merchandising and sales promotion

Merchandising is any special promotion such as an in-store demonstration, or sampling, where samples of the product are handed out in a store or delivered door-to-door. Merchandising is usually conducted over a short period of time and may be seen as a tactical promotional activity in the distribution channel.

Sales promotion is normally a long-term operation and can include the whole sales organisation, while merchandising is restricted to 'shot-in-the-arm' publicity. A sales promotion operation could include several separate merchandising operations, as may often be seen in the retail market with the promotion of cereals, toothpaste, certain drinks, soaps and detergents and other 'fast moving consumer goods' (FMCG).

### Competitions

These range far and wide and require some element of skill on the part of the competitors. A competition should be made easy to enter and should not be run over too long a period of time.

### Self-liquidating premium offers

Non-profit-making offers of products such as prints of pictures, towels, cutlery, holiday accessories, pans, small coffee tables, audio cassettes, quartz clocks. The item is offered for a number of wrappers, package tops or other labels plus a cash payment. The offer stimulates increased sales of the product which pay for the items.

### Multiple packs

Special offers in stores of small items such as chocolate, soap, toothpaste, biscuits, soft drinks, etc. Sometimes called 'Jumbo Packs'.

### Coupons and vouchers

Selected products carry a special coupon or part of the label is printed in the form of a voucher. These entitle the customer to purchase the next product at a reduced price. Retailers are empowered to accept these from shoppers to reduce the price of a particular product but not for the purchase of other goods.

### Gift coupons

One of the oldest forms of merchandising to secure regular purchases of the appropriate brand of product. Have been used with success by cigarette, tea, petrol, cocoa and other FMCG manufacturers.

### Trade characters

Quite a wide use is made of particular animals or characters. One of the most popular characters was the Esso petrol tiger. The slogan and its accompanying merchandising of 'Put a Tiger in Your Tank' was so popular with the motoring public that, when it was discontinued, there was a useful campaign to 'Bring back the tiger!'.

### Sampling

One of the best, if more expensive, ways of getting your product into the hands of customers. Often used in selected hotels where one or two samples of toiletries are left in hotel rooms for guests.

## Getting the best from sales literature

After personal representation, the next most important method of getting your sales messages over to prospective clients is with sales literature. Effective brochures depend as much on marketing analysis as on good writing and illustrations.

The manager responsible for the brochure briefs the designer. Don't use a printer's rep as the designer; you need objective advice. The briefing should define the general objective of the brochure: what it is intended to do and how it will fit in with the company's marketing scheme. The designer needs to become familiar with all other visual material issued by the company. Constraints such as name-style, logo, typeface, colours, and budget, are declared at the briefing.

Discuss with sales staff, marketing people, product designers, etc, to find out the categories of people and organisations who are likely to receive the brochure. If your brochure is to be read by people whose main language is not English, ensure that the sentences are short and of simple construction.

When the specific objectives have been agreed these should indicate the proposed sections, theme of each section, what facts, illustrations, etc are to be included; approximate length and any special points to be considered. The text is written, illustrations prepared, photographs taken, captions written, and a mock-up prepared. Circulate this mock-up and any photos and illustrations to appropriate people in the company and, unless there are strong reasons or new information for change, it should then be progressed to the printers for printing.

## Public relations

Every organisation has its various 'publics' and each group that comprises a particular 'public' has its impressions of the company, that might be correct or incorrect. Eight 'publics' can be identified and each has to be considered and communicated with in a distinct way:

- employees
- suppliers
- customers
- media
- communities
- government departments
- educational establishments
- shareholders

### Employees

Sadly, when substantial events are about to happen in an organisation, the employees are sometimes the last to hear about it. You don't build a company with products, you build it with people. And your employees are very valuable assets that do not appear in the final accounts of the company.

Talk to your employees through a staff newsletter, or periodic journal. Have a notice board on which news items about the company can be displayed. In the factories, have a wall newspaper with up-to-date information giving details of large orders, extensive contracts, and production achievements. News about the globe-trotting directors and senior executives may be of some interest, but of equal or greater interest will be news of other employees.

Above all, make someone personally responsible for keeping these notice boards and wall newspapers up-to-date. This means they must be inspected daily.

## Suppliers

It's an interesting point that we only contact our suppliers when we want something. We seldom take the trouble to visit a supplier just to find out what's new. Yet suppliers are often expanding, developing new products and ways of doing things. If we maintain a regular contact with our important suppliers, when there is anything that might be of interest to us, we shall probably be one of the first to be told.

PR contacts with suppliers should be developed, not only by people in the purchasing department, but also by those who do not normally contact them: people on the sales and marketing side. Frequently, new ideas and opportunities are discovered through such active PR links.

## Customers

These days, if you subscribe to something or buy something where it is necessary to give your name and address, you subsequently get deluged with offers in the post. But these are offers for sale. Few organisations just write to you to tell you what they are doing. Perhaps mounting costs and slimmer margins preclude this luxury.

When I handled the publicity for Moss Bros of Covent Garden, we had an excellent system for maintaining contact with customers. Anyone who purchased an item over a certain sum had their name and address recorded and filed in a central bureau. The customers were categorised according to the items purchased and, regularly, they received appropriate booklets by mail. These booklets were amusing or instructive but never selling anything. A book on ponies and horses would be sent to people who had purchased riding wear; an amusing story of Mr Warsash and his sartorial failings would be sent to men who had purchased suits, and so on.

The goodwill that can be built up by keeping in touch with customers is remarkable. Unfortunately, rising costs require us to question everything we do and I was responsible for changing the character of the purely PR mailing by increasing the content with 'stuffers'. These simple leaflets advertised various items or services available and were included to make up the weight of the package to equal that permitted by the postage.

## Media

When you develop contacts with media for PR purposes, you are talking with an entirely different set of people from those you deal with when placing advertising. What is of interest is news. If you want to stand a chance of getting your news published in the editorial columns, you must be professional in the way you offer it.

First, list all the newspapers, trade, technical and professional journals that could be of use to your company. Obviously, if you are in the engineering field, you have little interest in magazines for bakers, farmers, cosmetics, etc, so your list must be applicable to your industry.

Rank the publications in order of importance; the few which are of major importance, and then the remainder which will probably form the bulk of the list. Ordinary news items should be circulated to all on the list. This should be done on a regular basis using specially prepared A4-sized paper headed 'News Release', 'Information', or simply 'News'. The company's name and address should be printed discreetly at the bottom of the sheet and not at the top. Make your release easy to read and in need of the minimum editorial work so that it is capable of being published as it stands.

The layout of the release is important. Put the date at the top on the right-hand side. The headline should only identify the item and is not intended to be used by editors; they write their own. Paragraphs must be short and all, except the first, indented.

For style and treatment, be guided by news items in the leading papers; the subject of the story is contained in the first paragraph. When you prepare your news release, tell all in the first paragraph; don't tease the reader. If it's all there in a few words, it is likely to be printed. If the whole release has to be read to extract the story, it won't be read.

Keep your release to one page if possible. If you have to continue on a second sheet type 'more' at the bottom of the first page. Use continuation sheets with a printed heading, 'News Release Continued', and the same details printed at the foot. At the end of the news item type, 'ends'. Names and telephone numbers of contacts available during day and night, if necessary, are typed bottom right.

To cover all the points in the substance of a news release, I use the mnemonic TOADS. It stands for Topic, Organisation, Application, Details, Source. The main topic of the news item is given in the first paragraph and the company or organisation linked with the topic. The application of the topic and its advantages or improvement over existing products are given. Details that elaborate on the application are in one or more following paragraphs. The source from whom further information can be obtained is the last paragraph.

## Communities

Wherever the company has a branch or a factory, local employees should be encouraged to participate in community affairs. Your sales people should be able to join in community activities with your full support. Of course, such activities must not conflict with the main purpose of their jobs. Every time one of your employees is recognised in community affairs, he or she is often linked with the company. This builds an image of the company that pays dividends. When you need additional staff, planning permission to extend a building, approval for some particular project in the community, the fact that you are a 'good' company will help.

## Shareholders

Normally, shareholders are only written to because of statutory requirements, with, or without, their dividend cheques. The company would like their shareholders to hold on to the company's shares and also, when special issues of shares are made, for their current shareholders to be pleased to take up the offer. While the yield of shares is the greatest influence on their retention, a 'good' company with a good image and future prospects is also an attraction.

The occasional letter to shareholders, perhaps offering them special terms for company products, is well worth considering by the sales and marketing director with, of course, the approval of the board.

## Government departments

A liaison should be maintained with both central and local government departments. Being able to put a face to a name will be of great help to you when you want help from the appropriate official. When you want to develop your export activities, the amount of help and advice you can get from central government is impressive.

## Education

Many years ago, an electric cable manufacturer paid a small sum of money to a model railway manufacturer to have the name of the cable maker on every one of the railway wagons that carried a toy drum of cable. Now, no child is likely to be in the market for a drum of heavy duty electric cable, but it contributes to the image of the manufacturer. The name sticks long after the train set has been passed on.

Several companies supply schools, colleges and universities with extensive information and free materials about their industry. Not only does it help the students to understand some of the facts of industrial and commercial life, it also builds up an image of the company. When these companies make their rounds of the educational establishments looking for recruits, they tend to attract the best students.

## Language

You will appreciate that each separate 'public' has to be reached with a different language and in a different way. You cannot 'talk' to the media as you 'talk' to your employees; your communications with customers are different from your communications with government departments.

If you have a planned and continuous PR campaign it can be the most cost-effective means of projecting your company's image to the market. Do not be misled into thinking that it can be done 'on the cheap', or that PR is unpaid advertising. You should allocate approximately 10 per cent of your total appropriation to public relations.

# 15

# Pricing

To the extent that you price products and services unwisely, you will affect company profits and tend to increase the dissatisfaction of customers. Price can be set near to the ceiling or the floor; the factors that influence your choice are discussed. Of considerable interest to price-setters is the concept of elasticity of demand; you are shown how to use it. The problems of deciding whether or not to drop a losing product are explored with the aid of marginal costing.

## Importance of pricing

The price of a product has a direct impact on profit, yet price setting is not always well done in companies. In your present position you may, or may not, have a great deal of influence over the prices set for your products or services. If you have been appointed to a new post, you will probably be faced with existing price structures.

Nevertheless, you should know how price is structured and that it is a compromise between what the market will pay and the costs of producing it, storing it and getting it to that market. If you set the price toward what the market will bear, this would be a high price policy; if you set it toward the cost of production, this would be a low price policy. One of the main pricing problems is to decide at what point between the upper, 'market price' and lower, 'cost price' to set a price for a product. Several things will influence you.

## Influence of cost

It's almost too simple to ask, 'What does it cost?', 'How much profit do we normally make?' and 'How much do we need to sell it for?' to arrive at the price. There is no guarantee that prospective customers will pay what it costs to make your product, and companies sometimes find that the customer places a lower value on the product than its cost of production and distribution.

In 1985, two companies, one English, the other French, were competing to supply the American military market with a communications systems. The British system was superior; it was more advanced, more flexible, and had been designed with future needs of military communications in mind. The price reflected the superior quality. It is often said that the customer remembers quality long after he has forgotten the price, and that he can be persuaded to pay for quality.

But they didn't! The Americans bought the French version. Why? Because the British product had been over-developed and consequently its price, even though justifiable, was far too high. This illustrates one of the main reasons why some companies fail in their marketing endeavours: they try to sell a product that is better than the customer really needs, especially when its price is higher than the competition.

Some products are not marketed because the market sets a value on them lower than their cost of production. However, costs do not determine price and, if you do sell at or below cost, you must have some convincing reasons why you are prepared to subsidise such products.

## Influence of competition

The level at which you set price for a product can either stimulate or discourage competition. If you can differentiate your product and make it distinct from its competitors, you can have a significant price difference. The size of the difference will reflect the degree of product distinction you can create in the mind of the buyer.

## Influence of distribution methods

The closer you get to the end user, the more costly is distribution. A well established company will probably have the advantage of market coverage; an active, successful company will not only have market coverage but market penetration also. That is, it will have considerable experience in the chosen channels of distribution, with consistent repeat sales. You can have market coverage without having sold anything; it simply means that you have organised facilities to be able to supply demand as and when it arises. Market penetration is the character and extent to which you are selling in the selected channels.

Market share is quoted as a percentage of total market sales and can be in volume or value. Market penetration, though often used synonymously with market share, is a qualification of the share, describing distribution channels and methods, outlets, purchasing patterns and the strength of the hold on the market.

## Influence of public opinion

This is the opinion of buyers and users of your products. Products are purchased within certain 'price brackets' and these price brackets include products with similar characteristics and attributes. A low price for a product can indicate to a potential buyer that it is of insufficient quality and capability for what is required. The buyer will seldom refuse to consider a product solely on the grounds that its price is too low, but it can happen.

### Cheap plastics bearings

Some years ago when I was with the Vickers group of companies, I supplied plastics bearings to steel and aluminium rolling mills. These superseded the original phosphor-bronze bearings which had lubricating problems when under load. During one of my usual visits to the chief engineer of a steel mill in Newport, I saw in his office four plastics bearings propped against the wall.

'Hullo!' I exclaimed, 'what are those?'

'Oh!' said the engineer, 'they're from one of your competitors. We've had them for some time; we can't use them. Don't want to use them. They're about half the price of yours, so we can't risk it, but we've nowhere to put them.'

They couldn't use them because they were too cheap! The bearings could not be as good as those supplied by the Vickers organisation because they were half the price. To shut down a steel mill for maintenance is an expensive operation because of loss of output, in addition to the costs of shutting down. You can see the engineer's point. He wasn't going to risk the premature shutting down of a mill because he had installed cheap bearings. So they stayed in his office, unused ... until, one day, we failed with a delivery of bearings. The mill awaiting the bearings was stopped; tempers shortened, costs mounted. The engineer did what any sensible person would have done in the same circumstances: installed the cheap bearings to keep the mill going.

They kept going all right, and lasted longer than ours! The reason why they were 'cheap' was simple. We machined our bearings from huge blocks of fabric-bonded phenolicformaldehyde plastics, with considerable waste of material in the process. The competitor had invested in moulds so that they could mould bearings with practically no waste. The cost of the moulds was amortised over several years and they were able to offer a comparable bearing at about half the price.

My only criticism is that they should have priced them higher and more closely to ours, which would have given them a degree of respectability and comparability. They would not have been left lying around the factory office for so long; then, having got it, if ever it was necessary or desirable, they could have reduced their prices.

## Cheap cricket balls

Another pricing experience was when I was with the RIL group of companies. The chairman was keen on sports—indoor and outdoor—and decided that we should develop a cricket ball made from plastics instead of traditional leather. We already manufactured a very high grade leather substitute for footwear soling material and this was ideal for cricket balls.

However, cricket ball manufacture is another problem. Each ball has 92 stitches to hold the halves together and, apart from size, weight and the ability of the ball to pass a 'go, no-go gauge' for sphericity, there are little or no specifications. Our method of production was to make two halves, one half sewn with 92 stitches, and placed in the lower mould with a carefully weighed amount of plastics mixture. The second half was placed on top, the press closed and the assembled ball 'cured'. After a few minutes we had several dozen balls ready for play.

With the ball ready, the next task was to price and sell it because the factory was turning them out at an astonishingly high rate and we were getting rather full up with balls: we had balls everywhere. The basic cost of production was about three old shillings; a traditional ball was then selling at just under three pounds. I wanted to sell our ball at over two pounds because low grade composition balls ('compos') were under a pound. No cricketer would use his bat with a compo ball—it would damage it. Our ball was truly amazing for its qualities and was indistinguishable from balls made by the conventional method. It had been tried out at all levels of cricket by several personalities and had been surreptitiously used in a minor counties match.

I was forced to market it at nineteen shillings and sixpence. And, at that price, it stayed in the shops. The price did not indicate the quality of the ball and it was just another 'cheap compo ball' that was 'more expensive than necessary'.

## Pricing the first videos

Another example of pricing too low was with the introduction of the video cassette recorder (VCR). I was consulting with a company who were introducing one of the first VCRs on the market. Despite the extensive development and testing it was largely an unknown quality, especially in the hands of ordinary users. I thought that there should be a high percentage in the price for warranty and servicing. And, when marketing something new like this, it costs time and money to educate the potential user in its use and to accept it. I suggested that the initial market would be the educational and training departments of universities and colleges who, at that time, had the funds to purchase such equipment at my suggested price of £600. The company decided on a low price policy and priced it at around half this. In the event, the amount of servicing required during the first year or so was far in excess of what had been allowed for in the costings and it was not a profitable product launch, despite the reasonably high sales.

To the extent that you price unwisely, you distort the market, affect profits and increase the dissatisfaction of customers.

## Influence of profit

If you cannot sell a product at a profit then you must have sound business reasons for selling it. There are several examples of complementary products being sold at minimal or no profit in a highly competitive market so that profits can be made on the main product. Certain drawing office equipment is sold at very near to its cost so that profits can be made on the paper used in the equipment.

The Polaroid camera was originally sold in the USA at a low profit margin so that high profits could be made on the special film it required. A well known lighting company sells some of its bought-in fittings at a loss, because they round out a popular product line.

Profit is not only the reward for effort and risk, it is also the means to finance research, to develop new products, to cushion the effects of recession, to keep the company in business tomorrow when it might not be making profits.

Sales and marketing managers frequently have to rely on cost and management accountants to understand the importance of costs and levels of operation on price structure. While you must not try to turn yourself into an accountant, you should know what questions to ask and be able to understand the answers you receive from the financial people.

The task of pricing is not an easy one; it is one of the most difficult tasks in selling and marketing. It involves a degree of prediction. You have to look into the future and determine the likely effect of price on sales, on costs, on competition and on the market generally.

## Demand theory in practice

Other things being equal, the general tendency is that the lower the price of a product, the more you will sell. Some products are not like this. A good example is potatoes: if the price of potatoes falls, we don't buy more—we buy much the same quantities. Many products sell in the same volume year after year, irrespective of price.

Some products behave dramatically: price only has to fall slightly and there is a considerable increase in quantities sold. Strawberries, petrol, shirts, mini-computers, machine tools, video recorders, and many others have exhibited this behaviour, known as a high 'elastic demand'. An explanation is given in Figure 15.1. At price P1, quantity Q1 is purchased and, if the price is lowered to P2, an increased quantity, Q2, tends to be purchased.

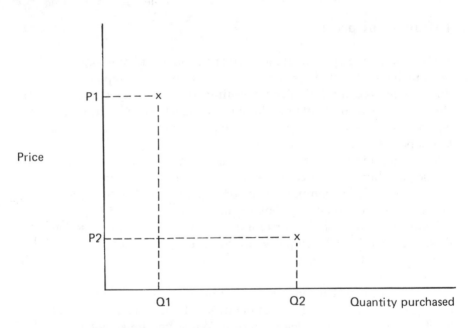

**Figure 15.1** *Demand and price relationship*

From this basic tendency, we make a jump: we say that it is possible to draw a line connecting all the various quantities likely to be purchased at various prices between P1 and P2. This gives a demand curve representing the quantities that would be purchased by the *same people at the same period of time*.

Obviously, this is theoretical: you cannot sell products at one price and then take them all back and offer them at a different price to the same people and see how many they would buy! In practice, to estimate a demand curve, a product is offered at different prices in different parts of the country at the same time. This indicates the quantities purchased at different prices but, by testing in different markets, other factors influence buyers and the results can only be, at best, reasonable estimates.

It is only possible to carry out such surveys with certain types of goods that are frequently purchased, such as FMCG: chocolate bars, soap powders, etc. It is not so easy to test with cars, furniture, typewriters, electric drills, and so on. With more costly products, particularly capital goods, you usually have only one chance to get the price right to get the order.

## Demand curve

Despite the difficulty of estimating likely demand at various price levels the implications can be used in pricing. An example is given in Table 15.1, from which the figures are plotted in Figure 15.2.

**Table 15.1**  *Specimen data—price and estimated sales*

| Price (£) | Estimated sales |
|-----------|-----------------|
| 10        | 40              |
| 9         | 45              |
| 6         | 70              |

With a company's previous sales figures and some intelligent analyses, it is possible to estimate a demand schedule and draw a demand curve even with only two reference points. The three points in Figure 15.2 can be joined and sales estimates made for prices in between.

## Determinants and conditions of demand

All the elements that cause demand are 'determinants' of demand, but all elements, other than price, are 'conditions' of demand. Examples of 'conditions' are: number of potential buyers, income or wealth of buyers, market size, advertising strength, prices of similar products, intensity of sales effort, product attributes. If price is changed, there is movement along the demand curve; if any of the conditions are changed (that is, anything other than price) there is a new demand curve either to the right or left.

An increase in demand caused by a change in one or more of the conditions creates a new demand curve, D2, to the right of the original one, D1. A decrease in demand through a change in conditions creates a new demand curve D3, to the left of the original curve, as in Figure 15.3. The

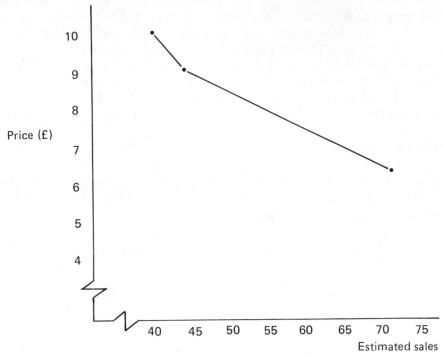

**Figure 15.2** *Table 15.1 as graph*

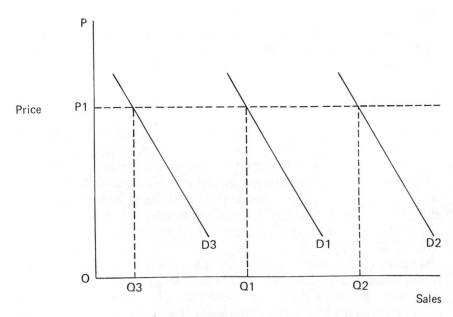

**Figure 15.3** *Demand curve[1]*

effect on sales, Q1, Q2 and Q3, at the same price level, P1, is clearly seen when there is a change in any of the conditions that create a new demand curve.

## Elasticity of demand

Consider the two demand curves in Figures 15.4 and 15.5. The slope of D1 is greater than that of D2 and this illustrates a very important topic for sales and marketing. Consider D1 and the two prices, P1 and P2, in Figure 15.4. The increase in sales, Q1 to Q2, is less than the decrease in price, P1 to P2. The opposite effect is seen with D2 in Figure 15.5. Price

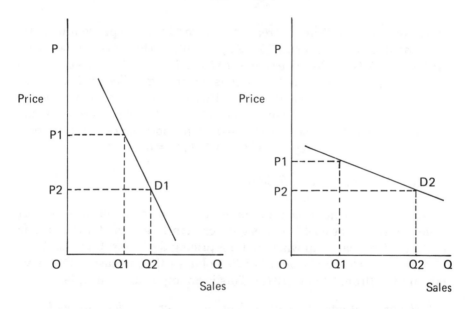

**Figure 15.4** *Demand curve*[2]     **Figure 15.5** *Demand curve*[3]

falls only slightly from P1 to P2, but the effect on sales is much greater, from Q1 to Q2.

This works in reverse, of course: if price is increased from P2 to P1, sales would fall from Q2 to Q1.

## Coefficient of elasticity

These two examples illustrate 'elasticity of demand'. It is the relationship between the proportionate (or percentage) change in quantity demanded and the proportionate (or percentage) change in price. The formula for determining the coefficient of elasticity of demand is:

*Proportionate change in Q divided by proportionate change in P*

Consider Table 15.2. There are two situations: when price is reduced, and when it is increased. If we have been selling at £7 and reduce the price to £5 (about 28 per cent reduction), sales increase by 15 (from 60 to 75), which is 25 per cent. The coefficient is $25/28 = 0.89$.

Table 15.2 *Specimen data—coefficient of elasticity*

| P | Q |
|---|---|
| £7 | 60 |
| £5 | 75 |

If we are selling at £5 and increase the price to £7, a 40 per cent increase, sales fall from 75 to 60, or $15/75 = 20$ per cent. In this case the coefficient is $20/40 = 0.5$. Over the price range of £5 to £7 two coefficients can be calculated, depending on whether price is increasing or decreasing.

It is more useful to calculate a coefficient half-way between the two prices and two quantities. This is called 'point elasticity'. Proportionate change in quantity is $15/\frac{1}{2}(75+60) = 0.22$; proportionate change in price is $2/\frac{1}{2}(7+5) = 0.33$. The coefficient is $0.22/0.33 = 0.67$.

## Practical use of the coefficient

When the coefficient of elasticity is less than 1, demand for the product is inelastic. When the coefficient is greater than 1, demand for the product is elastic. This can help when making pricing decisions. Consider Table 15.3. If price is lowered from £7 to £5, volume sales increase but turnover falls by £45 (from £420 to £375). This is an important principle:

*If the product has an inelastic demand, lowering price will tend to reduce total turnover despite sales increasing.*

These are not contrived figures. The principle applies to all demand situations. If you have a product with an inelastic demand, reducing its price increases sales volume but total revenue falls.

Table 15.3 *Specimen data—price, sales, turnover*

| Price (£) | Sales | Turnover (£) |
|---|---|---|
| 7 | 60 | 420 |
| 5 | 75 | 375 |

Supposing you have a fixed cost of £200 that has to be paid every week irrespective of how many products you make, whether you make 75, 60, or even none. Each product has £2 worth of labour and materials (variable cost). Lowering the price results in greater sales volume, but lower revenue and lower profit (Table 15.4).

It is not easy to estimate elasticity of demand. Obtain sales data for a period of years for a product, and adjust prices for inflation. Tabulate the sales achieved at each price level. Calculate the coefficients between each pair of figures. Observe whether there is any tendency that indicates elasticity or not.

**Table 15.4** *Table 15.3 amended, with additional data*

| Price (£) | Sales | Revenue (£) | Fixed cost (£) | Var. cost (£) | Tot. cost (£) | Profit (£) |
|---|---|---|---|---|---|---|
| 7 | 60 | 420 | 200 | 120 | 320 | 100 |
| 5 | 75 | 375 | 200 | 150 | 350 | 25 |

*Practical use of elasticity theory*

This property of elasticity of demand can be used in pricing. In the original schedule, Table 15.2, the coefficient of elasticity is 0.67. Using this, we can estimate likely sales if the price is set at £8:

| P | Q |
|---|---|
| £7 | 60 |
| £8 | x  (x assumed to be less than 60) |

We use point elasticity; thus, half-way point for price in this example is ½(7+8), and half-way point for quantity is ½(60+x). Therefore,

$$\frac{60-x}{\frac{1}{2}(60+x)} \div \frac{1}{\frac{1}{2}(7+8)} = 0.67$$

Turning the denominator upside down and multiplying:

$$\frac{60-x}{\frac{1}{2}(60+x)} \times \frac{\frac{1}{2}(7+8)}{1} = 0.67$$

Multiplying the numerators and denominators:

$$\frac{\frac{1}{2}(7+8)(60-x)}{\frac{1}{2}(60+x)} = 0.67$$

Multiplying both sides by ½(60+x):

$$\tfrac{1}{2}(7 + 8)(60 - x) = 0.67 \times \tfrac{1}{2}(60 + x)$$
$$450 - 7.5x = 20.1 + 0.335x$$

Collect the x terms on one side, figures on the other (change the signs when taking across the = sign):

$$7.835x = 429.9$$
$$x = 54.8$$
$$= 55 \text{ (to nearest whole number)}$$

This means that, assuming an elasticity coefficient of 0.67, setting price at £8 will achieve sales of about 55 and a higher profit (Table 15.5).

**Table 15.5** *Calculation of sales at a new price*

| Price (£) | Sales | Turnover (£) | Fixed cost (£) | Var. cost (£) | Tot. cost (£) | Profit (£) |
|---|---|---|---|---|---|---|
| 8 | 55 | 440 | 200 | 110 | 310 | 130 |

If you use this formula to estimate likely sales at a new price, you must keep the new price very close to the previous one because elasticity of demand changes over the length of the demand curve. Already, at £8, the coefficient would have changed from 0.67.

To illustrate this tendency for elasticity to vary over the demand curve, a demand curve is shown in Figure 15.6 which has been extended to cut the axes OQ and OP at X and Y respectively. When demand is almost at its maximum, at X, price is very near to zero: this gives a coefficient of elasticity of very nearly zero. When demand is almost nothing, at Y, this gives a coefficient approaching infinity. These facts are of particular importance in pricing. Over the whole range of demand, elasticity of demand becomes higher (very elastic) in the higher price range and lower (very inelastic) in the lower price range.

In real life, demand curves are not necessarily straight but, for all practical purposes, we can assume that the principle demonstrated applies to all demand curves.

## Should we drop it?

Sometimes a product loses money and yet it is not practical to increase its price. There is a natural tendency to want to drop it from the range.

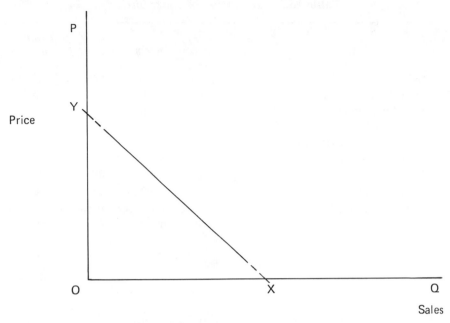

**Figure 15.6** *Demand curve⁴*

Contribution analysis will help you to compare the merits of products. Table 15.6 gives a projected revenue account for a company's four products.

**Table 15.6** *Specimen data—projected revenue account*

|  | 1 | 2 | 3 | 4 | Total |
|---|---|---|---|---|---|
| Sales (£) | 80,000 | 40,000 | 130,000 | 100,000 | 350,000 |
| Materials and labour | 30,000 | 20,000 | 50,000 | 40,000 | 140,000 |
| Production overhead | 20,000 | 12,000 | 30,000 | 25,000 | 87,000 |
| Selling expenses | 10,000 | 6,000 | 15,000 | 12,000 | 43,000 |
| Administration | 6,000 | 4,000 | 10,000 | 8,000 | 28,000 |
| Total cost | 66,000 | 42,000 | 105,000 | 85,000 | 298,000 |
| Profit (loss) | 14,000 | (2,000) | 25,000 | 15,000 | 52,000 |

Should product 2 be dropped? At first this seems to be sensible, but a marginal cost format, with every cost that can be attributed to a product identified and allocated (Table 15.7), shows the contributions made by the products. Contribution means the amount contributed to fixed over-heads and profits.

**Table 15.7** *Calculation of contribution*

|  | 1 (£000) | 2 (£000) | 3 (£000) | 4 (£000) | Total (£000) |
|---|---|---|---|---|---|
| Sales | 80 | 40 | 130 | 100 | 350 |
| Materials and labour | 30 | 20 | 50 | 40 | 140 |
| Variable production overhead | 6 | 5 | 9 | 7 | 27 |
| Marginal production cost | 36 | 25 | 59 | 47 | 167 |
| Variable selling expenses | 3 | 1 | 4 | 5 | 13 |
| Marginal cost | 39 | 26 | 63 | 52 | 180 |
| Contribution | 41 | 14 | 67 | 48 | 170 |

Fixed overheads (none directly attributable to any of the products):

| | |
|---|---|
| Production | 60 |
| Selling | 30 |
| Administration | 28 |
| Total | 118 |
| Net profit | 52 |

The net profit, £52,000, is the same. In such a marginal cost presentation, variable costs that cannot properly be allocated to a product are put in the general overhead section. In a full absorption cost presentation, as Table 15.6, general overheads have been allocated to the four products approximately according to turnover. Table 15.8 shows how the costs have been reallocated to products and to general overheads in Table 15.7.

**Table 15.8** *Calculation of general overheads*

|  | Original (Table 15.6) (£) | Marginal cost (Table 15.7) (£) | Transferred to general overheads (£) |
|---|---|---|---|
| Product 1 | 20,000 | 6,000 | 14,000 |
| Product 2 | 12,000 | 5,000 | 7,000 |
| Product 3 | 30,000 | 9,000 | 21,000 |
| Product 4 | 25,000 | 7,000 | 18,000 |
|  |  |  | 60,000 |
| Selling overheads |  |  |  |
| Product 1 | 10,000 | 3,000 | 7,000 |
| Product 2 | 6,000 | 1,000 | 5,000 |
| Product 3 | 15,000 | 4,000 | 11,000 |
| Product 4 | 12,000 | 5,000 | 7,000 |
|  |  |  | 30,000 |
| Administration—the total of £28,000 has been transferred |  |  | 28,000 |
|  |  |  | 118,000 |

If product 2 is dropped, the position is as shown in Table 15.9.

**Table 15.9** *Table 15.7 amended*

|  | 1 (£000) | 2 (£000) | 3 (£000) | 4 (£000) | Total (£000) |
|---|---|---|---|---|---|
| Sales | 80 | 0 | 130 | 100 | 310 |
| Materials and labour | 30 |  | 50 | 40 | 120 |
| Variable production overhead | 6 |  | 9 | 7 | 22 |
| Marginal production cost | 36 |  | 59 | 47 | 142 |
| Variable selling expenses | 3 |  | 4 | 5 | 12 |
| Marginal cost | 39 |  | 63 | 52 | 154 |
| Contribution | 41 | 0 | 67 | 48 | 156 |
| General fixed overheads: | Production |  |  |  | 60 |
|  | Selling |  |  |  | 30 |
|  | Administration |  |  |  | 28 |
|  | Total |  |  |  | 118 |
|  | Net profit |  |  |  | 38 |

By dropping product 2, total net profit has fallen from £52,000 to £38,000: this is the product's contribution of £14,000.

The marginal costing presentation, Table 15.9, is useful in other ways. For example, it shows that, if it were possible to double sales of product 1, profit would be increased by £41,000.

Although this analysis of total contribution is illuminating and demonstrates the folly of dropping a losing product (product 2) without further consideration, we need further data for sales management decisions. We need to know price and sales volume for each product and calculate *unit* contribution. This is given and calculated in Table 15.10.

**Table 15.10** *Calculation of unit contribution*

|  | 1 | 2 | 3 | 4 |
|---|---|---|---|---|
| Sales turnover (£) | 80,000 | 40,000 | 130,000 | 100,000 |
| Unit sales | 2,500 | 4,000 | 5,000 | 10,000 |
| Unit price (£) | 32 | 10 | 26 | 10 |
| Total contribution (£) | 41,000 | 14,000 | 67,000 | 48,000 |
| Unit contribution (£) | 16.40 | 3.50 | 13.40 | 4.80 |

From this data we can calculate the relative importance of the products in percentage terms (Table 15.11). Clearly, the price of product 2 is too low, because it contributes only 8 per cent of total contribution yet is 19 per cent of total sales volume and 11 per cent of total turnover.

**Table 15.11** *Calculation of percentage contribution*

| Product | % Volume | % Turnover | % Contribution |
|---|---|---|---|
| 1 | 12 | 23 | 24 |
| 2 | 19 | 11 | 8 |
| 3 | 23 | 37 | 39 |
| 4 | 47 | 29 | 28 |

The danger is that you cannot control the sales mix which, in this example, is 12 per cent, 19 per cent, 23 per cent and 47 per cent respectively for products 1, 2, 3, and 4. While product 4 provides 47 per cent of sales volume, product 3 provides nearly 40 per cent (39.4 per cent) of total contribution. If there is a change in the sales mix with a greater offtake of product 2 at the expense of the others, especially product 3, total contribution will fall.

It is vitally important for the sales manager to appreciate the effect of a changing sales mix and also the effect of similar sales effort on different products. The additional contribution from selling 250 units of each of the four products is:

| | |
|---|---|
| Product 1 | £4,100 |
| Product 2 | £  875 |
| Product 3 | £3,350 |
| Product 4 | £1,200 |

You must determine the contribution made by each of your products to your company's overheads and profit. We look at this subject again in Chapter 16 in the wider context of cost control.

## Marginal pricing

Marginal price is based on unit marginal cost. Table 15.12 shows the total marginal costs of the four products in Table 15.7 divided by the unit sales to give the unit marginal costs.

**Table 15.12** *Total marginal costs of products in Table 15.7*

| | 1 | 2 | 3 | 4 |
|---|---|---|---|---|
| Total marginal cost (£) | 39,000 | 26,000 | 63,000 | 52,000 |
| Sales | 2,500 | 4,000 | 5,000 | 10,000 |
| Unit marginal cost (£) | 15.60 | 6.50 | 12.60 | 5.20 |

If price is based on marginal cost there is always a danger that overheads will not be recovered. In this example, £118,000 overheads have to be recovered. On the current contribution figures, sales of the four products provide £170,000 toward overheads and profit (£118,000 + £52,000).

If the present sales mix (2,500 of product 1; 4,000 of 2; 5,000 of 3; and 10,000 of 4) is indicative of the general offtake of the company's products, then break-even figures are 118/170 of these = 69.41 per cent:

$$
\begin{array}{lll}
69.41\% \text{ of } \ 2,500 @ £16.40 & = & 28,458 \\
69.41\% \text{ of } \ 4,000 @ £ \ 3.50 & = & 9,717 \\
69.41\% \text{ of } \ 5,000 @ £13.40 & = & 46,505 \\
69.41\% \text{ of } 10,000 @ £ \ 4.80 & = & 33,317 \\
\hspace{1.4cm} \text{Total} & = & £117,997
\end{array}
$$

The assumption is that sales of all four products stay in the same ratio. Although this is unlikely, a thorough knowledge of costs, costings, contribution and profit will help the sales manager to channel the fire power of the organisation in the right direction.

If price is based on marginal cost it is essential to ensure that the overheads will be recovered at a level of sales that is less than the maximum possible. This is often at a level of 80 per cent of sales estimate. Because you do not have control over the sales mix, there is always a danger of under-recovery of overheads with marginal pricing. If a product is not contributing an adequate share to fixed overheads, increased sales of that product at the expense of others will cause insufficient contribution to be made to overheads. The special circumstances in which you might consider marginal pricing are:

- severe depression in the industry
- factory capacity that cannot be used for any other product
- seasonal fluctuations in demand
- when it is highly desirable to obtain a special order
- when forcing an entry into a market against strong competition

## Pricing policies

The pricing policy adopted will reflect the positioning of the product in the market, but with new products, three main policies will cover most situations:

*Value pricing.* Also known as 'skimming the market'. A high price is set for the product to 'cream off' all available demand at that level, which is maintained to allow customers who regard the product as important to 'upgrade' themselves into the high price bracket.

*Follow the demand curve.* Similar to value-pricing. A high price is set initially but there is a scaling down of price, mopping up all available demand at each price level. Instead of getting customers to upgrade themselves, promotion extends the appeal to a widening market.

*Penetration pricing.* The policy is to penetrate the market as quickly as possible to secure cost advantages through high volume or to dissuade competition.

These and other policies may be viewed as either a high-price or a low-price policy. You should consider adopting a high-price policy when:

- the product is well protected legally, or is unique
- considerable education or training is needed to use the product
- the size of the market is expected to be small, and not large enough to attract competition
- there is a very inelastic demand
- you have limited financial resources
- technical problems restrict output

You should consider a low-price policy when the converse of these apply.

# 16

# Marketing Cost Control

Sales and marketing managers should not try to become accountants, but they must know what questions to ask of the financial managers and, what is more important, they must understand the answers they receive. Of great impact on company profits is the control of credit; you are shown how to avoid borrowing your own money—and paying the bank for the privilege. Adequate cash budgeting and cash flow control will enable you to sleep more contentedly at nights.

## Initial financial controls

Start any job in sales or marketing management and you will be faced with two kinds of financial problems: expenditures, which you can authorise or influence, and costs, over which you have little or no control. You will have to cope with sales expenses, product costs at various levels of sales, price structures, discounts, incentives, commission schemes, advertising costs, cost of stocks, and cost of funding debtors, among many others.

A company's success is usually judged by such criteria as the ratio of profit to the amount of funds used to make it. Depending on how funds are defined and calculated, this ratio is variously called 'profit to funds', 'the primary ratio', 'return on capital employed' (ROCE), or 'return on investment' (ROI). All decisions you make will eventually affect this ratio, yet it does not readily translate into meaningful language.

If you sent an urgent memo to all members of your sales organisation telling them that the company had to increase the return on investment from 8 per cent to 12 per cent during the next year, what would happen? Can you imagine them all jumping out of bed each morning eager to get out into their territories to improve the ROI?

## What return on investment means

Figure 16.1 is a guide to the way that the ROI breaks down.

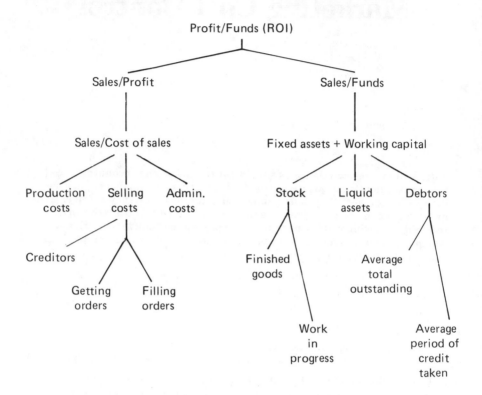

**Figure 16.1** *Breakdown of return on investment*

## Sales influence on finance

The main areas where you can affect the return on investment are in the costs of getting orders; filling orders; cost of goods in stock and, by implication, cost of work in progress; total outstanding debtors, and the time taken to pay. Each has its particular difficulties and, from the point when you exert your influence, each takes a different time to show results.

The costs of getting orders can be affected more or less immediately. You could review day-to-day selling expenses, making savings where possible, cut out waste if evident, and make appropriate economies. You could consider the advertising and promotion activities and determine whether some rationalisation is feasible without damaging your fire power. Similarly, the costs of filling orders such as warehousing, transportation and general distribution costs can be scrutinised. Invoicing and collection costs should also be assessed and performance improved, as outlined later in this chapter.

## Make your presence felt

If you are going to make an early mark in a new job as sales manager, or bring some new thinking to your present job, you must tackle those areas where your actions will be quickly evident. An area that causes more problems than most is debtors; it also takes a long time to achieve results by getting them reduced.

The more we sell, the more debtors we have. It is comparatively easy to get rid of creditors; the money is raised and cheques sent to clear the debts. The same cannot be done with debtors. You could send a letter to them all and ask, even demand, a cheque in settlement, but the likelihood of your receiving any substantial sums in payment is remote. Yet it is company money!

Turn your attention to company debtors as soon as you can, but remember that it is not an area where you will gain early recognition. I was talking with the financial director of a large multi-national organisation responsible for UK operations. He had been with the company for 12 years and, he said, 'It has taken me 10 years to get the debtors down to an acceptable level!'

## How to avoid borrowing your own money

You are unlikely to achieve any worthwhile change in the current level of debtors but you can initiate procedures to change future transactions. As soon as a sale has been made and delivered, what the customer owes is *your company's money*. The moment that payment passes from being due to being overdue, that money becomes a free loan to the customer! Some companies have a definite policy of slow payment to their creditors and are quite prepared to receive several letters demanding payment and threatening legal action because that money costs them nothing.

If your company is waiting for debtors to pay after the agreed settlement date, and operates with overdraft facilities or loans, it is borrowing its own money and *paying for the privilege!* Even if your company has no borrowings, it is being denied the use of its own money.

## Overdue debtors erode profits

Calculate the amount of money outstanding from your debtors as a percentage of (a) your total assets, and (b) your current assets. In many companies it is an unhealthy 25 per cent of total assets and as high as 40 per cent of current assets. If the cost of borrowing money is 20 per cent per year and the cost of the company's accountancy, credit control and chasing debts is 2 per cent of sales, Table 16.1 indicates the true percentage profit on sales if payment is delayed for the various periods.

**Table 16.1** *Percentage profit on sales if payment delayed*

| Company profit (%) | | | Payment received | | | |
| --- | --- | --- | --- | --- | --- | --- |
| | COD | 1 month | 2 months | 90 days | 4 months | 6 months |
| 5 | 3 | 0 | Loss | Loss | Loss | Loss |
| 10 | 8 | 6 | 5 | 3 | 1 | Loss |
| 15 | 13 | 11 | 9 | 8 | 6 | 3 |
| 20 | 18 | 16 | 14 | 13 | 11 | 8 |

## How to collect cash

Do not work on the basis of allowing the debtors figure to be a simple ratio of sales turnover, it would conceal too many variations. The length of the manufacturing cycle varies; the amount of cash tied up in materials, labour costs, fixed overheads, rates and the rest varies; the cost of 'factoring the invoices' (passing invoices to a collecting house) varies with risks involved; the age of different debts varies. A simple ratio would conceal all these and your basis for decision-making would be inadequate.

Classify customers into five colour categories and fix small coloured stickers on files, or code with letters, 'B', 'G', 'Y', 'O', and 'R'.

- *Blue.* 'Blue chip' organisations such as public sector institutions, clearing banks, oil companies, most multi-nationals.

- *Green.* These include all kinds of organisations, both well known and unknown; large and small companies, family businesses and those with a 'proven track record'.

- *Yellow.* Organisations who like to use your money as long as they can. They are not necessarily bad risks but need vigilance because they are content to borrow money at no interest while you re-borrow it from your bank at a price! It is very simple to be easy-going with this 'yellow peril' because you may have built up substantial business with them.

- *Orange.* Marginal companies that need careful monitoring of what they wish to buy and how long they hold on to your money. They are customers who can only be profitable to you if controlled.

- *Red.* Strictly cash with order, cash on delivery or by proforma invoice because these are people or organisations too risky for any other type of transactions.

After processing all existing customers, establish the amounts outstanding for each category, and what amounts in each category are overdue. You will be analysing the total debtors position in terms of relative risks.

## Terms of payment

Next, ensure that you know your own terms of payment: they may be printed on your invoices, but what happens in practice? What ought to happen? Adopt this procedure:

- Look at every type of invoice your company uses and note the terms printed on them.
- Obtain copies of recent invoices to a cross-section of customers and note whether the terms are varied in any way or, if terms are not printed on your invoices, what, if anything, is stated on the invoices.
- Find out the average credit taken by customers and whether there are any distinctions between different types of customers.
- With the five suggested categories of customers, ascertain the average time taken to pay by each category. You may need to analyse large individual customers for this.
- Analyse your total business to determine from where your turnover and profit arises. When you have listed those customers who supply 80 per cent of your profit, calculate the average length of time each one takes to pay.
- Find out the average time taken to pay in your industry.
- Determine the true profitability of each category of account.

From these investigations you will have three main items of data:

- what your terms are
- what your terms are in practice
- what your terms ought to be

## Credit rules

Construct credit rules in the light of this analysis and what your terms ought to be. Then inform your customers how you intend to conduct business in the future. You will not harass anyone or risk goodwill by telling people politely that you would like to have your money paid in line with your terms. Most of your pressure will be on the accounts departments of your customers and, although as a supplier you have to be careful with certain people in your customers' companies, it is unlikely to be anyone in the accounts department.

If you only get the business because you do not press for payment, then calculate the true profit from the transactions and consider amending the terms, or the price, to ensure that you are obtaining adequate profit in line with your general policy.

## Outstanding debtors

One method of assessing the debtor situation is to calculate the number of weeks' sales represented by the total sum owed to the company. Find out the total sales during a period, say a year, and calculate the average weekly sales. Divide the debtors' balance by this average weekly sales figure to obtain the average number of weeks that credit is outstanding. The two calculations can be combined:

$$\text{(Total debtors} \times 52)/\text{annual sales}$$

For the number of days, substitute 365 for 52.

This lumps together monies that have been owed for a week, a month, two months and so on. However, such measurements hide slow payers. A better measure is the number of days of sales outstanding (DSO). You work backwards to determine the company's DSO, as illustrated in Table 16.2.

Table 16.2 *Calculation of DSO*

| *Assume that:* | | |
|---|---|---|
| March credit balance outstanding: | 38,046 | |
| Less March credit sales: | 19,000 | |
| | 19,046 | = 31 days |
| Less February credit sales: | 8,082 | |
| | 10,964 | = 28 days (say) |
| Less January credit sales: | 10,599 | |
| | 365 | |
| Proportion of January sales (365/10,599) × 31 | | = 1 day |
| Days sales outstanding (DSO) | | = 60 days |

While this is a better measurement, it still hides slow payers and does not take into account the age of the individual debts.

## Cash collecting routines

Adopt the following routine procedures as soon as appropriate:

- Invoice the same day that advices of despatch are issued by the warehouse; no invoices are to be left over for the next day.
- Post monthly statements on a regular date by first-class mail, listing all invoices, including those not yet due for payment and any payments received.
- Five days—rigid—after payment is due, remind the customer that payment is overdue and, if you send a statement during the five days, endorse it with the words 'This statement contains items which are now overdue'.
- A week to ten days after, if the money is still outstanding, start chasing it. First make a phone call and establish that there are no queries on the invoice. Ensure that you get the person's name and initials. If one item, or a small amount, is disputed, acknowledge that there is a dispute and send an amended statement immediately showing the amount that is overdue for payment, and the amount that is in dispute.
- Put the substance of your phone conversation in writing addressed to the person with whom you have been speaking on the phone.

## How to collect cash more quickly

Here are some ways to collect money more quickly:

- Invoice immediately after the sale.
- Invoice more frequently.
- Improve the format of your invoices so that they are very easy for the customer to understand. Any layout open to different interpretations gives customers an excuse to delay payment.
- Obtain payment on account.
- Offer a discount for really prompt payment.
- Deposit cheques with your bank at least once a day.
- Offer a budget account and standing order payments.
- Look at the profit effect of factoring your invoices.
- Have large cheques specially cleared.

## Importance of cash flow

The purpose of business is to create customers, not to make money. If that were the main purpose of business many companies would make more money by selling their assets, because they are not used very profitably.

Profit should be used to measure success in satisfying customers and how quickly the money they owe is paid. Money outstanding reduces profit; delay in payment by customers reduces your available cash and affects your cash flow.

Control of business is achieved by keeping production and sales in balance with the available money. Too much production and you will be embarrassed with stock which has cost money for raw materials, components, and wages. Too many sales and not enough production—you will be embarrassed because you cannot deliver and you cannot make the profits available. Too many debtors, and you can get into difficulties.

As lubricating oil is to the motor car, so cash is to the business. If your car runs out of fuel it just stops; if it runs out of lubricating oil, it not only stops, it seizes up with its pistons jammed in the cylinders. If the business runs out of cash, much the same thing happens, but it's called bankruptcy.

## Cash flow example

Supposing you rented a small workshop in which to make wooden products, and engaged a workman at £100 a week to produce them: assume overheads for heat, light, power, rates, etc, are £50 a week. You sell the products for cash. The first week you purchase £100 of wood, pay £100 wages and £50 overheads. On the fifth day you sell your products for £320 cash. You have made a profit of £70 for the week (Table 16.3).

**Table 16.3** *Calculation of weekly profit*

|  | £ |
|---|---|
| Sales | 320 |
| Cost of sales: materials, wages, overheads | 250 |
| Profit | 70 |

To ensure that you have more wood for the following week you purchase another £100-worth on the fourth day. The situation is as shown in Table 16.4.

Because you intend to maintain production at the same rate, you have purchased more materials. Although you made a profit of £70 for the

**Table 16.4** *Table 16.3 amended with additional data*

| Days: | 1 | 2 | 3 | 4 | 5 |
|---|---|---|---|---|---|
| Sales (£) | | | | | 320 |
| Cash out: | | | | | |
|    Materials (£) | 100 | | | 100 | |
|    Wages (£) | | | | | 100 |
|    Overheads (£) | | | | | 50 |
| Cash out (£) | 100 | | | 100 | 150 |
| Cash flow, + or (−) | (100) | | | (100) | 170 |
| Cumulative cash | (100) | (100) | (100) | (200) | ( 30) |

week, you have a negative cash balance of £30. This is the difference between the cost of the second lot of wood and the profit of £70. You have used all your profit of £70, plus £30, for raw materials for the following week's working. The position for the second week is shown in Table 16.5.

**Table 16.5** *Table 16.4 amended*

| Days: | 1 | 2 | 3 | 4 | 5 |
|---|---|---|---|---|---|
| Sales (£) | | | | | 320 |
| Cash out: | | | | | |
|    Materials (£) | | | | 100 | |
|    Wages (£) | | | | | 100 |
|    Overheads (£) | | | | | 50 |
| Cash out (£) | | | | 100 | 150 |
| Cash flow, + or (−) | | | | (100) | 170 |
| Cash balance (£30) | | | | | |
| Cumulative cash | (30) | (30) | (30) | (130) | 40 |

At the end of the two weeks you have a cash balance of £40. To establish the profit made, include opening and closing stocks (Table 16.6).

**Table 16.6** *Calculation of fortnightly profit (£)*

| | | |
|---|---:|---:|
| Sales for the two weeks | | 640 |
| Opening stock | 0 | |
| Purchased | 300 | |
| | 300 | |
| Less closing stock | 100 | |
| Cost of sales | | 200 |
| Gross profit | | 440 |
| Wages and overheads 2 weeks' @ £150 | | 300 |
| Net profit | | 140 |

## Difference between cash and profit

A profit of £140 but a cash balance of only £40. This emphasises the difference between cash and profit. Any profit calculation must take into account the value of what is left in stock.

As sales manager, you are more concerned with the sales side but you can see that, if this customer does not pay on delivery but requires a month's credit, you need another £640 working capital. You could arrange to have the wood on monthly credit terms the same as you give your customer; you would still have to pay the wages and the day-to-day expenses.

## Over-trading

A problem arises if you are offered a big order: can you afford to accept it? More companies fold because of cash flow problems than for any other reason—and cash flow problems are problems of success, not of failure!

A big order means more money in raw materials, more work-in-progress, more people on production, more machines, more office staff. All these amounts have to be paid as incurred; not when the order has been delivered, the customer satisfied, and decided to pay. If you borrow money to finance the order, you have to pay interest on it.

# How to decrease profits

If your company is making 20 per cent profit per year and it borrows money at 12 per cent per year, the profit is reduced to 8 per cent.

Consider the woodworking business for the first six months' operation. You make and deliver £320-worth of goods every week, say £1,280 a month. The customer agrees to pay one month after receipt of the statement listing the previous month's deliveries. Thus, sales in month 1 are paid in month 3. The timber merchant requires payment on a cash-and-carry basis. £1,000 of your own money has been used to buy the woodworking machinery and other tools necessary for production. The bank is prepared to finance your working capital needs. You know that you make £70 a week—£280 every 4-week period. For the six months, your projected profit is £1,680. The cash flow projection for these first six periods is given in Table 16.7 (the letters in square brackets indicate where those figures appear in the revenue account and balance sheet).

You owe the bank money and, after the six months, you do not have the cash you thought you were going to have. Table 16.8 gives the revenue account for the period.

Tax will eventually have to be paid on this profit. If the tax-man asked

**Table 16.7** *Cash flow projection*

| (£) | 1 | 2 | 3 | 4 | 5 | 6 | |
|---|---|---|---|---|---|---|---|
| Sales | 1,280 | 1,280 | 1,280 | 1,280 | 1,280 | 1,280 | [A] |
| Wood | 500 | 400 | 400 | 400 | 400 | 400 | [B] |
| Wages | 400 | 400 | 400 | 400 | 400 | 400 | [C] |
| Overheads | 200 | 200 | 200 | 200 | 200 | 200 | [D] |
| Cash out | 1,100 | 1,000 | 1,000 | 1,000 | 1,000 | 1,000 | |
| Cash in | | | 1,280 | 1,280 | 1,280 | 1,280 | |
| Cash flow, +/(−) | (1,100) | (1,000) | 280 | 280 | 280 | 280 | |
| Bank interest | | (11) | (21) | (19) | (16) | (13) | [E] |
| Balance, + or (−) | (1,100) | (2,111) | (1,852) | (1,591) | (1,327) | (1,060) | [F] |

for it now, you would be in some difficulty because not only do you not
have any cash, but you owe the bank £1,060!

**Table 16.8** *Revenue account for the six periods (£)*

| | | |
|---|---|---|
| Sales [A] | | 7,680 |
| Opening stock | | 0 |
| Materials [B] | 2,500 | |
| Labour [C] | 2,400 | |
| Overheads [D] | 1,200 | |
| | 6,100 | |
| | 6,100 | |
| Less closing stock | 100 | |
| | | 6,000 |
| | | 1,680 |
| Less bank interest [E] | | 80 |
| | | 1,600 [G] |

The profit figure is transferred to the balance sheet (Table 16.9), which we
will 'strike' as at the end of these six periods.

**Table 16.9** *Balance sheet of the woodworking company as at the end of six periods (£)*

| | | |
|---|---:|---:|
| Fixed assets (machinery etc) | | 1,000 |
| Current assets: | | |
|    Stock | 100 | |
|    Debtors (two periods) | 2,560 | |
|    Cash | 0 | |
| | | 2,660 |
| Current liabilities: | | |
|    Creditors | 0 | |
|    Taxation | 0 | |
| Overdraft [F] | 1,060 | |
| | | 1,060 |
| | | 1,600 |
| | | 2,600 |
| Financed by: | | |
|    Owner's capital | | 1,000 |
|    Profit retained in company [G] | | 1,600 |
| | | 2,600 |

## Importance of proper funding

You've doubled the size of the company; you've made £1,600 profit. You can't go on holiday because you have no cash and you owe the bank £1,060!

If you could obtain wood on credit and pay when you are paid by your customer then you could use some of the cash that would be released. Tables 16.10, 16.11 and 16.12 show the situation if you acquire the wood on a month's credit.

**Table 16.10** *Cash flow projection, amended (£)*

| | 1 | 2 | 3 | 4 | 5 | 6 | |
|---|---:|---:|---:|---:|---:|---:|---|
| Sales | 1,280 | 1,280 | 1,280 | 1,280 | 1,280 | 1,280 | [A] |
| Wood | | | 500 | 400 | 400 | 400 | |
| Wages | 400 | 400 | 400 | 400 | 400 | 400 | [C] |
| Overheads | 200 | 200 | 200 | 200 | 200 | 200 | [D] |
| Cash out | 600 | 600 | 1,100 | 1,000 | 1,000 | 1,000 | |
| Cash in | | | 1,280 | 1,280 | 1,280 | 1,280 | |
| Cash flow, +/(−) | (600) | (600) | 180 | 280 | 280 | 280 | |
| Bank interest | | (6) | (12) | (10) | (8) | (5) | [E] |
| Balance, + or (−) | (600) | (1,206) | (1,038) | (768) | (496) | (221) | [F] |

**Table 16.11** *Revenue account for the six periods, amended (£)*

| | | | |
|---|---|---|---|
| Sales [A] | | | 7,680 |
| Opening stock | | 0 | |
| Materials (acquired) | 2,500 | | |
| Labour [C] | 2,400 | | |
| Overheads [D] | 1,200 | | |
| | | 6,100 | |
| | | 6,100 | |
| Less closing stock | | 100 | |
| | | | 6,000 |
| | | | 1,680 |
| Less bank interest [E] | | | 41 |
| | | | 1,639 [G] |

**Table 16.12** *Balance sheet of the woodworking company as at the end of six months (£)*

| | | | |
|---|---|---|---|
| Fixed assets (machinery etc) | | | 1,000 |
| Current assets: | | | |
|    Stock | 100 | | |
|    Debtors (two periods) | 2,560 | | |
|    Cash | 0 | | |
| | | 2,660 | |
| Current liabilities: | | | |
|    Creditors (two periods) | 800 | | |
|    Taxation | 0 | | |
|    Overdraft [F] | 221 | | |
| | | 1,021 | |
| | | | 1,639 |
| | | | 2,639 |
| Financed by: | | | |
|    Owner's capital | | | 1,000 |
|    Profit retained in company [G] | | | 1,639 |
| | | | 2,639 |

Even with a regular order of £320 a week and putting £1,000 of your own capital into the venture, you still need loan facilities of about £1,200 during the first 24 weeks. If the customer does not pay as agreed, you will be £1,280 out of pocket for as long as payment for the month's sales is delayed.

Look at the position in Table 16.10. At the start of third period you have an overdraft of £1,206. If the cheque for £1,280 does not arrive from the customer, you will be overdrawn £1,486!

This simple exercise should make you think very carefully about the essential need to keep cash flowing through a company. You cannot go on taking orders without calculating the implications on your cash situation and you should take an early opportunity of training all your sales personnel in these lessons.

## Spreading the fixed costs

To illustrate the impact of costs, assume you are to market a product that costs £75 for raw materials and labour and there is a fixed production overhead of £25. This fixed overhead is irrespective of the level of output and has to be paid every month. You pay 15 per cent commission to agents and support their efforts with an advertisement costing £50. The cost of one product is shown in Table 16.13.

**Table 16.13** *Cost of one product*

|  | £ | £ |
|---|---|---|
| Manufacturing cost | 75 | |
| Fixed monthly overhead | 25 | |
|  | | 100 |
| Advertising | | 50 |
| Total | | 150 |

The price is subject to 15 per cent commission. Thus, at £200, you receive a net £170 from which you deduct £150 to make a profit of £30.

The position is dramatically altered when two products are sold, because the fixed cost of £25 is spread over the two (Table 16.14).

**Table 16.14** *Profit from two products*

|  | £ | £ | £ |
|---|---|---|---|
| Sale of two units @ £200 | | 400 | |
| Less manufacturing costs: | | | |
|   Fixed | 25 | | |
|   Variable 2 @ £75 | 150 | | |
|   Total cost | | 175 | |
|         Gross profit | | | 225 |
| Less selling expenses: | | | |
|   Commission @ 15% | 60 | | |
|   Advertising | 50 | | |
|  | | | 110 |
|         Net profit | | | 115 |

Irrespective of how many products are made, there is a fixed cost of £25. If two products instead of one are made, each would only have to bear £12.50 of this fixed cost. If 25 are produced in the month, each one would bear only £1 of the fixed cost. Table 16.15 gives the production costs for 1, 2, 5, 10 and 25 units.

Table 16.15 *Cost of producing up to 25 units*

|  | 1 (£) | 2 (£) | 5 (£) | 10 (£) | 25 (£) |
|---|---|---|---|---|---|
| Fixed cost | 25 | 25 | 25 | 25 | 25 |
| Variable cost | 75 | 150 | 375 | 750 | 1,875 |
| Total cost | 100 | 175 | 400 | 775 | 1,900 |
| Unit production cost | 100 | 87.50 | 80 | 77.50 | 76 |

## Unit contribution analysis

Rather than compare profitability of products, which requires an arbitrary allocation of overheads to be made, it is better to compare the contribution each product makes towards total fixed costs and profit. Table 16.16 is a unit contribution analysis. Every one sold makes a contribution of £95 to the total of fixed costs and profit. In this example, the fixed costs are manufacturing overhead, £25, and advertising, £50—a total of £75. When one is sold, the contribution of £95 pays the fixed cost of £75, leaving £20 profit. Every additional product sold yields an additional contribution of £95. When the second one is sold, total profit is increased by the unit contribution of £95. Thus:

Profit on the first one:  £20
Profit when two are sold:  £20+£95 = £115 (as in Table 16.14)

Table 16.16 *Unit contribution analysis*

|  | £ | £ |
|---|---|---|
| Price of one unit |  | 200 |
| Variable costs: |  |  |
| Manufacturing | 75 |  |
| Commission 1·5% | 30 |  |
|  |  | 105 |
| Unit contribution |  | 95 |

Whenever you have to compare the performance of products, calculate the unit contribution.

Here is a summary of the calculations:

- *Fixed costs* (FC) are true fixed costs *plus* what are to be kept rigid for the time being—usually a year
- *Unit price* (UP) less discounts, commission, etc, is *net price* (NP)
- NP less *unit variable cost* (UVC) is *unit contribution* (U.CONT)
- U.CONT times number of units sold in total contribution (TOT.CONT)
- TOT.CONT less FC is *total profit* (TOT.PRFT)

Applying this to the example looked at:

| | | |
|---|---|---|
| FC is £25 + £50 | = | £ 75 |
| UP less commission is NP: £200 - 15% | = | £170 |
| NP - UVC is U.CONT: £170 - £75 | = | £ 95 |
| U.CONT times sales is TOT.CONT: £95 × 2 | = | £190 |
| TOT.CONT less FC is TOT.PRFT: £190 - £75 | = | £115 |

Allocate to the product all costs that can be reasonably attributed to it. In this example, in addition to the variable cost of manufacture, the commission of 15 per cent has been allocated to each product as a variable cost. However, advertising cannot be allocated in this way because it should be spread over all possible sales and regarded as an investment in product awareness for the future.

When unit contribution has been calculated, the break-even point can be determined. This is the number of products that have to be sold for the total revenue to equal total costs.

## Break-even calculation

The break-even figure is:

*Total fixed costs divided by unit contribution*

If net price (NP) is £200 less 15 per cent = £170, and the unit variable cost (UVC) is £75, then, in the example, the unit contribution (U.CONT) is £95. Fixed overheads and advertising (FC) total £125. Break-even (B/E) is therefore 125/95 = 1.3. We need to sell just over one product to break even.

If we took 8 adverts at £50 each = £400, total fixed costs would be £425. Break-even would be 425/95 = 4.47, which means that, when 5 products have been sold, the B/E point has been passed. It is also possible to construct a break-even chart with the X-axis for number of products and the Y-axis for costs and price (Figure 16.2).

### Inserting the fixed cost line

Select appropriate scales for the two axes. At £125 on the vertical scale, draw a line horizontal to the base to represent fixed costs. All other costs start from the point where this fixed cost line cuts the vertical axis at £125.

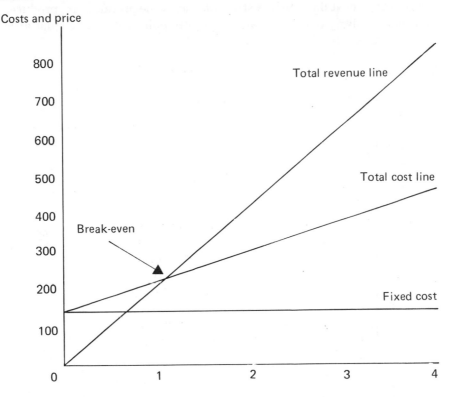

Costs and price

**Figure 16.2** *Break-even chart*[1]

### Inserting the total revenue line

Multiply the maximum production figure by unit price. In this example it is 4 times £200; the point is inserted at 4 units and £800. Connect this point with the origin.

### Inserting the total cost line

Multiply the maximum production figure by unit variable cost. In the example we have multiplied 4 by £105 (£75 production plus £30 commission) to get £420. The point plotted is £420 and 4. Connect this point with £125 on the vertical scale. All costs over the fixed costs must start from here.

The break-even point corresponds with the figure already calculated by arithmetic. It is more flexible to calculate break-even figures using arithmetic than by drawing graphs because it is easy to change figures and re-calculate. Where the break-even graph can be helpful is with the base line changed from number of products to months of the year (Figure 16.3). It is necessary to assume that production is evenly spread over the year and that the total cost line will be a straight line. If the products are produced and sold regularly over the year, break-even point takes place just after March: a good position to be in.

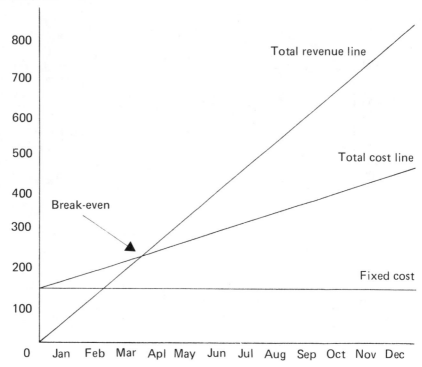

Costs and price

**Figure 16.3** *Break-even chart[2]*

Understand that break-even is a point on the road to profitability, not a main objective.

# 17

# Sales Meetings

'The meetings they hold here provide good clean fun; there isn't much time left to get much work done. The meeting is over, the members have gone, no further forward but all to press on.' You must get the most out of the time you spend in meetings, which are held for three main reasons. When reaching decisions, there are two main dimensions to consider: quality and acceptance.

## Meetings, meetings, always meetings

Have you ever been to a meeting and, after an hour or so, as you walk out a colleague asks, 'What was that all about?'?

It is not unusual to attend a meeting which consumes far too much time for the little it achieves: interminable discussion and argument; innumerable points of view; subjects have been thoroughly explored but few plans of action formulated. By the time the meeting ends, the reason for it has receded into the background.

I used to work with a group of companies that had a particularly difficult chairman. Many of his decisions were based on whim rather than reason and it was no surprise to me to hear of the company's collapse some two years after I had left and gone on to other things. Of the many memories I have of that time, one is of the meetings we had, especially with the chairman. They went on and on, sometimes all day, and voluminous minutes were prepared, circulated and had to be followed up at the next meeting.

The solution was simple: there were always two editions of the minutes: one for the chairman, and one that we used to work with. He was happy, and we could get on with things.

One Christmas, at the annual dinner and dance, two of the executives sang a song parodying the old Western Brothers music hall tune. The advertising manager had written special words; the opening lines were:

> The meetings they hold here provide good clean fun,
> There isn't much time left to get much work done.
> The meetings are over, the minutes remain,
> But the damned things get altered again and again.
> >Keep the minutes clean chaps,
> >Keep the minutes clean.

On hearing this, the chairman moved swiftly down the hall to the stage and took in every following verse, which made pungent comment and poked fun on the many incidents that embellished our life in the company. I must say, matters were never quite the same after that.

When you hold a meeting, keep it as short as necessary; everyone knows why it has been called, and what they have to do as a result.

## Three reasons for having a meeting

We hold sales meetings for three main reasons:

(1)  to carry out training

(2)  to transmit information

(3)  to solve a problem

### Training

Before you hold a training meeting, inform everyone that it will have specific objectives and at the start of the meeting restate the objectives.

Only experienced lecturers can retain the interest of a group of people for longer than about 10-15 minutes; and even the most amusing and interesting speaker can only hold an audience for limited periods. Therefore, if you are not an experienced speaker, break up your presentation with charts, slides, overhead projector work, participative discussions, and so on. If you are experienced in public speaking, you will know the dangers of over-talking and will organise your presentation accordingly.

### Dissemination of information

Only use a meeting to pass on information if there is no better, more convenient, method. Make sure that the right people attend such a meeting and that they know exactly what they have to do with the information.

Giving confidential information verbally to a selected few is better than committing it to writing but, if the information is complicated, break into two parts. Give one part verbally and circulate the remainder in writing. This second part should not be intelligible to anyone who has not been at the meeting so, if it is seen accidentally, the whole information should still be confidential. Do not label the written part 'Confidential'; this always invites unwanted interest.

## Problem solving

Problems can be located in only two places—in the work situation and in people. Problems in the work situation can be further subdivided into those located in plant, machinery and equipment, and problems located in procedures, methods and ways of working. Problems with people can be subdivided into those located in individuals and those in groups. Figure 17.1 illustrates this.

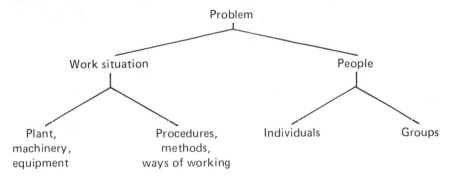

**Figure 17.1** *Problem breakdown*[1]

Locating the source of a problem is not a particularly simple task because different people see the same problem caused by different reasons. Nevertheless, your first task in a problem-solving meeting is to agree on the source of the problem. If agreement cannot be obtained on one of the four possible locations, you have to consider each in turn and possibly explore up to four possible courses of action.

Supposing that sales are falling and you have called a meeting to discuss what might be done to arrest the decline. The source of the problem can only be in the product (itself or competitive products); the way in which it is being offered for sale (or competitive offers); one individual (which may be you of course!); or in a group of people. If you can agree on the source, or sources, of the problem, corrective action is easier.

### Market problems

We can apply this analytical approach to the market generally. Suppose that the company has a problem in the marketing of its products. Adapting Figure 17.1 we have Figure 17.2.

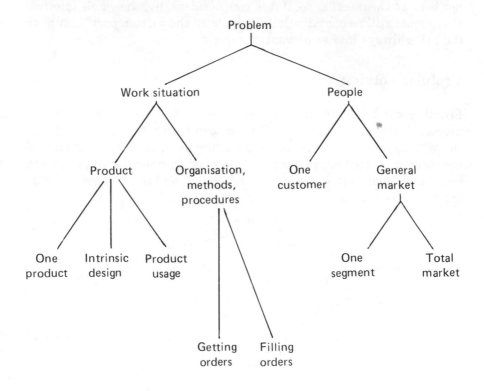

**Figure 17.2** *Problem breakdown[2]*

Narrowing down the possible causes of the problem in this way guides the discussion of the meeting toward decisions and actions. The scheme of analysis will prevent people from digressing into side issues, but help them to contribute to the main problems, and introduce relevant points.

This particular problem may be seen by the meeting to lie in the way in which the company is trying to obtain orders, and they may feel that publicity is not sufficiently persuasive. The analytical approach can be extended to consider publicity (Figure 17.3).

This analysis is not intended to be exhaustive and it will need to be modified to suit your company. It helps to channel the discussion in the meeting towards areas where corrective action can be agreed.

*Quality and acceptance decisions*

When the source of the problem has been located, a decision has to be

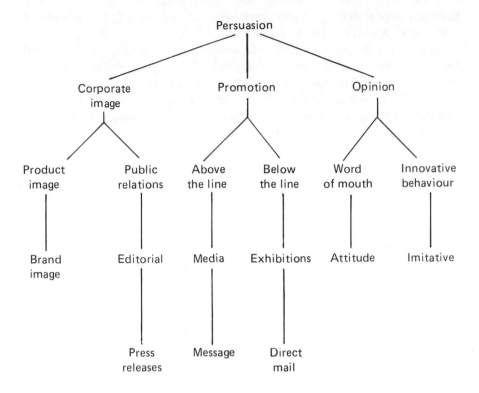

**Figure 17.3** *Analysis of publicity*

made. Decisions are of two types: quality decisions, and acceptance decisions. Quality decisions are those which may be regarded as good decisions and will solve the problem. However, the word 'good' is open to argument here. Decisions can only be judged retrospectively. You cannot say 'This is a good decision', only, 'That *was* a good decision'. For this reason the word 'quality', rather than good, is used to describe a decision which, when implemented, will be efficacious. Acceptance decisions are those which will be accepted by the people involved in the problem.

To illustrate this important topic, suppose that during a meeting of your sales force, the dates of their annual holidays are to be agreed. You want to avoid too many people being away at any one time so you start with the first person on your left and you say, 'You take the first two weeks in June'. To the second you say, 'You take the second two weeks in June'. Continuing, you look round the room, allocating two weeks successively to each person. Before you get very far, you will hear a plaintive voice from your right, 'I'm not going to get my summer holiday until November!'.

But this would be the 'best' decision, the quality decision: there would only be one person away in any two weeks. The trouble is, your sales force will not accept it; so you try again.

'Tell me when you are taking your annual leave,' you say. And you find that half want to go the last two weeks in July, and the other half want the last week in July and the first week in August!

If you look back at the diagram in Figure 17.1 you will agree that your problem is located in the group of people. The diagram is enlarged in Figure 17.4 to include the decision-making activity.

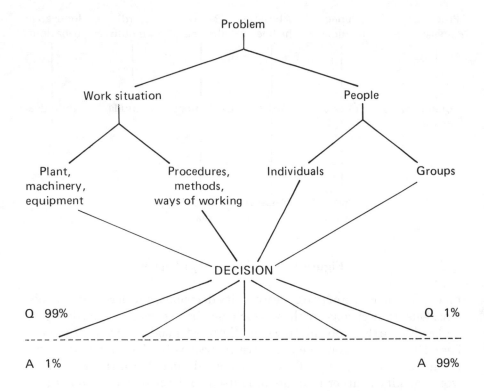

**Figure 17.4** *Problem breakdown[3]*

The deeper you think the source of the problem lies in the work situation, the more you can move your decision to the left: that is, it can be a quality decision. The more you consider the problem to be located in people, especially in groups of people, the more you have to decide to the right: that is, you must make an acceptance decision.

Quality decisions are relatively easy; *you* can take these decisions because you are not likely to upset people. Acceptance decisions can be very difficult, especially if a high degree of acceptance by those involved is needed. You cannot make acceptance decisions lightheartedly or you will have a revolt on your hands. If the decision has a very high acceptance factor, the group will probably have to take the decision.

The majority of decisions tend to fall in the middle, where quality and acceptance are of equal importance. Who takes the decision then?

## Your standing with the group

Of help will be your standing within the group of people. You can either be in a strong position or in a weak position. If you are 'on top of your job', well thought of, have been working well with the group, and have their respect and allegiance, you are in a strong position: you can take a $Q = A$ decision and use your leadership power to gain acceptance.

If, however, you are in a weak position—perhaps sales have not been going too well, you haven't seen the people for some time, one or two things have gone wrong—you cannot take a $Q = A$ decision, and it is better for the group to take the decision and for you to apply your skill of chairmanship to upgrade the quality of their decision.

# Decisions on problems

The majority of meetings are held to solve problems. Here are eight sections to guide you in the conduct of such meetings.

(1) Understand the language

(2) Get all the facts

(3) Locate the source of the problem

(4) State the problem in objective terms

(5) Determine quality and acceptance of the decision

(6) Consider possible solutions

(7) Screen the solutions

(8) Select and agree the decision

## Understand the language

When I am conducting a training session on problem-solving, I get agreement from the group on the first things that have to be done before we can start to consider the problem. There is nearly always unanimous agreement that the first thing to do is to get all the facts. I agree, and tell them that I have a simple problem I would like them to tackle. I emphasise the ease with which it can be solved and that all the facts will be shown on the overhead projector. 'Let's see how quickly you can solve this problem,' I say, as I place the transparency on the projector. On the screen are shown a dozen Chinese characters. There is usually some laughter and I apologise and turn the transparency round the other way.

The lesson of this lighthearted approach is serious. Even with all the facts, problems cannot be solved if the language is not thoroughly understood. And not simply the language of the country, but the language of the particular subject, trade or industry. All the people at your problem-solving meeting must understand the language being used and the meaning of the various terms in a problem.

## Get all the facts

The difficulty in getting all the facts is that, often, we do not know how many facts there are. When we meet to solve problems, we are considering symptoms; in the same way that a doctor considers the symptoms, explores with suitable questions, and narrows down the possible causes before prescribing treatment.

Look at Figure 17.5. Sometimes a symptom is caused by more than one problem, and problems themselves can have more than one root cause.

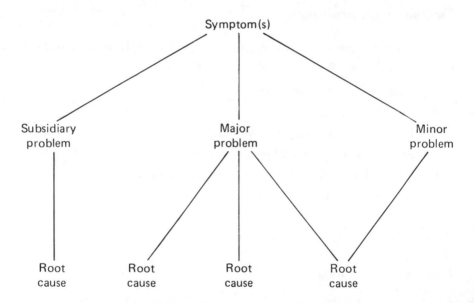

**Figure 17.5** *Problem breakdown[4]*

Getting all the facts will help but, if you are not sure you have them all, use conjecture to fill in gaps in your knowledge. Fall back on the 'What if...' question to supply possible facts.

## Locate the cause of the problem

If you do not get agreement on the location of the problem, you are unlikely to get unanimous support for corrective action. If opinions in the
meetings are strongly divided as to the cause, then you must develop possible courses of action for each.

## State in objective terms

This is stating the problem without subjective opinions, without adjectives that indicate what someone thinks about the statement. Where possible, the problem should be stated in quantitative rather than qualitative
terms.

## Determine quality and acceptance

The more it is agreed that the cause of the problem is rooted in people and
groups of people, the greater the degree of acceptance needed in the solution. You cannot impose 'good' decisions or 'right' decisions on groups of
people if they will not accept them.

Suppose the meeting has agreed five possible courses of action which
are, in order of merit:

A   B   C   D   E

The people who have to carry out the action may have an entirely different view of the order of merit and consider E to be the best decision. If
their order of acceptance of the decision is:

E   D   B   C   A

the 'best' decision will be B. This gains the highest combined quality and
acceptance of the decision.

## Consider possible solutions

Possible solutions are not probable solutions; they are possible. Sometimes, people's preferences get in the way of their agreeing as to what is
possible because they have already rejected the particular solution.
Remind the meeting that a solution is the result of a decision taken and
agreed in the meeting. A decision cannot be prejudged; it has to be implemented before it can be evaluated.

Often, complicated problems can be solved by simple solutions but
these are not readily seen at the beginning. Meetings tend to want to
devise complicated solutions for such problems. Make sure that all possible solutions are recorded for consideration.

*Screen solutions*

When a meeting makes a lot of progress, ideas flow, much discussion takes place, and solutions are sometimes tabled more in enthusiasm than in cold, logical deliberation. Screen the possible solutions.

Be very wary of solutions that have been transferred from other situations: 'We had this problem a couple of years ago. What we did was....' This is not a good basis for accepting the solution. What happened in another place, in another time, is unlikely to be the same in the current climate.

Decisions supported by facts, or their interpretations, that are agreed by the meeting, should be considered as possible decisions. If the facts are disputed, then any decision based on them is suspect.

If a trend has been observed, then solutions based on that trend should receive consideration, especially if any exceptions to the trend have been satisfactorily explained.

*Select decision*

Some solutions are incompatible and therefore mutually exclusive. If one solution is to increase newspaper advertising and another is to reduce it and increase below-the-line activities, you cannot do both.

Some solutions can be combined. You could increase the number of sales people in a territory and alter the territory; special discounts could be offered and a specific direct mail campaign launched; certain large accounts could be transferred to a national accounts executive and a new product range given to the previous sales person who serviced those accounts.

Determine the cost of all solutions; establish how practical they are; how many could be combined; the degree of acceptability by those who have to carry them out, and by management; the likely outcome of implementing them; the possible reactions of competitors; the support in the meeting for the decision.

# Before the meeting

Before you call the meeting:

- Decide if a meeting is the best method of achieving the objective.
- Put the objectives in writing.
- Consider who is likely to be affected by the decisions reached at the meeting and decide who is to attend.
- Collect all the information necessary.

- Select specific items for discussion.
- Anticipate difficulties, delays, awkward members, and prepare documents and courses of action to overcome the difficulties expected.
- Prepare the agenda with not more than five objectives.

## During the meeting

(We assume that you will take the chair at the meeting.)

- State the purpose of the meeting.
- Outline the objectives it is hoped to achieve.
- Develop participation by contrasting differing viewpoints, but do not impose your views on the group.
- Direct the discussion toward the objectives.
- Occasionally summarise discussions, stating clearly the points of agreement and disagreement.
- Periodically test the feeling of the members on points of disagreement to see how strongly held are the views. If you detect a 50/50 split, avoid accepting a proposition too early; subsequent discussion can modify viewpoints previously strongly held.
- Watch the clock and note reactions of members who appear to be losing interest—discussions can drag on too long. Problems of today tend to become half their size next week. A change in direction of discussion and then a return to the original topic can often secure agreement where a sustained frontal attack fails.
- Restate the conclusions agreed so that all members understand.
- Where opinion is irrevocably divided and a vote has to be taken: if a degree of formality has to be introduced into the proceedings, a motion has to be proposed and seconded, after which, it is 'before the meeting'. Once a motion is before the meeting it can be discussed at length and cannot be withdrawn without the consent of the meeting. An amendment, proposed and seconded, can be made to a motion that is before the meeting. If adopted, it becomes part of the motion which, in its final form, is a substantive motion. If there are several amendments, the chairman decides their priority. A motion that has been proposed, seconded (amended or not) and agreed, becomes a resolution.
- Written reports can be received and, if approved, adopted. Oral reports can only be received.

- Points of order may be raised at any time, when properly relating to matters of procedure:

  'Chairman, on a point of order, did we not agree to the contrary at our last meeting?'

  'Chairman, may I raise a point of order? We cannot all vote on this motion because four of the members were co-opted, and not elected, to the committee.'

  The following is not a valid point of order:

  'Chairman, on a point of order, the speaker is quite wrong in his facts because...'.

- References, or remits, back to a sub-committee are sometimes made with reports if the main meeting does not adopt them in their presented form or if the report needs clarification.

## After the meeting

- The secretary of the meeting prepares 'minutes' which have three functions: record of the proceedings (when approved and signed at a subsequent meeting); authority to act when a decision has been agreed that someone should do something; a link between meetings to evolve policy.

- Minutes must be an accurate account of the substance of the meeting. They should not deal with opinions, discussions, irrelevant talk, or anything that does not qualify, condition or otherwise modify the agreed resolutions and decisions. They should be brief.

- Minutes should follow the agenda of the meeting.

## Specimen agenda

Most discussion is likely to be on the matters arising from the previous meeting and the specific items for the current meeting. List the items with the easiest to decide first; the more difficult items may need to be the subject of a special meeting.

### Specimen agenda

| | |
|---|---|
| Present | Chairman is first; remainder in alphabetical order. If the secretary is not a member of the committee, insert in brackets '(in attendance)'. |
| Apologies | Secretary reports apologies received. |

| | |
|---|---|
| Minutes of the meeting held on... | Previous meeting's minutes should have been circulated so that members of that meeting who are now present can agree the minutes, which are then signed by the chairman. |
| Matters arising | Points that are not separately itemised under the next heading are discussed. |
| Specific items | Each item must have a heading: New Products; Future Advertising Campaign, New Database, etc. |
| Any other business | For items to be discussed at current meeting or to be placed on agenda for next meeting. |
| Date of next meeting | Also the location, time and any specific points. |

## Tips for better meetings

- Hold them early in the day and don't allow phone calls to interrupt the proceedings.
- Pay particular attention to seating; chairs should not be plastics-covered but fabric-covered and firm.
- If you know you are going to have a difficult person at the meeting, sit that person on your right or left. It is then easy to use a gesture with your hand when making a point and physically shield him from the rest of the group. If that person is allowed to sit opposite you, the meeting will often be split into two with the difficult arguments coming from directly opposite you.
- Get everyone to contribute to the discussion but don't put people on the spot by asking, 'What do you think, Jane?' or, 'You haven't said anything for some time, David. What's your view?'.
- Place your watch on the table in front of you so that people can see you intend to run to time; start on time; finish when you say you will.
- Be as permissive as you can but don't be afraid of bringing members back to the main theme by asking, 'What is the point you are making?' or, if you wish to be more abrupt, 'What is the point you are trying to make?'.
- A meeting should develop 'acceptance' decisions and, in so doing, will upgrade the quality of those decisions. Avoid letting members know what you think before they have made their views known.
- If you possess non-confidential information, perhaps constraints or conditions laid down by the directors, which are crucial to the

subject of the meeting and will condition members' views, tell them.

● Summarise the discussion of each topic so that members have a clear understanding of the views of the meeting.

● Remember that researches have shown that the longer the discussion allowed on a topic, the less information members will use on which to base their decision. Boredom and tiredness tend to erase all but the most easily remembered data.

# 18

# Marketing Planning

**There are four things to consider in marketing planning: where the company is now, where we would like to be, what we have to do to get there and whether or not it is feasible. To help you with your own planning, a specimen plan is given from an actual company.**

## Importance of the marketing plan

The company's selling activities must be related to the company's production capabilities and both controlled within the bounds of what is feasible as far as finance is concerned. You will know how easy it is for a company's operations to get out of hand and how lack of sufficient cash causes severe embarrassment. It is therefore essential that management organises and controls company operations according to an agreed plan.

Company operations are usually planned for a year, with the sales plan part of, or following on from, the marketing plan. The marketing plan is developed from a rigorous analysis and compromise between market potential and production capabilities, and then between these two and financial opportunities and restraints.

## Four basic points

There are four basic questions to be answered when preparing the marketing plan:

(1) Where are we now?

(2) Where would we like to be?

(3) What do we have to do to get there?

(4)  Is this feasible?

If it is not feasible because of financial or resource limitations, the second point must be modified. Equally important is, is it feasible in terms of control?

# Planning and control

Planning and control of the plan should be considered together and not as separate entities. The marketing plan is usually for the company's activities over the following year. Keep in mind the people who will be implementing and controlling the plan; you will only be as good as the people to whom parts of the plan are delegated.

# Marketing planning check-list

Whenever you prepare a marketing plan, use this check-list to remind you of the various things to look at. It will not provide you with everything you have to do but it lists groups of 'trigger words' to make you think of things appropriate to the product and market you are considering. There are seven sections. The first section is the current position of the company and the market generally; the next five sections deal with the product, price, place, promotion and service; the last section is concerned with objectives.

## 1. Current position

*Company*

    Total sales in volume and in value.
    Total gross profit, expenses, and net profit.
    Percentage of sales, for expenses, advertising, etc.
    Percentage of sales in each market segment.
    Volume and value of sales by area, month, product, etc.
    Sales per thousand consumers, per factory, in segments.
    Market share of total market and of segments.

*The market*

    Number of actual and potential buyers by area.
    Characteristics of consumer buyers—income, occupation,
        education, sex, size of family, etc.
    Characteristics of industrial buyers—primary, secondary, tertiary,
        manufacturing, type of industry, size.
    Characteristics of users if different from buyers.
    Locations of buyers, or users.

When purchases made—time of day, week, month, year, frequency
of purchase, size of average purchase, what is typical?

How purchases made—by specification or competitively, by
sample, inspection, impulse, rotation, system, cash, credit, in
bulk, by contract, by tender.

Attitudes, motivation to purchase, influence on buying decision,
the decision-making unit in organisations.

Product uses—primary and secondary.

## 2. The product

*Company*

Quality, materials, workmanship, design, method of manufacture,
manufacturing cycle, inputs-outputs.

Technical characteristics, attributes that may be considered as
selling points, buying points.

Models, styles, sizes, ranges, colours, etc.

Essential or non-essential, convenience or speciality.

Similarities with other company products.

Relation of product features to users' needs, wants, desires.

Development of branding and brand image.

Degree of product differentiation, actual and possible.

Packaging used, functional, promotional, materials, sizes, shapes,
construction, closure, re-usable.

*Competition*

Competitive and competing products.

Main competitors and leading products and brands.

Comparison of design and performance with leading competition.

Comparison of offerings of competitors, images, value.

*The future*

Likely future product developments in the company.

Likely future developments in industry.

Future product line or range contraction, modification, expansion.

## 3. Price

*Company*

Pricing strategy and general methods of price structure.

High or low policies, and reasons why.

Prevailing wholesaler, retailer margins in consumer markets or
middlemen margins in industrial markets.

Discounts, functional, quantity, cash, reward, incentive.

Pricing objectives, profit objectives, financial implications such as cash flow, cash budgeting, break-even.

## Competition

Prices and price structures of competitors.

Value-analysis of competitors' products compared with own products.

Discounts, credit, leasing, etc, offered.

## The future

Developments in costs likely to affect price structures.

Possibilities of more or less costly raw materials or labour.

Possible competitive price attacks.

## 4. Place

## Company

Current company distribution structure.

Distribution channels and methods.

Total number of outlets (consumer or industrial) by type.

Total number of wholesalers or industrial middlemen broken down into areas and by type.

Percentage of outlets of each type handling product by area.

Attitudes of outlets by area, type, size.

Degree of co-operation, current and possible.

Multi-brand policy, possible or current.

Strengths and weaknesses in distribution system, functionally and geographically.

Number and type of warehouses, location.

Transport and communications.

Stock control, delivery periods, control of information.

## Competition

Competitive distribution structure, strengths and weaknesses.

Market coverage, penetration and saturation.

Transportation methods used, delivery periods, specific selling conditions.

## The future

Likely possible developments in industry as a whole or from one or more competitors.

Probable changes in distribution system of company.

Future likely changes in outlets.

## 5. Promotion

*Company*
Size and composition of the sales force.
Calls per day, week, month, year, by sales force.
Conversion rate of orders from calls.
Selling cost as a percentage of value and of volume of sales achieved.
Internal and external sales promotion.
Recruiting, selection, training, and control of sales force.
Methods of motivating sales force.
Remuneration schemes.
Advertising expenditure per thousand readers, per thousand circulation, viewers of main and all media used.
Methods and costs of merchandising.
Public and press relations, exhibitions.

*Competition*
Selling activities and methods of selling and advertising.
Strengths and weaknesses of selling and advertising.
Review of competitors' advertising themes, media used.

*The future*
Likely developments in selling, promotion and advertising.

## 6. Service

*Company*
Extent of pre-sales service, customer service, after-sales service, product service.
Survey of customers' needs.
Installation, education in use, inspection, maintenance, repairs and provision of spares and accessories.
Guarantees, warranty period, returned goods, complaints.
Methods, procedures for carrying out service.

*Competition*
Services supplied by competition.
Types of guarantee, warranty, credit provided.
Advantage of competitive offers over company offers.

*The future*
Possible developments that might require revision of policy.

## 7. Marketing objectives

*Company*
> Short-term objectives for current year in light of current political and economic situation.
> Construction of standards for measurement of progress towards achieving objectives, management ratios that may be translated into control procedures.
> Breakdown of turnover into periods, areas, segments, outlets, etc.
> Which personnel required to undertake what actions, responsibilities, when, and how.

*Competition*
> Likely competitive reactions—company responses.

*The future*
> Long-term objectives, related to products, price, place, promotion, personal selling, service.

# Computer databases for marketing

A database is the heart of a sales and marketing operation. It covers sourcing of materials, sales people, territories, types of customers, remuneration and commission, competitive activities, and everything necessary for managers with computers to do their jobs more effectively.

An adequately constructed database can quickly yield data on monthly, weekly and daily sales, monies due and outstanding from debtors, location of potential customers for different products and even broken down into possible offtake and usage.

Databases differ in their ease of use, speed of operation, especially in accepting new data, and flexibility in supplying answers. What is required for competitive marketing is access to information whenever it is needed and not necessarily as the programmer has designed it.

## Hierarchical databases

Hierarchical databases have their information organised for the convenience of the computer, in files, records, and fields. A file is typically a floppy disk used for, say, customers for various products. A record is a unit of data such as name and address of a particular customer on file. A field is a component of a record—customer name, or address, or product.

When using a hierarchical database you must specify which fields, on which records, on which files. Information is divided into categories and smaller sub-categories, each level with pointers telling the computer where to find the next sub-category.

A simple database might contain a company's customer records with products purchased, sales people and engineers servicing them. If the main task is to keep track of customers, the field containing the name of the customer will be at the top of the hierarchy with a pointer to the record of products, etc.

This operates well if you only want information on customers and sales. If you want information on productivity of the sales force or profitability of customers, the hierarchical database has difficulties because sales people service more than one customer and therefore selection and elimination of duplications is time-consuming.

## Network databases

Network databases are an improvement because they remove one of the constraints of the hierarchical database, sub-category records being indicated by one, and only one, pointer from a higher to a lower level record. In network databases pointers can lead anywhere and each record can be connected to any number of other records.

To create a list of customers, a chain of pointers leads from customer to customer. To record sales of a product, a chain runs from the name of the product through the fields where the sales are kept.

Updating a network database is faster because the multiplicity of pointers means that an amendment need only be routed through a single record; all the appropriate changes are made automatically by means of the pointers. However, pointers in the network database must be meticulously maintained as records and files are updated, amended or deleted.

Supposing you wanted to know how many of your fork joints had been sold by salesman Andrews. The database offers alternative ways of providing the data: start at Andrews and search the chain of fork joints, or start at fork joints and search the chain of Andrews. If the number of fork joints sold by Andrews is less than the number of salesmen who have sold them, then it is quicker to initiate a search with Andrews. With a large number of sales people and products, the difference in time of access is dramatic but there is no way that the network database provides help in selection of method.

## Relational databases

Relational databases are a great improvement because they do not use pointers. Data is organised into tables; tables are the files; rows are the records; columns are the fields.

Considerable skill is necessary to develop tables for the relational database. The data in each column is broken up into its smallest useful form and indexed for access. You could have a table indexed by customer, with address, the various products purchased, and the actual products bought each month. Although 'location' is dependent upon the customer's name, the quantity purchased each month is only found by specifying both the product and the customer. The table would need to be divided into a separate table and indexed on both fields. Thus, the data in each column is dependent on its index. A table indexed by customer lists their names, addresses and post codes. Because the post codes are dependent on location, the table should be split into two: one indexed by customer, listing addresses, the other indexed by address, listing the post codes.

These tables are flexible and simple to manipulate but speed is sacrificed unless the tables are expertly constructed and the data broken down into smaller and smaller tables.

**Relational database tables**
Here are some simple tables:

### Structure of relational product database

| P | Product | Gross margin |
|---|---------|--------------|
| P1 | Fork joints | 0.36 |
| P2 | Flat slabs | 0.35 |
| P3 | Round ends | 0.41 |
| P4 | Small butts | 0.30 |
| P5 | Thin wedges | 0.33 |
| P6 | Blue rims | 0.26 |
| P7 | Red balls | 0.29 |

| S | Salesman | Sal & exes | Area |
|---|----------|------------|------|
| S1 | Andrews | 15.23 | M |
| S2 | Archibald | 14.33 | S |
| S3 | Brown | 14.55 | B |
| S4 | Burrows | 15.66 | F |
| S5 | Daniels | 14.22 | A |
| S6 | Hutton | 16.21 | D |
| S7 | Macdonald | 15.32 | R |
| S8 | Postlewaite | 14.12 | V |

| S | P | Turnover |
|---|---|---|
| S1 | P1 | 264,890 |
| S1 | P2 | 133,400 |
| S1 | P4 | 382,680 |
| S1 | P7 | 371,300 |
| S2 | P2 | 1,382,000 |
| S2 | P7 | 784,000 |
| S3 | P3 | 1,200,340 |
| .. | .. | ... |

# Specimen marketing plan

The following marketing plan for STU Ltd is based on an actual company; the name, figures and some of the identifiable products have been altered to preserve anonymity. It illustrates how the company approached the market which was in a depression, and is offered as a guide to your own planning.

*Marketing Plan for STU Ltd for year 19X1*

### Key points

- To market the existing, new and improved STU products nationally throughout the UK.
- To provide a full customer service for size variations from standard STU listed products in order to:

  (a) Remove the burden of special order problems from dealers.

  (b) Develop a greater control over the specials market.
- To stimulate and maintain the flow of STU products being placed by users with existing, reputable dealers.
- To develop direct sales with organisations, laboratories and OEMs where it is considered that dealers cannot adequately handle new products.
- To test market new and improved STU products regionally and nationally prior to full commercial launch.
- To ensure that present business in traditional, fast-moving STU products is not solicited, or diverted away from existing, reputable dealers.
- To ensure that the STU dealer network receives continuous encouragement from all sales staff.

- To reduce stock holding from 6 per cent of sales to 2 per cent of sales turnover over five years and locating stocks in more convenient locations.

- To reduce outstanding debtors from the level of over 4 per cent to 2½ per cent of sales turnover over five years.

**STU Ltd sales estimates for 19X1**

|   |   | Sales (£) | Gross contribution (£) |
|---|---|---|---|
| 1. | Filters | 291,800 | 98,000 |
| 2. | High performance liquid chromatography (HPLC) | 217,100 | 131,000 |
| 3. | Other chromatography | 175,500 | 68,250 |
| 4. | Laboratory accessories | 119,500 | 41,283 |
|   |   | 803,900 | 338,533 |
| 5. | New products | 35,250 | 12,800 |
|   |   | 839,150 | 351,333 |

In view of the adverse conditions prevailing in the market at the present time and the possibility of legislation that might affect STU's operations, a minimum projection based largely on achieving 80 per cent of budget has also been prepared.

**Projected profit and loss accounts for STU Ltd for 19X1**

|   |   | Maximum (£) |   | Minimum (£) |
|---|---|---|---|---|
| Sales |   |   |   |   |
| Existing products |   | 803,900 |   | 643,120 |
| New products |   | 35,250 |   | 28,200 |
| Total |   | 839,150 |   | 671,320 |
| Variable costs: |   |   |   |   |
| Existing products | 465,367 |   | 371,948 |   |
| New products | 22,450 |   | 17,963 |   |
| Warehousing, etc | 16,028 |   | 12,822 |   |
|   |   | 503,845 |   | 402,733 |
|   |   | 335,305 |   | 268,587 |
| Promotion |   | 90,000 |   | 90,000 |
| Total contribution |   | 245,305 |   | 178,587 |
| Fixed expenses |   | 201,000 |   | 201,000 |
| Profit (loss) before tax |   | 44,305 |   | (22,413) |

*continued*

In view of the proposed capital expenditure over the next five years:

*Proposed capital expenditure for five years*

| | £ |
|---|---|
| 19X1 | 23,000 |
| 19X2 | 28,000 |
| 19X3 | 37,000 |
| 19X4 | 33,000 |
| 19X5 | 20,000 |

it is desirable to present a five-year forecast of sales and cash flow. This is set out on following pages.

**5-year forecast based on maximum budgeted sales, £000**

*Profit and Loss Account*

| | 19X1 | 19X2 | 19X3 | 19X4 | 19X5 |
|---|---|---|---|---|---|
| Sales: | | | | | |
| Existing products | 804 | 922 | 1,033 | 1,136 | 1,261 |
| New products | 35 | 39 | 47 | 54 | 66 |
| | 839 | 961 | 1,080 | 1,190 | 1,327 |
| Cost of goods | 488 | 559 | 628 | 692 | 771 |
| Warehousing, etc | 16 | 18 | 21 | 23 | 25 |
| Promotion | 90 | 90 | 95 | 95 | 95 |
| | 594 | 667 | 744 | 810 | 891 |
| Contribution | 245 | 294 | 336 | 380 | 436 |
| Fixed expenses | 201 | 220 | 234 | 245 | 254 |
| | 44 | 74 | 102 | 135 | 182 |

*Cash Flow Statement*

| | 19X1 | 19X2 | 19X3 | 19X4 | 19X5 |
|---|---|---|---|---|---|
| P & L A/C | 44 | 74 | 102 | 135 | 182 |
| Add depreciation | 16 | 19 | 31 | 31 | 31 |
| Capital expenditure | (23) | (28) | (37) | (33) | (20) |
| Stocks | (50) | (48) | (43) | (36) | (27) |
| Debtors | (36) | (38) | (38) | (30) | (33) |
| Flow, + or (−) | (49) | (21) | 15 | 67 | 133 |
| Balance, + or (−) | (49) | (70) | (55) | 12 | 145 |

**5-year forecast based on minimum budgeted sales, £000**

*Profit and Loss Account*

|  | 19X1 | 19X2 | 19X3 | 19X4 | 19X5 |
|---|---|---|---|---|---|
| Sales: |  |  |  |  |  |
| Existing products | 643 | 738 | 826 | 909 | 1,009 |
| New products | 28 | 32 | 37 | 43 | 53 |
|  | 671 | 770 | 863 | 952 | 1,062 |
| Cost of goods | 390 | 448 | 502 | 553 | 617 |
| Warehousing, etc | 13 | 15 | 16 | 18 | 20 |
| Promotion | 90 | 90 | 95 | 95 | 95 |
|  | 493 | 553 | 613 | 666 | 732 |
| Contribution | 178 | 217 | 250 | 286 | 330 |
| Fixed expenses | 201 | 220 | 234 | 245 | 254 |
|  | (23) | (3) | 16 | 41 | 76 |

*Cash Flow Statement*

|  | 19X1 | 19X2 | 19X3 | 19X4 | 19X5 |
|---|---|---|---|---|---|
| P & L A/C | (23) | (3) | 16 | 41 | 76 |
| Add depreciation | 16 | 19 | 31 | 31 | 31 |
| Capital expenditure | (23) | (28) | (37) | (33) | (20) |
| Stocks | (40) | (39) | (35) | (29) | (21) |
| Debtors | (29) | (31) | (30) | (24) | (27) |
| Flow, + or (−) | (99) | (82) | (55) | (14) | 39 |
| Balance, + or (−) | (99) | (181) | (236) | (250) | (211) |

**5-year forecast based on adopted sales estimate, £000**

*Profit and Loss Account*

|  | 19X1 | 19X2 | 19X3 | 19X4 | 19X5 |
|---|---|---|---|---|---|
| Sales: |  |  |  |  |  |
| Existing products | 725 | 832 | 932 | 1,025 | 1,140 |
| New products | 32 | 36 | 43 | 50 | 61 |
|  | 757 | 868 | 975 | 1,075 | 1,201 |
| Cost of goods | 440 | 505 | 567 | 625 | 699 |
| Warehousing, etc | 14 | 17 | 19 | 21 | 23 |
| Promotion | 90 | 90 | 95 | 95 | 95 |
|  | 544 | 612 | 681 | 741 | 817 |
| Contribution | 213 | 256 | 294 | 334 | 384 |
| Fixed expenses | 201 | 220 | 234 | 245 | 254 |
|  | 12 | 36 | 60 | 89 | 130 |

*continued*

**5-year forecast based on adopted sales estimate, £000** (continued)

*Cash Flow Statement*

|  | 19X1 | 19X2 | 19X3 | 19X4 | 19X5 |
|---|---|---|---|---|---|
| P & L A/C | 12 | 36 | 60 | 89 | 130 |
| Add depreciation | 16 | 19 | 31 | 31 | 31 |
| Capital expenditure | (23) | (28) | (37) | (33) | (20) |
| Stocks | (45) | (43) | (39) | (32) | (24) |
| Debtors | (33) | (35) | (34) | (27) | (30) |
| Flow, + or (−) | (73) | (51) | (19) | 28 | 87 |
| Balance, + or (−) | (73) | (124) | (143) | (115) | (28) |

## The Promotion Budget

|  | £ | £ |
|---|---|---|
| Trade advertising | 20,500 | |
| Public relations | 3,000 | |
|  | | 23,500 |
| Direct mail literature | 5,700 | |
| Postage | 18,000 | |
| Direct mail house costs | 3,500 | |
|  | | 27,200 |
| Marketing research | | 5,000 |
| Symposium | | 2,000 |
| Exhibitions | | 14,000 |
| Production costs | | 16,300 |
| Contingencies | | 2,000 |
|  | | 90,000 |

*Promotion by Product Group*

| Group 1: | £ | £ |
|---|---|---|
| HPLC | 33,500 | |
| Electrophoresis | 4,000 | |
| Other chromatography | 9,500 | |
|  | | 47,000 |
| Group 2: | | |
| Avonkote | 4,800 | |
| Phase separators | 8,000 | |
| Indicator papers | 4,500 | |
| Other laboratory accessories | 6,500 | |
|  | | 23,800 |
| Group 3: | | |
| Sturga | 5,400 | |
| Stuglass | 7,400 | |
| Other filter products | 6,400 | |
|  | | 19,200 |
|  | | 90,000 |

### The market

The market for the company's products are mainly chemists and scientific workers in laboratories. Approximately 75,000 such contacts are accepted as existing in the UK.

Segmentation is based on geographical locations and nature of the activity and specific scientific interests.

### Field activities

- A high customer and prospect awareness to be engendered regarding:

  (a) STU range of products

  (b) Developing laboratory techniques

  (c) Availability of supplies and deliveries

  (d) Technical service

- Continuing strong links with appointed dealers to be maintained and direct sales to be negotiated on understanding by dealer of relief from problems of special orders.

- Continual feedback from market segments on product application techniques and development, particularly relating to new products. Test marketing of new products will be the agreed responsibility of product managers who will organise sales force briefings and subsequent progress assessment meetings on a regional and national basis.

- The field sales organisation will be increased to 12 during the year on the basis of each sales person being responsible for areas of approximately 15,000 square miles.

- Distribution will continue by using the postal services and contract road transport for larger orders. During the year experimental local stocks will be held.

### Development

The following abilities in the company will be developed:

(a) Competence of those staff who have contact with customers to deal with all types of enquiry.

(b) Efficiency and effectiveness of clerical and stores staff.

(c) Accuracy of sales forecasting.

(d) Adaptability to changes required for test marketing and selling of new products.

(e) Provision of facilities to permit all staff to carry out their responsibilities to a very high level.

## Pricing

All STU products will be sold at list prices without discounts except in those cases where it can be proved to the national sales manager that business would otherwise be lost to competition.

Prices of unlisted size variants will be in accordance with company procedure set out in the sales manual, and what the market will accept.

Invitations to tender at prices below STU list prices will be passed to approved dealers or declined.

During the year it is expected that there will be fairly substantial price increases of which we will be able to give about two months' notice.

## Marketing research

The limited attitudinal research and some product-oriented research will continue to be carried out during the year. A sum of £5,000 is included in the promotion budget for these purposes.

## Competition

The main competitive suppliers are:

| | |
|---|---|
| Anachem | M & B |
| Biorad | MN |
| Gelman | Merck |
| Hypersperes | Millipore |
| Kodak | Pharmacia |
| LKB | Shandon |
| Lichrosorb | Whatman |
| Lyphan | Wright |

All staff should ensure that head office receives immediate reports on any activities of competitors. In particular, we would like to see, on a regular basis:

(a) literature and price lists

(b) personnel changes

(c) promotion activities

(d) any specials

(e) samples

(f) new entries into the market

# 19

# Sales and Advertising Planning

**Sales people are the front-line troops; advertising and publicity, their weapons. Following on from your marketing plan, your sales activities must be adequately planned and directed. You are shown how to plan and then how to implement the plan into action: plan the work, work the plan.**

## Sales activities planning

A sales manager has many activities to carry out to achieve the agreed objectives, but means are limited: not everything can be done. Choices have to be made, resources committed and, once committed, they are often impossible to change. The sales force committed to the north cannot cover the south at the same time. Money spent on television cannot also be spent on press advertising.

Decisions are needed on how many full-scale demonstrations it would be prudent to have on customers' premises; whether a direct mail campaign should be combined with technical visits or with telephone calls; extra discounts or extra promotion?

You have to select the products on which to concentrate; which to give a high, and which a low degree of attention. You allocate available resources to a range of activities; this requires planning.

## Sales planning form

The sales planning form, Figure 19.1, has a number of suggested activities and a couple of spare lines for additions. You may need to revise the list to suit your company's requirements more closely. At the top of the form insert products ranked in order of importance.

Year _____

Products _____

| | | | | | | | | | | |
|---|---|---|---|---|---|---|---|---|---|---|
| 1. Rep visit | | | | | | | | | | |
| 2. Manager visit | | | | | | | | | | |
| 3. Technical visit | | | | | | | | | | |
| 4. Direct mail | | | | | | | | | | |
| 5. Telephone sale | | | | | | | | | | |
| 6. Demonstration | | | | | | | | | | |
| 7. Bench mark | | | | | | | | | | |
| 8. Commando attack | | | | | | | | | | |
| 9. Rep promotion | | | | | | | | | | |
| 10. Customer promotion | | | | | | | | | | |
| 11. Samples | | | | | | | | | | |
| 12. Discount | | | | | | | | | | |
| 13. Sales bonus | | | | | | | | | | |
| 14. Sales contest | | | | | | | | | | |
| 15. Price attack | | | | | | | | | | |
| 16. Service | | | | | | | | | | |
| 17. Merchandising | | | | | | | | | | |
| 18. Sell out | | | | | | | | | | |
| 19. Advertising | | | | | | | | | | |
| 20. Exhibition | | | | | | | | | | |
| 21. Mini-exhibition | | | | | | | | | | |
| 22. Trade show | | | | | | | | | | |
| 23. Press release | | | | | | | | | | |
| 24. Sales meeting | | | | | | | | | | |
| 25. | | | | | | | | | | |
| 26. | | | | | | | | | | |

**Figure 19.1** *Sales planning form*

Mark the squares where you intend to direct the sales effort for the year. As you gain experience, insert numbers to indicate the degree of importance of the particular activity; the higher the rating, the more resources allocated to the activity for that product. The following notes will help you to plan your activities.

(1) Rep visit. Most important means of maintaining contact with customers and prospects but you may be able to sell some of your less important products without personal visits—perhaps by phone and direct mail.

(2) Manager visit. A number of key customers must be visited by local and national managers. But, which products are more important?

(3) Technical visit. For many products, technical visits are necessary in addition to routine visits by field sales people. Product usage might indicate the need for such technical back-up. Special usage of the product in one company would indicate opportunities for introducing the usage in other companies.

(4) Direct mail. Personal visits cannot be made to all customers for all products. Informative literature and direct mail shots are the next best way to maintain contact.

(5) Telephone sale. Encourage greater use of the telephone to sell products, progress enquiries, seek information, make appointments or simply to maintain contact with good customers. Long-standing customers may welcome the occasional phone call; potential customers can often be stimulated with planned phone calls. To avoid sales personnel using the phone as a substitute for face-to-face calls, issue a telephone selling manual and require reports on phone calls.

(6) Demonstration. Many products have to be demonstrated before customers will purchase. A demonstration is only one part of the total selling process and often a considerable amount of pre-planning and follow-up is required. Plan the number of demonstrations for products you think are necessary but which can be handled effectively by your organisation.

(7) Bench mark. With some technical products, after a general demonstration, it is necessary to organise a special on-site application with the prospective customer's own plant and equipment. Considerably more planning and attention is essential for bench marks.

(8) Commando attack. Occasionally it is desirable to concentrate your sales attack on a small area of the total territory. Sales people are brought in from other areas and, after a thorough

briefing, selected prospective customers are 'attacked' to achieve specific objectives.

(9) Rep promotion. Not only does the market need sales promotion, sales personnel need to be stimulated from time to time with cash and non-cash incentives. Here are some reasons for using incentives: year-round effort can be sustained over slack periods; introducing a new product; slow moving products can be given a boost; new accounts can be opened; selling an agreed product mix rather than only the items customers want to order; resurrecting dormant accounts; increasing number of calls; obtaining market and competitive information; obtaining larger orders; eliminating small orders; reducing selling costs; clearing old stocks; collecting due and overdue debts.

(10) Customer promotion. Simple cash incentives such as attractive early settlement terms; discounts for larger orders; visits to head office; special visits to overseas factories and places of interest, with suitable hospitality provided.

(11) Samples. The quickest way to get users to try your product. Have a special budget in your costings for samples to cover your estimated needs for the year.

(12) Discount. When you give discounts, you are giving away part of your profits. Nevertheless it is a powerful method of selling and buyers are frequently pressing for extra discount. Price structures should allow for this. Unless heavy discounting is a feature of the market, do not use this as a general sales aid.

(13) Sales bonus. This may be for customers and for sales personnel. For employees, the bonus can be money, travel, gifts, or paid leave. Seek professional advice on the tax problem of incentives.

(14) Sales contests. Contests for sales personnel should be based on percentages, not actual figures. This enables areas of different size and potential to be compared. Devise the contest so that every sales person has an equal chance of winning. If you run a sales contest for actual users of a product, it is advisable to include middlemen. Award prizes to those who handled the product in the distribution channel to the winning users. Use the results for publicity purposes.

(15) Price attack. Not a favourite form of sales activity because it invites counter-attacks. However, where a product is being phased out, or where sales are difficult because the product is inferior to what is available on the market, a short, sharp attack with a price cut does have some merits.

(16)  Service. Often overlooked. If your product requires periodic servicing, remember that the service engineer is with a user every day and can be a powerful influence for replacement sales. An incentive scheme through service engineers linked with the rep on the territory is a sound way of maintaining sales. Some products can be linked with ancillary services: microwave ovens and cookery classes; word processors and training; computer hardware and software; clothes and dry cleaning services. (See Chapter 12.)

(17)  Merchandising. Most consumer, and some industrial, products can be promoted at the point of sale: display cards, counter literature, window displays, mock-ups, dummy products, working models, and so on.

(18)  Sell out. Sometimes it is necessary to help middlemen and dealers to sell the products. It is no use selling in to a stockist if the goods stay on the shelves. By helping the staff of middlemen to sell your products you maintain your sales levels.

(19)  Advertising. General advertising will have been planned, media schedules agreed, space and time booked, but have a budget for tactical advertising in individual areas. Take advice from personnel on the spot. Remember, however, that advertising is a highly professional activity and is not a play-thing for amateurs. If you allocate a small budget to be used by sales people in their areas, it will be as much a motivation as it is a selling aid.

(20)  Exhibitions. Exhibitions need long lead times and careful planning (see Chapter 14). Allow a minimum of one year to organise a major show unless it is an overseas activity—in which case you need longer.

(21)  Mini-exhibition. The only difference from a major exhibition is the time-scale. You still need a long lead time. Do not think that because it is only a small exhibition you can cut the organising time in half.

(22)  Trade show. What is written about exhibitions applies even more to trade shows because professionals, people in the trade, and competitors, visit them. Allow sufficient time not only to impress your industrial buyers but also to worry your competitors with the design, impeccable planning and organisation of your exhibit. Treat it as publicity.

(23)  Press releases. Send these regularly to all the trade, technical and professional press. Where appropriate, send really news-

worthy items to major newspapers. The secret of good press relations is regular issue of news releases with one person named as the company's contact or source of information. Press releases which are published during spells of ordinary advertising create impact on the market. Use them for anything that might remotely be considered as news. Approximately two-thirds of the editorial content of all trade journals is taken from well-written press releases. (See Chapter 14.)

(24)  Sales meetings. Stimulate and sustain morale with short, regular sales meetings relating to a product, the market generally, other selling experiences, competitive activity and future company plans. They are part of the selling activity and not an interruption of it. (See Chapter 17.)

## Sales action plan

The plan designed to achieve the company's sales objectives is completed with the aid of Sales Planning Form (Figure 19.1).

Specific actions are now planned, each activity is transferred to a sales action form (Figure 19.2), and expanded. State the objective in terms of results to be achieved. Insert exactly what is to be done, by whom, when, at what cost, and the total cost. Estimate and update as necessary.

To control the selling activities, calculate the likely return if the objective is achieved; allow for contingencies by using 80 per cent of this return as the estimated yield of the activity. Compare this with the total cost of the activity.

All activities should show a positive yield but it is not always possible to estimate this. The return may be spread over a considerable future period, too costly to find out with any degree of accuracy, or it may be non-cash benefits that cannot be translated into value. Consider:

>  Activity:      Advertising
>  Objective:    To increase the awareness of product $X$ in electrical
>                     and mechanical engineers in the Midlands
>  Cost:          £5,000

It would cost about twice this amount to determine whether the objective had been achieved, because you would need to ascertain the degree of awareness before and after the advertising campaign. Consider:

>  Activity:      Sales contest for sales personnel
>  Objective:    To stimulate sales during a normally slack period
>                     of the year
>  Cost:          £1,000

Product _____ Activity _____

Objective _____

_____

Ref _____ Date _____ Prepared by _____

| | What | Who | When | Cost |
|---|---|---|---|---|
| 1. | | | | |
| 2. | | | | |
| 3. | | | | |
| 4. | | | | |
| 5. | | | | |
| 6. | | | | |
| 7. | | | | |
| 8. | | | | |
| 9. | | | | |
| 10. | | | | |

Total cost:

Estimated percentage achievement:

Follow up:

**Figure 19.2** *Sales action form*

If you work on a net profit of say, 5 per cent, then you need to obtain an increase in sales turnover of £20,000 to pay for the activity. If you achieve only 80 per cent increase in sales, £16,000, the promotion will have cost your budget £200 but you will have sold products in the market that you might otherwise not have sold. Therefore, do not be too rigid in assessing cost and yield solely in terms of cash. Non-cash benefits can have a lasting effect in the market. Consider:

Activity:      Sales training for the sales force
Objective:     Sales people will open more sales successfully, the results being reported at their monthly regional meetings with their managers

This is not an easy objective to measure but, as with all training, it is highly desirable to relate it to some purpose or aim, if not an objective. You cannot necessarily relate it to improved sales. (See Chapter 5.)

Sales Action Form is given as a guide only; one page is unlikely to be enough for all activities. An exhibition, for example, will need several pages. Use continuation sheets with the product and activity at the top, and spaces for 'what', 'who', 'when', and 'cost'. Number each specific point of the activity for easy reference.

Collect the separate pages of activities into a loose-leaf file and transfer the dates under 'when' to your diary. Co-ordinate all the activities so that there are no clashes between personnel. Don't forget to delegate. (See Chapter 20.)

## They never come back

For future selling activities, there are current customers, current products, new customers, new products. What about old customers? Especially those who used to be good customers but left for one reason or another.

They say good boxers never come back; once they've faded after their glory and prizes, they never return to the ring. Old customers never come back; once you've lost them, they've gone for ever. Or have they? Good boxers may not come back, but sometimes good customers do. The problem is how to get them back.

Prepare a plan that will safeguard your present turnover and give you opportunities of recapturing lost customers. Consider the situation in Table 19.1: six segments A, B, C, D, E and F, in order of priority.

*Segment A:* Current customers, present products. This is your bread-and-butter. Don't allow other work to interfere with your turnover from this 'A' segment but build your plan around it. However, if you concentrate entirely on this segment, sooner or later you will find sales declining.

**Table 19.1** *Specimen data—products and customers*

|  | Current customers | New customers | Old customers |
|---|---|---|---|
| Present products | A | C | F |
| New products | B | D | E |

A small part of the market is always being lost; one customer moves away from the area, and another, and another; tastes change and customers prefer to buy elsewhere; a competitor gets in with a cut-price product, and so on.

At least 60 per cent of the selling hours available must be spent on this segment. In a 40-hour week, 25 hours is for selling the present range to current customers.

*Segment B:* Current customers, new products. It's common sense to offer new products to present customers; they can be introduced on the same call when selling the current range and obviously, there is no extra travelling involved. Extend each call by up to, say, half-an-hour a day to plug new lines—2½ hours a week.

*Segment C:* New customers, present products. Prospective customers have to be dug out from suspects. This takes time: only thorough pre-approach work will indicate whether the suspected customers are genuine prospects and for 'C' or 'D' category. Every 'A' or 'B' member called on should be asked: 'Do you know anyone else who might be interested in this range?'. Allocate 5 hours a week on segment C prospecting and selling.

*Segment D:* New customers for new products might also be new customers for present products. Regard this as a separate segment and allocate 5 hours a week looking for new prospects who could buy the new products.

*Segment E:* Old customers, new products. There are about 2½ hours a week left for this segment.

You can forget segment F. Trying to sell 'old hat' to old customers is a waste of time; the old product range may be why they quit.

All this can be programmed as shown in Table 19.2.

## Daily work plan

Five hours on existing customers selling the present range but extending each call to introduce the new line. Find out how long sales people spend on average with each buying customer and divide 5 hours by this average time to determine how many customers can be seen each day. Compare

**Table 19.2** *Analysis of Table 19.1*

|            |   | Segments |   |   |   |
|------------|---|----------|---|---|---|
|            | A | B        | C | D | E |
| Monday     | 5 | ½        | 1 | 1 | ½ |
| Tuesday    | 5 | ½        | 1 | 1 | ½ |
| Wednesday  | 5 | ½        | 1 | 1 | ½ |
| Thursday   | 5 | ½        | 1 | 1 | ½ |
| Friday     | 5 | ½        | 1 | 1 | ½ |

with current practice to see if any conflicts need resolving. In other words, you have to 'sell' this scheme to the sales force; do not just implement it.

Allocate two hours a day for prospective new customers (segments 'C' and 'D'). Sales people will have to decide before the call whether they will open their presentation with the existing range or new lines.

When sales people are making visits to areas where there are old customers, they should devote half-an-hour per day to introducing new products to 'E' members. This experience will improve their approaches to other previous customers.

*Weekly plan*

No plan ever works out exactly as intended and you might prefer to use numbers of calls rather than hours. Once you have your basic plan, adapt it to fit the market, the number of customers and potential customers, and the selling process involved with your products.

Build the weekly call plan around the 'A' and 'B' segments but appreciate that tomorrow's customers—'C' and 'D' segments—require some action today. Old boxers may never come back but old customers can if the approaches made by your sales people are focused accurately and timed well. The shot-gun won't work; take careful aim with a high-powered rifle and control the number of shots so as not to affect current sales adversely.

# Campaign planning

Single ads do not work; you need several to achieve synergy—the total effect being greater than the sum of the individual ads. A campaign establishes recognition, like an old friend or a familiar face one sees in a crowd. The smaller your budget the more important it is to plan a campaign that transmits the same message every time. You may have the same ad, or two or more that communicate the same idea in different ways. A unifying link is essential. This could be the name in the same typeface; the same illustration; the same approach.

Never approve an advertisement in isolation. Ask for outlines of proposed future ads. Ask for some headlines for suggested print ads; a paragraph or two for proposed TV and radio ads; a few illustrations for future posters. This will ensure that your advertising is developed as a campaign and not just one shot for approval.

When considering the proposed campaign, look for consistency of attitude, of presentation, of 'feel', of treatment, and check that all the ideas belong to the same family. Look for visual similarity. This can be obtained in many different ways: the same spokesman or personality; same product photograph; same demonstration; same typeface; same treatment, such as a comic approach; same memory device, such as the Colgate toothpaste 'ring of confidence' that pops onto people's faces to identify properly cleaned teeth. Even the same position in a particular publication creates familiarity.

Listen for similarity of sounds. Familiar ads have familiar sounds; sometimes music or a jingle, a doorbell chime, or the same unique voice that announces, or sings the praises, of the product.

When considering any medium, look at seven specific aspects: frequency; penetration of the target market; circulation; readership; profile; secondary media; cost.

## Frequency of ads

How often does the medium appear? Is it issued daily, weekly, monthly or less frequently? How quickly can the content be changed? A cinema manager with a weekly change of programme does not advertise in monthly magazines. The more frequently the copy has to be changed, use the more frequently published medium—daily or weekly, rather than monthly.

## Penetration of the target market

Penetrate the target market but minimise the wastage of advertising to people who do not form part of your market. Getting the message to the right market is more important than the message itself. The most powerful, persuasive message will fail if it is directed to the wrong target.

## Circulation figures

Use circulation figures rather than 'readership' figures when comparing costs of publications. Audited circulation figures are factual; readership figures are the result of occasional market surveys of samples which are then statistically projected for the whole market.

## Readership of publications

There are two aspects of readership: the estimated number of readers of the same issue of a publication, and their social grade. Generally, readers of *The Times* are different from those of *The Sun* or *The Daily Mirror*. But there is also 'cross-readership'—readers who read more than one publication. A percentage of *Times* readers also read the *Financial Times* and the *Daily Telegraph*; some of the *Sun* readers also read the *Mirror*, and so on. Surveys are obtainable on readership indicating sex, age, income group, social grading, degree of cross-readership, for most of the important and large circulation publications.

## Profile of readership

The profile of readers includes the proportional breakdown into the social grades. For major publications and many technical and specialist publications, profiles by jobs, titles, etc, are available from the publishers.

The standard social grade classifications used by market research organisations indicate the relative amount of disposable income that people have and how they might spend it. These classifications are important to advertising operations because the varying tastes and preferences of people have been conditioned by their education, living standards, employment, etc. This influences what they will buy.

> A. *Upper Middle Class* (3% approx). Head of the household is a successful business or professional man, senior civil servant, airline pilot, university professor or similar, and may even have a substantial private income. Live in country or suburban areas in large detached houses or in towns in expensive flats or houses.

> B. *Middle Class* (13% approx). Senior people near to the top of their chosen business or profession. Adequately well paid and regarded as 'well off', but their life-style is generally respectable rather than luxurious.

> C1. *Lower Middle Class* (22% approx). Small traders, non-manual workers, and so-called 'white-collar workers'. In the main these are supervisors, administrators, clerical staff and often 'middle management' people.

> C2. *Skilled Working Class* (31% approx). Manual workers who possess skills that are normally acquired after serving an apprenticeship. Often referred to as the 'blue-collar' workers.

*D. Semi-skilled and Unskilled Working Class* (19% approx). All manual workers who are generally unskilled, or need a minimum of skills to carry out their daily jobs.

*E. Lowest Subsistence Levels* (11%). Old Age pensioners who have only a state pension, widows and their families, casual workers and those who, through sickness or unemployment, are dependent on social security and other state schemes, or have very small private means.

Note that 'disposable income' and 'discretionary spending power' of individuals in the groups varies tremendously. A member of the upper middle class (A) may have high disposable income but many commitments, and therefore relatively little spending power. In contrast, a member of the skilled working class (C1) such as a specialist printer, can be paid at a rate double that of a university professor. The discretionary spending power of the printer is very great but it is likely that he will spend his money in an entirely different manner from that of the professor.

The distribution of the classes in the UK, shown in Table 19.3, does not change very much over the years.

**Table 19.3** *Distribution of social grades in the UK*

| Social grade | All (000) | (%) | Adults Over 15 Men (000) | (%) | Women (000) | (%) |
|---|---|---|---|---|---|---|
| A | 1,352 | 3.1 | 668 | 3.2 | 684 | 3.0 |
| B | 5,796 | 13.4 | 2,838 | 13.7 | 2,958 | 13.1 |
| C1 | 9,674 | 22.3 | 4,444 | 21.4 | 5,230 | 23.2 |
| C2 | 13,505 | 31.2 | 7,061 | 34.0 | 6,444 | 28.6 |
| D | 8,254 | 19.1 | 4,093 | 19.7 | 4,160 | 18.5 |
| E | 4,719 | 10.9 | 1,677 | 8.1 | 3,042 | 13.5 |

## Secondary media

The main media schedule will be a selection of publications that contain the fewest number of different media to reach the target market. Secondary media support the main media. Thus, you might have a campaign in daily newspapers and local posters near to stockists where the product is available.

A typical combination advertising an FMCG such as a food product would be: television commercials, posters near to supermarkets, point-of-sale displays in the store. A technical, repeat purchase product could have trade press ads supported by direct mail to the users. Each medium has a specific task to carry out. Don't restrict your publicity to one medium.

## Cost

Define your target market, decide how many times each person should have an opportunity of seeing or hearing your ad, then compare the costs of doing this in different media.

The same sized ad in different sized publications will have different attention values. A medium sized ad will look small on a large page, and big on a small page. Here are suggested 'standard' sized ads for similar attention value:

| | |
|---|---|
| Text papers | 20 cm/TC (triple column) |
| Tabloids | 15 cm/DC (double column) |
| Large periodicals | 1/4 page |
| Small periodicals | 1/2 page |
| Pocket magazines | WP (whole page) |

The following formula gives the cost of reaching the 20 per cent of thousands of 'readers' (circulation is used here) who, on average, see an advert.

$$\frac{Cost \; of \; comparable \; sized \; advertisement}{20\% \; of \; 000s \; of \; circulation}$$

Use readership figures when advertising to specific target markets such as, say, the AB social grade.

Table 19.4 gives four worked examples, two tabloids and two large (text) newspapers.

**Table 19.4** *Media analysis — newspapers*

| | SCC* (£) | 15DC (£) | 20TC (£) | Cost per 20% (£) |
|---|---|---|---|---|
| Tabloid X (2,183,917) | 48.50 | 1,455 | | 3.33 |
| Tabloid Y (1,930,723) | 38.00 | 1,140 | | 2.95 |
| Text A (1,379,166) | 35.00 | | 2,100 | 7.61 |
| Text B (290,365) | 23.00 | | 1,380 | 23.76 |

*SCC = single centimetre column

Do not evaluate media purely on the grounds of comparative cost. The type and quality of readership of the media are very important. The narrower the readership, the more costly, but the more focused on a target market.

## Developing media strategy

When you consider the great number of daily and weekly newspapers, the free circulation papers, the weekly, monthly and quarterly periodicals, the continual broadcasting of commercials on television and radio, the multiplicity of outdoor billboards and the amount of advertising that drops through your letter box or falls out of periodicals, you will not be surprised to know that the number of advertising messages we are subjected to every day runs into many thousands. We don't see all of them because we don't have the opportunity, and the majority we do 'see' are quickly forgotten or do not even register with us.

This is the environment in which your media plan has to operate, so it is essential to start with a media strategy. Developing a media strategy means planning how to spend the advertising money where potential buyers will see your messages. Answers to the following questions will supply the strategy objectives for your media plan. Whom do you wish to reach? Where can they be reached? When do you want to reach them? How best can they be reached? How often should they be reached?

### Whom do you wish to reach?

Prepare a profile of the type of people you wish to reach. If you are advertising to consumers, describe age, sex, occupation (rather than social grade), education, experience, salary bracket, life-style if known, buying habits, and so on. If you are advertising to industrial organisations, describe type of industry, technological level and type of products manufactured, whether purchases of your kind of product are decided by buyers or technical people, size and value of average purchase, frequency of purchase.

### Where can they be reached?

Potential consumer buyers are not gathered in one locality but spread throughout the country. Industrial buyers are often grouped into localities; engineering tends to be in one area because of its original link with coal; furniture makers, motor car manufacturers, and others, are found in various identifiable localities. Consumers can be reached through geographical channels; industrial buyers can be reached mainly through technical channels but sometimes in geographical areas.

## When do you want to reach them?

Decide when you want to reach them. Ads to consumers for holiday-wear won't work in the middle of winter; you don't want to reach industrial buyers with publicity for your water softening additives before they have installed a water-softening plant. Carefully consider your product and its market and decide when is the best time to appeal to them. (Refer to the section on seasonal effects in Chapter 10, and Tables 10.14 and 10.16.)

## Size, value and frequency of purchase

This indicates whether potential buyers tend to buy your type of product on impulse or whether there is a lot of comparison and deliberation. The longer this purchasing stage, the earlier you should transmit messages to your audience. This applies to consumer and industrial products and helps you in deciding when you should transmit your messages.

## How best to reach them?

A lot will depend on the product and its use. If the product requires explaining, demonstrating, or the customer has to be educated or trained in its use, you will only be able to reach potential buyers with your name and the type of product with simple, short messages. Does the message need colour or action? Does the message need to be directed first to trade channels or to end users? Will it be more efficacious to 'push' it through the channel (direct the messages to the trade and rely on middlemen to push sales) or 'pull' it (advertise to the end user and stimulate sufficient interest in the product for end users to seek out the product)? Would television be more suitable than newspapers? Might it be more effective to develop a regular series of press releases to appropriate media than to use ordinary advertising space?

## How often should they be reached?

How often do you need to reach them in order to impress your message on their minds? On average, about 20 per cent of readers of a publication will notice any particular ad. The number of times you want to reach your audience will thus be related to the number of times you give them the opportunity of seeing or hearing it, and the impact of the particular ad.

# Advertising research

Here are some observations from an advertising research conducted into readership of a cross-section of nearly 50 industrial publications.

- Just under 5,000 readers of over 40 industrial publications reported that, on average, they spend about 1½ hours looking at one issue of a publication.
- Over 70 per cent of readers spend more than one session reading a particular issue of a publication.
- Readers who read the most editorial matter also read the most ads.
- The most well-read advertisements (bracketed figures are the number of times mentioned converted into relative 'weights'):

  Are very informative of the product (89)
  Are large in size (81)
  Show the product being used (71)
  Have people with the product (70)
  Headline the product's benefits (57)
  Have colour (52)
  Bleed (the print appears to go over the edge(s) of the page and there is no margin (10)

- When colour is used, 20 per cent more readers notice the ad than when in black and white. The best ways of using colour are:

  Dramatising the way the product works
  Focusing attention on product features
  Highlighting design or structure of product
  Emphasising key words
  Linking headline with body matter
  Indicating an attention route for readers
  Portraying tables and graphs

Adverts repeated several times indicate no significant variation in readership scores per appearance of a particular ad. Table 19.5 gives the reported readership percentages of four groups of ads (1,000 ads repeated once; 150 repeated twice; 50 repeated three times; 25 repeated four times).

**Table 19.5** *Readership percentages for repetition of advertisements*

|         |            | Original insertion | Number of times advert repeated | | | |
|---------|------------|--------------------|-----|-----|-----|-----|
|         |            |                    | 1   | 2   | 3   | 4   |
| Group 1 | 1,000 ads  | 21%                | 21% |     |     |     |
| Group 2 | 150 ads    | 22%                | 22% | 20% |     |     |
| Group 3 | 50 ads     | 22%                | 25% | 22% | 22% |     |
| Group 4 | 25 ads     | 22%                | 24% | 23% | 24% | 23% |

Advertisements with headlines attracted about 25 per cent more readership than ads with no headlines. Advertisements with the name of the advertiser in the headline or combined with the name of the product achieved about 30 per cent more readership than ads with no headlines.

Readership differences are indicated for different types of headlines as follows (the best = 100):

- Objective, editorial-type statement in third person (100)
- Statement of possible reader need (100)
- Headline without immediate connection with product being advertised or, where product is stated, reader has to work out the connection (96)
- Unanswered questions of the teaser type (93)
- Statement including 'you' or 'yours' linked with the reader's plant, equipment, procedures, profit, money, or other possession (88)

Provided that there is a dominant, single illustration in the advert, there is little difference in readership of advertisements with a prominent, medium or unobtrusive headline.

Whole page ads with half-page illustrations average very high readership and, when used with long copy, have greatest readership (= 100) (Table 19.6).

**Table 19.6** *Readership of advertisement with text and illustration*

| Length of copy | Size of illustration | | |
| --- | --- | --- | --- |
| | Under ½-page | ½-page | Over ½-page |
| Up to 100 words | 64 | 71 | 76 |
| Up to 250 words | 66 | 85 | 83 |
| Up to 500 words | 88 | 100 | 70 |

Informative copy about the product's performance gets high readership; ads trying to get readers to respond in some way (additional information, free catalogue, prices, estimates, etc) have lowest readership ratings:

- Informative. Product copy. What it is, what it does, how it helps the users, case history if appropriate, 'news' items (100)
- Institutional or corporate. Copy relating to prowess, capabilities, skills, experience, research, quality, service, of company (85)
- Selling. Soliciting enquiry copy, offering service, assistance, visit, despatch of free literature (74)

The content of ads that readers like to have is on applications of the product being advertised, as can be seen from the following (the best = 100):

- Applications of the product (100)
- Technical data (40)
- Properties of the product (30)
- How the product is manufactured (24)
- How the product can be used (21)
- Sales, distributor, service information (6)

## Checking your media plan

When you have prepared a draft of your plan, check it against the following points:

(1) There should be a statement of the media objectives which fit in with the creative strategy and marketing plan.

(2) The media schedule should be set out on paper wide enough to display the total campaign, with columns showing size, frequency, cost per insertion, and headed in months and subdivided into weeks. The five main media should have the dates, or marks, indicating insertions. You can see at a glance the weight of advertising every month.

(3) The overall press and periodical plan should be based on a minimum of size changes per publication. If you have many different sizes and shapes of advertisement you increase the costs of production and could affect the creative presentation.

(4) The pattern of publicity may be at a continuous level with approximately the same numbers of ads appearing each month; or could be in discrete periods with nothing in between. The best arrangement is a pulsing or wave pattern. You maintain a basic low level of advertisements and, periodically, have bursts of ads in a variety of media.

(5) Basing your calculations on circulation or viewers, and allowing for an average of, say, 20 per cent to notice your ad, will you reach the potential number of individuals required by the marketing plan?

   If your plans require you to reach, say, 50 per cent of 150,000 electrical engineers, then taking two successive whole-page ads in an appropriate publication with a circulation of 40,000 means that the ad might be seen by 8,000 with the first showing, and a further 8,000 on the second showing—but many of these will be duplicated notings. Even if the second assumed 8,000 were all new readers, your reach of 16,000 will have been far short of the required 75,000.

By taking some purely arbitrary figure, say 50 per cent, who are always new noters, of the 20 per cent average noters per issue, then for a journal with a circulation of 40,000 you have:

| | | |
|---|---|---|
| 1st insertion | 8,000 | 20% circulation |
| 2nd insertion | 4,000 | 10% |
| 3rd insertion | 4,000 | 10% |
| 4th insertion | 4,000 | 10% |
| ... ... ... ... | ... | ... |
| 9th insertion | 4,000 | 10% |
| After 9 insertions | | 100% circulation |

If less than 4,000 new noters see your ad each issue, you would need more insertions to reach the circulation of the publication. If the new noters per issue were not 50 per cent but only 25 per cent of the 8,000 (2,000 = 0.05% of circulation) then, with the first insertion achieving an estimated 20 per cent of the circulation, you would need 17 insertions to reach total circulation: the original insertion plus 16 (0.8/0.05 = 16).

Very careful advertising research is needed for accurate reading and noting figures: this example has been given to indicate how the media reach is considered.

(6)   Don't be misled by the 'cost per thousand', whether it is cost to reach all adults, all women, all smokers, households, A, B and C1 housewives, or whatever. It is a measurement of cost, not of effectiveness.

(7)   If you have to decide on grounds of cost, go for frequency of ads rather than for size or anything else. All the success stories of advertising are rooted in frequency. Frequency means repetition. Repetition helps people to remember. On this basis, two half-pages are better than one whole page; four quarter-pages are better still. Sometimes four quarter-pages in the same publication will have greater attention value than a whole page. Naturally, the smaller the size the less you can say and, bearing in mind all that has already been mentioned, you try to get the maximum effect with a series of compromises.

(8)   Repetition of the transmitted message is vital to get it received by the target audience. Reinforcing the transmitted message helps the reception process. Don't be afraid of using different media at the same time. Direct mail shots, local radio

announcements, and posters, can back up press and TV advertising. Repetition makes the audience remember.

(9) The people responsible for constructing the media plan must work closely with those responsible for developing the creative themes. Media and copy are not separate considerations. They have to work together. The media planner should attend all major meetings where copy and illustrations are discussed.

(10) If you have to cut the advertising budget, restrict the number of publications, or reduce the number of insertions, ask: What do we lose if we do not have this particular insertion? It is as difficult to estimate how much you would lose as to say what you would gain but, sometimes, this negative approach sheds a little light on the situation.

# 20

# Managing People

*Theories and hypotheses are eschewed; practical advice is given on how to direct and control other people to achieve the results for which you are responsible. Two of the more important activities of managing are considered in detail: accountability and motivation.*

## Crux of your job

In a nutshell, management is getting something done through other people. Your job is sales management, therefore your job is getting sales through other people. This means you have to delegate; here are some principles to guide you.

## Principles for delegation

- Each task needs to be clearly defined with the performance standards that have to be achieved.
- The person accepting the task is responsible for carrying it out, and is accountable to you: how and when you are to be informed of progress must be stated when the tasks are delegated.
- The authority given must be adequate for the tasks to be done and must be thoroughly understood by the subordinate.

## Responsibility

The question of responsibility, and whether or not you can delegate it, is often the subject of much argument. It is said that you cannot dodge the issue and make someone else responsible for something for which you have accepted responsibility. This is both true and untrue; true in the broader sense but certainly not true when you consider the practicalities.

You have the responsibility of obtaining a certain sales turnover and achieving an agreed profit for your company with a sales expenses budget. If sales come from thousands of customers all over the country you cannot possibly obtain all of them yourself; you need help. You divide the country into areas, appoint sales people, and make them responsible for getting sales from their respective areas to agreed levels. You are still responsible for obtaining the company's total sales turnover, but you delegate parts of that responsibility to other people.

Responsibility is nothing more than the obligation to carry out a task. And in this sense, not only is it possible to delegate responsibility, it is essential if you are to become an effective manager.

## Seven ways to succeed

Selling is a lonely job. Although sales people are continually talking with customers and prospective customers, they move from call to call without the advantage of social discourse with anyone in the company; they are alone. If you continually ignore your sales people, you will automatically develop morale problems.

Selling is a partnership between the people in the field, face-to-face with the customers, and those at headquarters. If sales people do not succeed in reaching sales quotas, it is a failure of the partnership, not a failure of the sales people alone. This is why the selection procedures discussed in Chapter 4 are so important to you. Sales people fail if:

- they are not developed and grow
- they do not receive regular inputs of training
- they are expected to do all their own planning
- they are not supported by you and the company
- they are not motivated
- they are not regularly appraised
- they are not told how well they are doing

### Development

Sales people do not necessarily want to stay in the same selling job all their lives; they want to develop into supervisors, area managers and headquarters staff. If sales are so important to a company, then a well-developed sales person with skills in addition to the ability to sell should be top management potential.

## Training

Training is a line management responsibility. Continually assess the skills of your people and, with their help, determine their training needs. Ongoing training should be part of every sales person's normal duties. Make full use of the sales skills survey form discussed in Chapter 5.

## Planning

If the main task of the sales person is to maximise the time spent face-to-face with customers who can place orders with the company, any time spent planning is time not spent doing the main task. Provide a comprehensive planning service for their territories.

## Support

Securing sales is a partnership between you and the sales people, which means that they represent the customer to you, and you to the customer. Give full support with sales literature, documentation, sales leads, letters, deliveries as required by the customer, by-return answers to queries and requests, follow-up telephone calls, visits when asked, and so on.

## Motivation

In order to play the part, sales people must look the part. All representatives of the company should dress in an acceptable manner. What is acceptable will depend on the company, its industry and its management. If they look like well turned out sales people they will be motivated to act like sales people.

Achieving sales is a team effort between the person face-to-face with the buyer and the managers. Sales people cannot be motivated unless they know what is expected of them; this means that their managers must communicate and involve them in setting quotas and goals. Field managers and supervisors should also work closely with people in the field developing plans for working the territory. Accountability is maintained with check-points which tell the sales person when performance is running above or below standard.

## We all want praise

Give praise when it is earned; guidance, constructive help and support when it is needed.

'Look what I did at school today, Mummy!'

'I've finished painting the spare room, come and have a look.'
'I've finished your cardigan, is that all right?'
'It's a new recipe; do you like it?'
'I thought we did very well today, don't you?'

We all want praise. We have done the job and we look around for someone to pat us on the back; irrespective of class, age, sex or type.

Sincere praise, even a little flattery, motivates people. Whenever a receptionist or telephone operator has been pleasant and efficient with me I usually say, 'Thank you. You sound very efficient', or, 'Thank you. You've been most helpful, thank you.' It works wonders. But it must be sincere, and you only give praise when it is due.

Convince your subordinate managers of the power of praise. Some may think that to give praise is to invite complacency; it doesn't. If praise is consistently given to people who deserve it, an absence of praise will be noticed immediately and can also be a motivating tool.

If you do not give praise where it is due, sales people may not even realise that they have done something well—and won't do it again! The next time you have the opportunity, praise one of your staff; and practise giving sincere praise to people outside the company. Giving praise, sincere praise, is an acquired skill.

## Money does not always motivate

Motivation of people is only partly achieved with money. After a certain level, further offers of reward achieve less motivation. People need and enjoy to be given recognition for work done. When this is given with panache, it stimulates them. Suppose you are the sales manager of one of a group of companies and, at a social gathering, the chairman of the group introduces his wife to you and says to her, 'James is one of our best managers. He has a bright future'. Would you feel downcast, depressed? Of course not. You've just received a little flattery.

It can be done obliquely. You're on the phone to a customer and one of your sales people is in the office with you. You say to the person on the phone, 'Look, what I'll do is ask our best man to come and see you. He's an expert on flow pumps and has a world of experience. You tell him your problems and he's the best one to advise you. I'll contact him today and get him to phone you'. You then tell the salesman in your office, 'You heard that. Will you phone him later today and make an appointment to see him as soon as possible? It's right up your street—after all, you're the expert on flow pumps'.

You say to one of your sales people, 'Y'know, Jean, you're one of our hardest working reps—and always consistent. I wish the rest were like you'. What is Jean going to feel, especially when she is back with her family? Probably, she will say, 'Do you know what my boss said today?'.

## Be sincere

Motivate people by knowing thoroughly what they are doing, and complimenting them on specific points. When an appropriate opportunity arises, pass approving remarks about them to other people, as the chairman did to his wife about the manager. But do it with care, especially when you have a sales person who is a little below standard. Say, 'This next period's going to be tough, John. We've a lot of ground to make up but it's well within your capabilities. If you can use the same tactics you did with that splendid effort in Cheltenham, we'll be home and dry. Now, how can we best help you?'.

## Regular appraisal

The best method of regularly appraising your staff is by using job specifications as illustrated in Chapter 3. Never give the impression that you are looking for trouble or a scapegoat. The standards in the job specification should have been set by agreement with the person concerned. If the intended results have not been achieved, maybe they were set too high or in the wrong direction. Tend to use the word 'we' when appraising your staff; you are appraising a partnership. 'We haven't done so well this month, Peter. Where have we gone wrong? Is the quota too high or haven't we called on sufficient good prospects?'

## How well are we doing?

If you require a driver not to exceed a speed limit, a speed indicator is necessary. If you are coaching high-jump athletes to achieve a certain height, you let them know their progress: you certainly don't keep them in the dark. If you require your sales people to achieve certain levels of activity and productivity, it is necessary to keep them informed of how they are doing.

You should do this with regular informal discussions and not leave it to the periodic appraisals with the job specification which may be too far apart for corrective action.

Don't leave individuals in the dark about the rest of the team: circulate all results as percentages of achievement to everyone. This will enable comparisons to be made between territories that are not comparable, and between groups of large major accounts and small territories. Inevitably, you will have to face the fact that sometimes a reprimand has to be given to an employee.

## Poor performance

Poor performance by a sales person is partly your fault and something you will have to share with that person. Therefore, you do not reprimand people for poor performance; they need corrective action.

- Never take corrective action with a person in front of others.
- Recognise that the person probably needs coaching and counselling rather than corrective action, and any failure could be the result of faulty instructions.
- Compliment the sales person on whatever you think appropriate before raising the subject of poor performance.
- Do not criticise, but explain in what ways the person could do better.
- Ask how the person thinks the situation could be improved and listen carefully to distinguish between effort and results. No one, except perhaps you, can be held responsible for thinking that sales are possible where, in fact, they are not.
- Do not over-correct. The fact that you are 'on top of the job', know what is going on, and have raised the issue, is usually sufficient to motivate the person into renewed efforts.
- Do not criticise without offering a constructive alternative: your task is to build confidence, not destroy it.

## Reprimanding

Reprimanding must only be done face-to-face, although I am not entirely convinced that you should sit behind your desk and require the person to stand in front of you. It is better that the two of you sit in similar chairs, round a small coffee table. That person is a human being and may only be partly to blame for being in the present position. Take the following steps:

- Choose a quiet place for the interview and ensure that there will be absolutely no interruptions during the meeting.
- Give the person as little advance notice as possible. Do not arrange for a reprimand meeting to take place in a month's time. Hold it when it is convenient for the person concerned and use your skill to avoid letting the person know why the meeting is being called. If you develop the habit of continually getting people to see you about all sorts of matters, you will not create unnecessary fear in the person.
- Make sure you have all the pertinent facts and, where appropriate,

have these in a file on your desk and not interposed between the two of you. They must not be used as a set of charge documents, but to back up the facts you have ascertained. They will only need to be shown to the person if necessary.

- State the facts and the substance of your complaint and ask the person for his or her views. Listen carefully to what you are told and decide whether it agrees with the facts you have.

- Remain calm and poised, irrespective of what you are told, and do not react. It is not a contest. Listen, and look the person in the face but occasionally lowering your eyes and head slightly toward the coffee table or floor. This will give you a human and understanding appearance.

- Respect the person's integrity and assume that you are getting honest responses. If you know, really know, from the evidence you possess, that the person is deliberately lying, do not react but listen carefully. Be sure that you possess evidence on paper and it is not simply one person's word against another.

- When you are sure that you have received the sales person's explanations, and perhaps an admission of guilt, maybe an apology, say what action you propose to take. This might be in the form of an admonishment, or a warning, or suitable punishment that fits the misdemeanour. Serious crimes will, of course, call for serious actions and require you to seek guidance from the company's legal advisors before you take any action.

## Replacement planning

Planning replacements for your sales organisation is investing in your future strength. If you wait until replacements are necessary, there will be the inevitable delay before new people are competent. During this period, you could lose valuable business to your competitors. Make use of sources for likely people and potential candidates, as discussed in Chapter 4. In this way you can act swiftly to fill vacancies when promotions, resignations or terminations occur. Also, develop the possible replacements by giving them specific tasks similar to those they will experience when actually doing the job. This will help their transition when moving into the vacancy.

If you have field managers, ensure that they are trained in replacement planning. The sales people who report to them should all be potential candidates for promotion. This means that standards of performance and development must be agreed with the field managers and made known to the sales people so that they are aware of opportunities for advancement in the company.

## Promotion criteria

You, your immediate subordinates, and your field managers should know what it takes to succeed in the company's sales organisation. Devise criteria by studying your best sales people for the main abilities and characteristics they have in common. These could be enthusiasm, personal skills, resilience, vocabulary, ability to converse, and so on. Have an example that clarifies each characteristic and settle on these as promotion criteria. These are circulated to your managers and executives for use when considering candidates for possible promotion in the future.

## Planning and control

Planning and control go hand in hand. If we have an objective of obtaining a certain sales turnover in the next year, our plan will be *how* we intend to use our resources to achieve the objective. Without a plan we would have to resort to 'designing on the shop floor', which means we would move confidently but aimlessly from crisis to crisis.

Involving the field sales people in planning is often necessary with industrial products and this 'bottom up' approach to planning builds commitment in the sales organisation and gives a measure of credibility to sales forecasts. Make sure you avoid the dangers of using the sales force in this way, as discussed in Chapter 9.

## Product/market knowledge

Everyone in the sales organisation should be as familiar with the features and benefits of competitive products as they are with their own. This is good product knowledge but, as you will have read in Chapter 11, it is not sufficient; you must consider the product/market.

All your staff should be knowledgeable about their customers' business, what customers do, what they use your company products for, and to whom they sell. If you do not introduce your sales people to competitive offers, your customers will. All your sales people must know the competition 'backwards'. Refer to the relevant parts of Chapter 11 and make sure that they understand and agree the positioning of all competing products.

Also reconsider the section on the purchasing-selling interface discussed in Chapter 2. Your sales people should know the purchasing structure and procedures of your main customers.

If some products tend to be sold at the expense of others, the reason may be that the product is easy to sell, has more commission, or may be a more established product and your people know more about the product and its uses. Provide product knowledge and application training for other products whose sales you wish to increase and, perhaps, adjust the commission scheme to favour these products. Consider the points regarding commission arrangements discussed in Chapter 6 if you are thinking of altering them.

## Account planning

If your management philosophy for major and minor accounts follows the suggestions in Chapter 2, you should encourage sales people to give careful thought on the handling of large accounts. Take an interest in the way they handle them, and ask specific questions to demonstrate that you know what they are trying to achieve with potential major accounts. When, subsequently, their large accounts have to be transferred to some-one responsible for 'national accounts', if you have followed the advice in Chapter 2, the person losing the account will regard this not so much as a loss but as an opportunity to achieve further success.

## Exposure and feedback

Try to develop a balanced approach to your subordinates, colleagues and superiors in the organisation by exposing your thoughts and ideas, and obtaining feedback on theirs. By giving little hint of what you think, and asking for little comment in return, you will develop a very reclusive personality; your people will not be able to get close to you and, worse still, you will not be able to do your job properly.

However, if you habitually put forward your thoughts at the expense of finding out what other people think, this might be seen as ego-striving, and an over-confidence in your own opinions. Others will feel that there is little point in telling you what they think and they will harbour feelings of resentment and insecurity. They will tend to perpetuate the situation and even withhold important data from you, because you don't really want to know.

By contrast, if you are continually asking for other people's opinions and ideas, and have an aversion to revealing your own thoughts, you will also generate feelings of mistrust in others. You would be guilty of creating a screen that would be difficult to penetrate because you never let on what you think. This gives rise to feelings of anxiety and hostility in others and, at worst, may create secret feelings of disgust.

Strive for an open style of management: considerable exposure of your thoughts and opinions balanced with a sincere desire to learn of others' ideas and judgements. Take care to couple this interest in other people's thoughts and suggestions with a high degree of sensitivity. Cultivate a climate of reciprocal candour and trust and, with this style of management, you will be able to stimulate and realise considerable creative potential in your staff.

## Some definitions

An understanding of the meanings of words used in managing will help you to clarify your thoughts when issuing instructions to others. Here are some definitions of words we often hear and use.

*Definition:* Statement containing the essential attributes of the thing being described, without qualification, without assessment, without reflection.

*Management:* Organising people to get something done.

*Good management:* Achieving the aim with the most economic use of the determined resources. (You may find a definition nearly the same as this, but which uses 'the available resources'. This means using what resources are there; you may not need all of them and must determine how few you need to do the job.)

*Organisation:* An arrangement of people to get something done.

*Planning:* Activity that enables a person to decide how to use the determined resources.

*Control:* The activity that ensures that what is planned is done.

*Task:* The work done to achieve an objective.

*Objective:* Measurable result to be achieved in a period of time.

*Aim:* That which has to be achieved. (A work aim has to be achieved because of a contractual responsibility; a personal aim is a self-imposed responsibility.)

*Measurement:* Counting the number of units in something (any competent person, using the same measuring method, should get the same answer).

*Assessment:* A judgement without defined units and based on a personal opinion. (All assessors tend to get different results.)

*Evaluation:* A judgement using defined units. (Sometimes we assess something before it occurs, and evaluate it after it has occurred.)

*Work:*    Any activity by which you discharge a responsibility.

*Responsibility:*    Obligation to carry out a task.

*Authority:*    The right to use determined resources to discharge a responsibility.

*Privilege:*    Authority beyond what is needed to discharge one's responsibility.

*Span of co-ordination:*    The number of subordinates to whom you can delegate.

*Delegation:*    Authorising someone to do something for you.

*Policy:*    The extent and limits of the use of resources which are used to discharge a responsibility.

*Accountability:*    The means by which one contracting party informs the other of the progress being made in carrying out the task that has been assigned and accepted.

# Appendix I
# What Kind of a Marketing Animal Are You?

Sales and marketing theory has been widely explored all over the world, especially in the USA; how well theory has been translated into practice is another matter. What is even more important is sales effectiveness. This audit will help you to determine how effective your organisation is in its sales and marketing efforts.

To each of the following questions or statements there are two responses. Insert in the brackets a *total of five marks* to the two statements indicating your response, that is, 5-0, 4-1, 3-2, 2-3, 1-4, or 0-5. Although you may not be in the situation described, consider how you would respond if you were.

1. Company sales and marketing personnel understand the importance of serving the needs of customers in the markets in which the company is operating.

   1

   X. This applies to all, or practically all, sales and marketing personnel.

   X   Y
   ( )   ( )

   Y. Although this may be known, it is not generally practised in the company; we concentrate on achieving sales and profits.

2. The aim of the company is to sell current and new products to whoever will buy them.

   2

   X. An increasing number of key executives realise that this is not the best marketing approach and we are trying to improve our methods.

   X   Y
   ( )   ( )

   Y. While this may be realised as not the best method of marketing our products, little is being done to change the way we have been doing things for years.

3. Management understands that there are many

different market segments but we sell to all with one
main strategy.                                          3
  X.  We know that segmentation is important and we   X   Y
      are expanding our knowledge of marketing and   ( )  ( )
      how our methods must change to cope.
  Y.  In the main, our products do not readily lend
      themselves to having different strategies for
      different segments.

4.  Company markets have been segmented, with products/
    services oriented to those segments.                 4
  X.  Management appreciates the necessity of making   X   Y
      sure that all products are related to the needs of  ( )  ( )
      customers in particular segments.
  Y.  The segments have been selected according to
      various characteristics in the industry.

5.  The company conducts its business activities knowing
    that the total market is a number of different product/
    market segments but not necessarily making specific
    approaches to those segments.                       5
  X.  Management is actively introducing these   X   Y
      concepts of marketing into its operations.   ( )  ( )
  Y.  The company does not conduct business in this
      way, but has a healthy turnover and profit.

6.  The market segments in which the company operates
    have been selected for their long-term growth and
    profit potential.                                   6
  X.  Yes, management thinks in terms of serving the   X   Y
      needs of well defined markets that have good   ( )  ( )
      growth and profit records.
  Y.  No, most of the markets have been selected by
      the sales organisation as a result of their
      experience.

7.  New products are developed in the company without
    using any direct reference to present and likely
    customers.                                          7
  X.  Nevertheless, products are developed more with   X   Y
      an eye to their use by current and potential   ( )  ( )
      customers than to their profit potential.
  Y.  New products are introduced as and when useful
      ideas emerge and to maintain a complete product
      range with as few gaps as possible between
      products whose sales are declining and the new
      ones.

8. New products are developed in tandem with reference
   to the company's existing customers.

          8

       X   Y

   X. While the company must retain the right to
      ( )  ( )
   decide whether or not a product is marketed, it
   knows that a product will have a better chance
   of succeeding if the needs, wants and desires of
   customers are considered when the product is
   being developed.

   Y. Management is reluctant to involve customers
   when we are developing our products because we
   prefer to introduce new products which we have
   ascertained from our surveys and soundings will
   sell.

9. The company concentrates on selling its products and
   services to its immediate customers.

          9

       X   Y

   X. Although management takes a long-term view of
      ( )  ( )
   its channels of distribution the bulk of the
   efforts are in selling to, and servicing, immediate
   customers.

   Y. While admitting that marketing is important,
   management considers that there is too much
   talk of marketing and not enough of selling.
   Selling at a profit is what keeps firms in
   business.

10. Management takes an overall view of marketing and
    fully appreciates that any changes in suppliers,
    channels, customers, environment, will affect the
    company's marketing activities.

          10

        X   Y

    X. Yes, it is realised that marketing is a total
       ( )  ( )
    company activity requiring support from every
    major and minor function, from research and
    production to the lowliest sales person in the
    organisation.

    Y. Although management understands that
    marketing is important, we are more concerned
    with our actual customers.

11. Is there high-level integration and control of the sales
    and marketing functions in the company?

          11

        X   Y

    X. Sales and marketing functions are represented
       ( )  ( )
    on the board.

    Y. Marketing is viewed as a staff function in the
    quest for sales turnover.

12. If you were asked whether marketing management

worked well with management of research, manufacturing, finance, purchasing, distribution and sales, would
you say:

12

X.  There is effective co-operation and any conflicting issues are resolved in the best interest of the
company.

X    Y

( )   ( )

Y.  There are complaints that marketing people are
unreasonable in the demands and costs they
place on the other departments.

13. When did your company last undertake a marketing
research study of its products, customers, buying
influences, competition, distribution channels and
methods, or other activities?

13

X.  Within the last year.

X    Y

( )   ( )

Y.  More than a year ago, or do not know.

14. Does your company possess adequate marketing
information?

14

X.  We know the sales potential and profitability of
the different market segments, customers,
products, areas, channels and order sizes.

X    Y

( )   ( )

Y.  We try to determine the cost of getting sales and
devote some effort to measuring the cost-
effectiveness of different marketing activities.

15. With regard to the annual marketing plan:

15

X.  We do little or no formal marketing planning.

X    Y

( )   ( )

Y.  We develop a detailed annual marketing plan
and a long-term plan that is updated from time
to time.

16. If you were asked to condense your company's marketing strategy to a mission statement, would you:

16

X.  Say this would be fairly easy to do because the
company's strategy is clear, well-reasoned and
based on current data.

X    Y

( )   ( )

Y.  Say this would be a little difficult because the
current strategy is not clear.

17. Suppose that you were faced with an unexpected
increase in activities during the financial year and
these required additional funding, would you:

17

X.  Say that life would become somewhat difficult
because there is little or no contingency
planning?

X    Y

( )   ( )

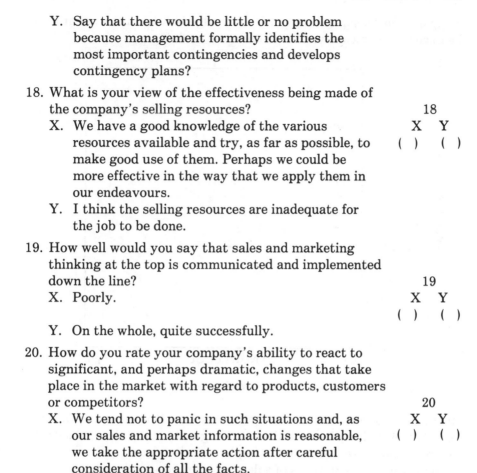

Y.  Say that there would be little or no problem
because management formally identifies the
most important contingencies and develops
contingency plans?

18. What is your view of the effectiveness being made of
the company's selling resources?

18

X.  We have a good knowledge of the various
resources available and try, as far as possible, to
make good use of them. Perhaps we could be
more effective in the way that we apply them in
our endeavours.

X    Y
( )   ( )

Y.  I think the selling resources are inadequate for
the job to be done.

19. How well would you say that sales and marketing
thinking at the top is communicated and implemented
down the line?

19

X.  Poorly.

X    Y
( )   ( )

Y.  On the whole, quite successfully.

20. How do you rate your company's ability to react to
significant, and perhaps dramatic, changes that take
place in the market with regard to products, customers
or competitors?

20

X.  We tend not to panic in such situations and, as
our sales and market information is reasonable,
we take the appropriate action after careful
consideration of all the facts.

X    Y
( )   ( )

Y.  We have procedures which provide us with
current sales and market information and can
respond fast to such changes.

We can consider a company's sales and marketing operations in terms of
their *knowing* what to do, and their *doing* it (Figure A1).

Of the two dimensions, the more important is implementation: it isn't
what you know, it's what you *do* about what you know. Many people with
limited knowledge succeed because they do a lot about what they know;
they make every little bit of knowledge they possess work for them.

If you have boundless energy and work hard, you will be successful
simply because you are *doing* something—even if your knowledge is limited. Many companies achieve high turnover and profits without having
a very extensive knowledge of sales and marketing; the energy of the
employees more than makes up for the lack of knowledge. However, a

company that possesses adequate knowledge but does little about it can be likened to someone who is 'all talk and no do'.

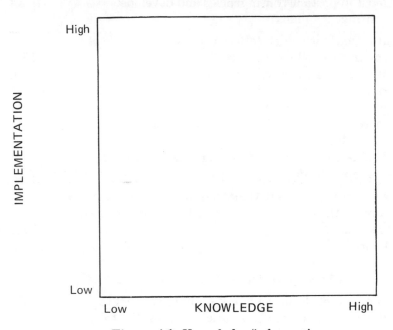

**Figure A1** *Knowledge/information*

Real success stems from an amalgam of the two. Knowledge, of the market, of competition, of sales and advertising techniques, is combined with vigorous and sustained action to implement decisions.

There are four main types of sales and marketing animal:

- *Lion:* Energetic and possessing high sales and marketing knowledge.
- *Beaver:* Energetic but possessing low knowledge.
- *Tortoise:* Lethargic but possessing high knowledge.
- *Sheep:* Lethargic and possessing low knowledge.

*Lion.* Company operations should be most effective where knowledge of sales and marketing is extensive and the company actively exploits this knowledge in the market. Lions will always be willing to look at new ideas in marketing and selling. They also know that continuing prosperity of a company is dependent on its product range and how this is maintained to reflect the changing market.

*Beaver.* These companies always work hard and what they lack in know-how, they make up in energy. These companies are selling rather than marketing. They are not so much concerned with marketing skills and techniques but achieve success through the sheer power of their sustained selling efforts. The danger is that the concentrated energies devoted to immediate objectives may blind such animals to the longer-term problems.

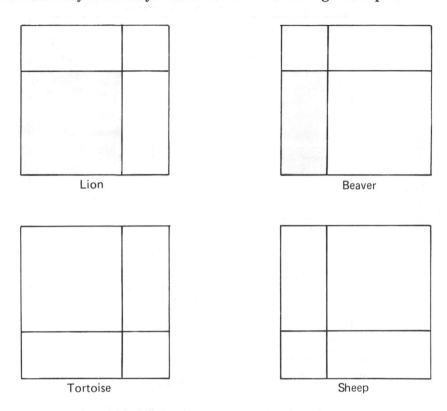

**Figure A2** *The main types of marketing animal*

*Tortoise.* The tortoise often possesses all the trappings of marketing orientation but little of the substance. A shell of knowledge has been built up housing a slow-moving organisation that reacts to unfamiliar stimuli by withdrawing into traditional postures. Such companies are unable to respond to market changes or competitive attacks and tend to rely on their tradition of quality and service.

*Sheep.* Worse than the three fabled monkeys who saw nothing, heard nothing and said nothing, sheep know little and do little. Selling is flaccid and marketing is largely a closed book to management of such companies. Their activities in the market-place are as adventurous as sheep who flock together and follow one another without question. Success is marginal and largely due to the kindness or failings of others rather than to their own energies.

In the ideally-managed company, implementation of marketing, selling and advertising techniques should keep pace with their understanding and assimilation as shown in Figure A3.

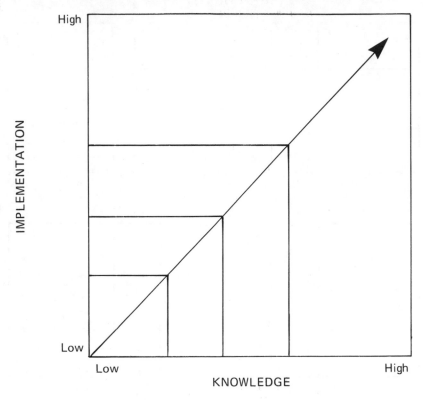

**Figure A3**  *Knowledge/implementation[1]*

## Calculate your sales and marketing audit scores

The scores of your responses indicate two measures: what your company knows about sales and marketing and how far it is implemented. In other words, what you know, and what you do about what you know.

The total of the ten Xs in brackets, (...), is your reported knowledge. The total of the ten Ys in brackets is implementation. Transfer the scores of Xs and Ys from your answer sheets to this table and total the brackets (...).

|   | X | Y | *Sales and marketing audit* |
|---|-----|-----|---|
| 1 | .... | ( .... ) | The scores in the table below indicate the |
| 2 | ( .... ) | .... | average scores obtained by over 5,000 |
| 3 | ( .... ) | .... | managers reporting on company sales and |
| 4 | ( .... ) | .... | marketing practices. |

|    | X | Y |
|----|------|------|
| 5  | .... | (....) |
| 6  | (....) | .... |
| 7  | .... | (....) |
| 8  | (....) | .... |
| 9  | .... | (....) |
| 10 | (....) | .... |
| 11 | .... | (....) |
| 12 | (....) | .... |
| 13 | (....) | .... |
| 14 | .... | (....) |
| 15 | .... | (....) |
| 16 | (....) | .... |
| 17 | .... | (....) |
| 18 | (....) | .... |
| 19 | .... | (....) |
| 20 | .... | (....) |
| TOTALS | (....) | (....) |

*Sales and marketing audit*

The average for knowledge was 24. The average implementation was 28. This means that, at the 50% mark, the average manager scored a 24 × 28 audit, or, only (24 × 28)/(50 × 50) = 27% effective marketing power was being used. 73% was not used by the average manager!

The standard deviation (SD) is used to indicate how close, or how far, you are from the average. If you are within *twice* the SD of the average, you are not significantly different from the average manager with regard to marketing ability.

Knowledge is from 14 to 34. Implementation is from 17 to 39.

| Knowledge | Percentile | Implementation |
|-----------|------------|----------------|
| 12 | 1 | 16 |
| 14 | 10 | 18 |
| 17 | 20 | 20 |
| 20 | 30 | 22 |
| 22 | 40 | 26 |
| 24 | 50 | 28 |
| 25 | 60 | 30 |
| 26 | 70 | 33 |
| 28 | 80 | 36 |
| 30 | 90 | 38 |
| 34 | 99 | 39 |
| SD  5 |  | 5.5 |

Transfer the totals of your KNOWLEDGE (X) and IMPLEMENTATION (Y) and also their percentile rankings to the graphs in Figure A4. On the upper graph, plot your totals for KNOWLEDGE (X) and IMPLEMENTATION (Y). On the lower graph, plot the percentile rankings for each of them.

Ideally, you should have as large an area as indicated. Deviations of size and shape should be related to the four main types (Figure A2).

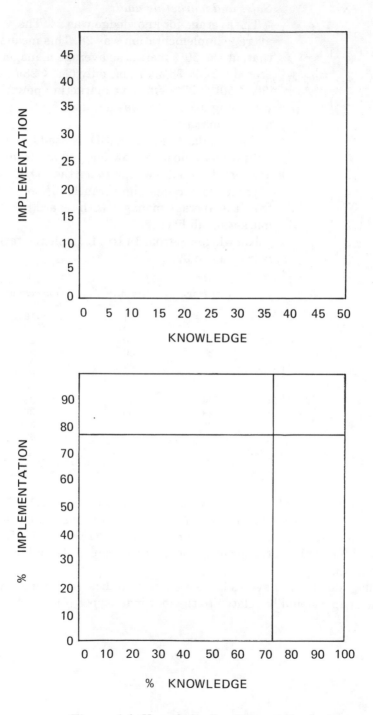

**Figure A4** *Knowledge/implementation²*

# Appendix II
# Specimen Job Specifications

Job specifications of three sales executives in one company are reproduced here for consideration. The absence of specific standards makes
these a little difficult to use as management tools, but the general
approach is useful. The limits of financial control are given for the first
two; you may care to consider what constraints you would apply to the
third.

*Specimen job specification*

| | |
|---|---|
| *Title:* | Sales Manager |
| *Reports to:* | Sales Director |
| *Job Description:* | Planning, implementing and controlling the sales operations for the company's products |

*Job Specification:*

a.  Establishing the sales potentials for products marketed by the
    company.

b.  Estimating the shares of these potentials that can be achieved.

c.  Estimating the costs of achieving these figures broken down by:
    Area and distribution pattern.
    Selling activities.
    Promotion activities.
    Advertising activities.
    Servicing requirements.

d.  Submitting annual and quarterly budgets for approval.

e.  Achieving the agreed sales and profit forecasts within the
    budgets.

f.  Reviewing the area performances periodically with local managers and agreeing changes necessary to achieve objectives.

g.  Defining jobs of field managers in terms of agreed, attainable standards.

h.  Working for approximately 40 per cent of total working time in the market to monitor company selling activities, to maintain day-to-day contact with company personnel, to assess the value of any training undertaken.

i.  Contributing to overall company policy by submitting reports on any aspects thought to need attention.

*Financial Control:*  Absolute control within the agreed quarterly budgets, with the constraint that not more than 35 per cent of one quarter's budget is committed in any one month, nor more than 10 per cent of quarterly total in any one week.

## Specimen job specification

*Title:*                 Sales Promotion/Advertising Manager
*Reports to:*            Sales Director
*Job Description:*       Planning, implementing and controlling advertising and sales promotion for the company.

*Job Specification:*

a.  Establishing the sales promotion and advertising requirements of the company's products in various market segments.

b.  Submitting annual appropriation and general media policy for approval.

c.  Implementing and controlling the approved appropriation with internal and external staff by:

> Determining, in liaison with the company's advertising agents, the most effective media mix.
> Supervising all external professional services to the company.
> Keeping all sales and relevant staff informed of current and future advertising and promotional campaigns.
> Liaising with appropriate company departments in the preparation of all advertising and promotional material.
> Monitoring the effectiveness of advertising and promotion.

d. Defining the jobs of each member of the advertising and promotion staff in agreed, attainable standards.

e. Reviewing the performance of advertising and promotion staff regularly.

f. Organising the internal and external training of staff within the agreed budget.

g. Contributing to overall company policy by submitting reports on any aspect thought to need attention of management.

*Financial Control:* Absolute control of the approved advertising and sales promotion appropriation—an agreed percentage of which is for contingencies to be used with the agreement of the sales director.

## Specimen job specification

*Title:*  Regional/Area Sales Manager

*Reports to:*  Sales Manager

*Job Description:*  Planning, implementing and controlling regional/area selling operations for the company.

*Job Specification:*

a. Establishing the area's market potentials for company products.

b. Estimating the shares of these potentials as sales potentials that can be achieved with the area sales staff; preparing sales forecasts broken down by products and time.

c. Estimating the costs of achieving these forecasts broken down by:

> Areas.
> Selling costs.
> Sales and promotion costs.
> Advertising costs.
> Servicing costs.

d. Submitting annual budgets and monthly budgets for approval.

e. Achieving the approved sales forecasts within agreed expense limits by allocating tasks to sales personnel.

f. Reviewing performances monthly with the sales manager and modifying plans as necessary to achieve agreed figures.

g. Approving variations of prices, discounts, etc, within the limits laid down by the sales manager.

h.  Defining the jobs of all regional/area staff in attainable standards.

i.  Monitoring performances of staff against standards and establishing any training needs.

j.  Spending at least 80 per cent of working time in the field, monitoring, supervising and ensuring that company policies and procedures are followed; evaluating the results of any training.

k.  Maintaining enthusiasm and a high level of morale in all staff.

l.  Reviewing performances of staff every six months with the sales manager.

m.  Recommending career development activities for staff.

n.  Contributing to company policy by submitting reports on any aspect thought to need attention of management.

*Financial Control:*

*(Left blank for you to consider what constraints you would apply to the regional/area sales managers.)*

# Index